GW01605617

WORLD WAR II · TIME-LIFE INTERNATIONAL (NEDERLAND) B.V.

BY ROBERT T. ELSON

AND THE EDITORS OF TIME-LIFE BOOKS

PRELUDE TO WAR

WORLD WAR II

Editorial Staff for *Prelude to War:*
Editor: Charles Osborne
Picture Editor]Designer: Charles Mikolaycak
Staff Writers: Philip W. Payne, James Randall
Researchers: Josephine Reidy, Doris Coffin, Clara Nicolai, Suzanne Wittebort
Editorial Assistant: Cecily Gemmell

Correspondents: Elisabeth Kraemer (Bonn); Margot Hapgood, Dorothy Bacon (London); Susan Jonas, Lucy T. Voulgaris (New York); Maria Vincenza Aloisi, Josephine du Brusle (Paris); and Ann Natanson (Rome). Valuable assistance was provided by Carolyn T. Chubet (New York) and Villette Harris (Washington, D.C.).

Cover: Members of the infant Nazi party jam a battered truck that will take them to a rally in the Westphalian town of Herne. Impoverished as they were in the '20s – the swastika is crudely painted on pieces of cardboard – these Nazis, and others throughout Germany, already displayed the swaggering military bearing that many of their countrymen found both reassuring and compelling.

The Author: ROBERT T. ELSON has a long career with Time Inc., including assignments as LIFE Magazine's deputy managing editor and Washington and London correspondent for the TIME-LIFE News Service. He is the author of the two-volume *Time Inc: The Intimate History of a Publishing Enterprise.*

Introduction: GORONWY REES, born in Cardiff in 1909, was educated at Oxford, where he became a Fellow of All Souls in 1931. After working as a leader writer for the *Manchester Guardian* and as an editor at *The Spectator,* he joined the army in 1939. Returning to Oxford after the war, he went on to become Principal of the University College of Wales and to publish numerous books, including a study of the Depression.

The Consultants: A. E. CAMPBELL is Professor of American History at the University of Birmingham, England. He was formerly Fellow and Tutor of Modern History at Keble College, Oxford, and has served as Visiting Professor at several American universities. He is the author of *Great Britain and the United States: 1895-1903.*

O. EDMUND CLUBB is a former United States Foreign Service officer who served with distinction in the Far East. He has taught at Columbia University and New York University, and was a senior research associate with the East Asian Institute. His books include *20th Century China* and *China & Russia: The 'Great Game.'*

COL. JOHN R. ELTING, USA (ret.), is a military historian, author of *The Battle of Bunker's Hill* and *A Military History and Atlas of the Napoleonic Wars.* He edited *Military Uniforms in North America: The Revolutionary Era* and served as associate editor for *The West Point Atlas of American Wars.*

HANS-ADOLF JACOBSEN, Director of the Seminar for Political Science at the University of Bonn, is the co-author of *Anatomy of the S.S.* and editor of *Decisive Battles of World War II: The German View.*

HENRI MICHEL, research director at France's National Center for Scientific Research, is also President of the International Committee for the History of the Second World War. An officer of the Legion of Honor, his book, *The Second World War,* won the French Academy's Prix Gobert in 1970.

JAMES P. SHENTON, Professor of History at Columbia University, has lectured frequently on educational television. He is the author of *History of the United States from 1865 to the Present* and *Robert John Walker: A Politician from Jackson to Lincoln.*

First European English language printing, 1979.

ISBN 7054 0522 2

CHAPTERS

PICTURE ESSAYS

CONTENTS

INTRODUCTION TO THE BRITISH EDITION

When the First World War ended on November 11, 1918, there was almost universal rejoicing that at last the blood-letting was over, and an almost equally universal determination that such a catastrophe should never occur again. Yet only 20 years later, the world was faced with an outbreak of war on an even greater scale than in 1914. *Prelude to War* traces, by word and illustration, the process that led to a second terrible conflict, and the book addresses its subject so vividly that, even though we may deplore the fatal process, we may at least hope to understand it.

The story of the years between the two wars is told from an American viewpoint that may appear a trifle strange to a British reader: it gives unexpected prominence, for example, to the American Depression during the 1930s and its effect on world events, and to the role of such peacemakers as President Woodrow Wilson, who pledged that war would henceforward be rendered impossible. It is an entirely valid viewpoint, however, for Wilson's attitude of optimism was shared by democratic nations throughout the world. Here in Britain it seemed that nothing could be allowed to endanger the peace secured in 1918. And to this end, we ignored the signs of Nazi and Fascist aggression and adopted a policy of appeasement that was, from the start, doomed to failure.

Looking back, how can one explain so rapid an extinction of all the hopes that had been born out of the horrors of what, in Britain, we are still accustomed to speak of as the Great War? What factors combined to produce an illusion of peace? One was the belief that the utter revulsion against the mass slaughter of 1914-1918 in itself constituted a moral force no government could afford to ignore. Another was that in the League of Nations, the Versailles Treaty had, for all its faults, created an instrument powerful enough to deter any potential aggressor. And a third factor was Europe's almost miraculous recovery from the anarchy of the immediate post-war years and an unprecedented economic boom that did much to repair the ravages caused by the war.

During the 1920s, the prospects for peace, progress and prosperity had never seemed brighter. In Central and Eastern Europe, revolutionary outbreaks were suppressed, sometimes ruthlessly. Reliable governments were established, currencies stabilized, and the Locarno Treaty seemingly guaranteed that Germany and France would never fight each other again. Under the statesman Gustav Stresemann, Germany entered on a policy of fulfilling the terms of the Versailles Treaty, and the burden of reparations which it imposed on the Germans was more than balanced by large American loans.

Compared with the almost miraculous process of recovery, the existence of a revolutionary regime in the Soviet Union, the growth of Japanese power in the Far East, and the establishment of Mussolini's Fascist dictatorship in Italy represented clouds no larger than a man's hand. And in Germany, Adolf Hitler having failed to bring off a coup in Munich, seemed permanently condemned to the role of an obscure Bavarian politician commanding the allegiance of only a handful of fanatical followers.

Yet the recovery was essentially fragile. The bitterness and resentment left behind by the war and by the Versailles Treaty had never been genuinely healed; and after the Wall Street crash in America in 1929, the economic boom gave way to world-wide depression. In Germany, the financial collapse and the subsequent withdrawal of American loans introduced a period of calamitous mass unemployment and, as a consequence, all the country's suppressed resentments found expression in their most extreme form. By 1933, Hitler had emerged from his Bavarian obscurity to become Chancellor of a new, thousand-year Reich, pledged to release Germany from the restraints imposed at Versailles and to assert the dominance over Central and Eastern Europe that he believed to be rightly hers.

The outbreak of the Second World War should perhaps be dated not from Germany's invasion of Poland in 1939, but from Adolf Hitler's entry into the German Reichs Chancellery in 1933. From that moment Europe's rush towards the abyss became like that of the Gadarene swine; it was accelerated and encouraged by the indecisions, self-deceptions, and the mutual mistrust and misunderstandings of the Western democracies in face of the danger represented by National Socialist Germany. By a series of daringly conceived and brilliantly executed strokes, Hitler quickly released Germany from the "shackles of Versailles", reoccupied the Rhineland, withdrew from the League of Nations, achieved the Pan-German dream of *Anschluss* with Austria, destroyed Czechoslovakia and thereby opened the way to the further expansion in the East, which was the ultimate and fundamental aim of his policy.

Mussolini, emboldened by his fellow-dictator's success, advanced his own imperial dreams by the invasion of Abyssinia while, in the Far East, Japan was equally encouraged to engage in the invasion of China. In Spain, the Civil War afforded yet another opportunity for Germany and Italy to show their contempt for the democracies by openly flouting Anglo-French attempts to impose a policy of non-intervention.

The real tragedy of war, of course, lies not in the world of politics, diplomacy or military strategy, but in the miseries it inflicts on the huge, anonymous mass of suffering humanity. *Prelude to War* faithfully and graphically records the steps that led to a world-wide conflagration, and it helps to explain why, by the summer of 1939, war had come to seem unavoidable to an entire generation.

Goronwy Rees

Goronwy Rees

WHEN THE SHOOTING STOPPED

The shell-blasted moonscape of a World War I battlefield lies silent and deserted after the 1918 Armistice emptied the trenches.

DISQUIETING SIGNS AMID THE CELEBRATIONS

Reprieved by defeat and lucky to be alive—the War had cost Germany 1.8 million men—this teenage German soldier was typical of those surviving.

At work in her Paris apartment on November 11, 1918, American novelist Edith Wharton heard the bells of nearby Saint Clothilde ring at an unfamiliar time. Soon they were joined by the chimes of Saint Thomas d'Aquin, Saint Louis des Invalides, Notre-Dame, the Sacré-Coeur—then all the city's bells. As she later wrote, the message of the ringing took a moment to sink in: "We had fared so long on the thin diet of hope deferred," she noted, speaking for everyone in the city that day, "that for a moment or two our hearts wavered and doubted. Then, like the bells, they swelled to bursting and we knew that the War was over."

In the trenches of the Western Front, there was, at first, no sound at all—and very little afterward. When the word came down from headquarters, most men could not seem to comprehend right away that the killing had really ended. Then a few of the victors cheered. Here and there soldiers on both sides climbed from their trenches and apprehensively approached one another. Some simply stared; others shook hands and exchanged souvenirs, though the supply-starved German soldiers in the sectors opposite British and American lines had little to offer in exchange for the cigarettes pressed on them. Then the troops headed home.

Out of the silence of the battlefield, and the joyous clamor in Paris—and London and New York—there came a great surge of hope that for a brief time seemed to envelop much of the world: perhaps, in the wake of four years of unprecedented destruction, mankind would at long last learn to live in peace, forever. As farmers returned to their fields and refugees to their homes, the leaders of the victorious nations met to hammer out the shape of a world without war.

Reasonably enough, the defeated shared little of this optimism. For them, the long war and its shattering denouement brought chaos and hunger and despair. Among many returning veterans, especially in Germany, it brought something worse. Looking at the destruction around them, they refused to accept the fact of their battlefield defeat. Almost before the ink was dry on the treaty of peace, they were looking for ways to redress the blow to their warriors' pride.

Joyful citizens of London, festooning a double-decker bus, celebrate the news of peace with what Winston Churchill called "triumphant pandemonium."

SIGNAL CORPS
U.S.A.

French refugees and demobilized soldiers trudge homeward toward Sedan—a garrison town on the Belgian border—which was devastated by shell fire.

German warplanes, stripped of their wings and stacked on end in a jumble of useless weaponry, await the torch demanded by the terms of the Armistice.

Ingenious French peasants use an abandoned tank as a tractor to help a team of horses, in preparation for the first postwar planting of their fields.

German troops back from their defeat march proudly and defiantly through Berlin's Brandenburg Gate—traditional victory arch of the Kaiser's Empire.

1

Death warrant in a ceasefire
An eerie silence along the trenches
A diet of pine cones and nettles
A façade of fourteen pillars
The visionary and the tiger
An operatic exit from the palace
An olive branch from Lenin
Old hatreds inside new borders
Slow train through a ruined land
A fateful phone call to Berlin
The final ordeal of Woodrow Wilson
Peace package with a burning fuse

"A PEACE RESTING ON QUICKSAND"

The train crept to a stop deep in a forest. Mist shrouded the oaks and beeches around the clearing. The time was 7 a.m., the date November 8, 1918. World War I was ending. World War II was beginning.

From the train's rear car, its green satin upholstery a relic of the days when it had been the private railroad coach of Emperor Napoleon III of France, the passengers could see another car on a siding. They did not know where they were but they knew this was the end of a nightmare journey—a journey they hoped would end the fighting.

A French Army officer appeared at the door to inform the newcomers, six Germans, that Marshal Ferdinand Foch, Supreme Commander of the Allied forces, would receive them at 9 a.m. For Matthias Erzberger, spokesman of the group, the prospect of waiting only added to his discomfort. His stocky frame ached, his hat was crushed, and somewhere along the way he had lost his glasses.

To reach this place, he and his companions had traveled for 18 hours or so, starting by automobile caravan from German Army Headquarters in the Belgian town of Spa. Just outside Spa, Erzberger had suffered a bad pounding when the automobile in which he was riding failed to take a curve, crashed into a house and was rammed by the vehicle next in line. The shortened caravan had gone on, jolting over roads pocked by battle and obstructed by trees felled to cover a German retreat. The party had arrived at the designated point of crossover into enemy territory hours late, after nightfall, and in a drizzling fog. The caravan had inched along, with a bugler on the lead car's running board blowing short blasts. At last a French escort emerged from the fog to lead them to a rail depot and a train that took them to their unknown destination, the forest of Compiègne.

Awaiting the audience with Foch, Erzberger reflected that seeking an armistice was a strange mission for a civilian, even one who was a leader in Germany's moderate Catholic Center Party. But the new parliamentary government in Berlin that had loosened the autocratic rule of Kaiser Wilhelm II did not altogether trust the military, and the High Command was only too happy to avoid the onus of bearing the white flag. Erzberger recalled Field Marshal Paul von Hindenburg's last words to him as he left Spa: "God go with you, and try to get the best you can for our country."

A few minutes before 9 a.m. the Germans walked across a

line of duckboard that had been laid between the tracks and entered Foch's headquarters, a former dining car on France's peacetime rail network. Then, ramrod-straight at the age of 67, Foch appeared, accompanied by Britain's First Sea Lord, Admiral Rosslyn Wemyss.

Foch was icily formal: "What brings these gentlemen here? What do you wish of me?"

Erzberger said they had come to receive the Allied proposals for an armistice.

"I have no proposals to make," said Foch.

A moment of consternation followed; one of the Germans asked how he wanted them to express themselves.

"Do you ask for an armistice?" replied Foch. "If you do, I can acquaint you with the conditions under which it can be obtained."

They asked for an armistice.

There was complete silence while an aide read out the terms. Foch sat like a statue, occasionally pulling at his mustache. The Admiral toyed with his monocle. As the Germans listened, they were stunned, for the first time comprehending the magnitude of their defeat.

Germany was to begin at once to evacuate all the territory it now held—most of Belgium and Luxembourg and a sixth of France—plus Alsace and Lorraine, the provinces it had annexed from a beaten France after the war of 1870-1871. Allied forces would move into Germany to occupy the left bank of the Rhine and the chief bridgeheads on the right bank. The German Fleet was to steam to the British naval base at Scapa Flow in Scotland to be interned. Germany was to turn over 150,000 freight cars, 5,000 locomotives and 5,000 trucks. War materials to be surrendered included 1,700 bombers and fighter planes, 5,000 pieces of heavy and field artillery, and 25,000 machine guns. No mention was made of the soldiers' own rifles. "They fought well, let them keep their weapons," Foch later commented.

There were more terms, 34 in all. When the reading ended, Erzberger asked for an immediate cease-fire, citing the revolutionary ferment sweeping his homeland. Foch refused; there would be no cease-fire until the Germans accepted the terms. They had 72 hours in which to decide.

Three days later, at 5:20 a.m. in the same railroad car, Erzberger signed the Armistice—and in so doing his own death warrant. Within three years he would be gunned down by embittered fellow Germans, a pair of fanatically nationalist ex-Army officers.

The intransigence of Foch and the bloody fate of Erzberger are vivid examples of the forces released at the end of the first great conflict that led—it now seems inevitably—to the second. These forces, compounded of vindictiveness and pride, in both the Germans and their conquerors, were to gather momentum even as the guns fell silent.

The cease-fire took effect at 11 a.m. on November 11, 1918. It was announced by wireless and word of mouth up and down the line of battle that extended from the Swiss border all the way to the English Channel. An eerie silence fell. "Peace came so suddenly we were stunned, asking ourselves was it possible, were we dreaming," wrote a French officer. "Walking along the trenches some hours after the Armistice I was surprised to see all our soldiers at listening posts or in shelters as if the war were still on."

In contrast was the celebrating in the cities. In London it began with Parliament's adjourning for a thanksgiving service in Saint Margaret's, official church of the House of Commons, but soon it mounted to wild excess. "Total strangers copulated in doorways and on the pavements," wrote the British historian A. J. P. Taylor. "They were asserting the triumph of life over death." In Paris, 20,000 people massed in front of the brilliantly lit Opéra and joyously sang the *Marseillaise.* In the United States, shrieking factory whistles added to the clamor of jubilant crowds.

The Kaiser heard the news en route to exile in Holland; he had been forced to abdicate two days before. The leaders of the three major powers aligned against Germany marked the Armistice in their own ways. In London, Prime Minister David Lloyd George, too exuberant to wait for formalities, came out of his 10 Downing Street residence at 10:55 a.m. and kept shouting to startled onlookers: "At 11 o'clock this morning the War will be over!" In Washington, President Woodrow Wilson gave government workers the day off and wrote out a statement pledging Americans to assist in establishing "a just democracy throughout the world." In Paris, 77-year-old Premier Georges Clemenceau reported the Armistice terms to an assemblage of the Chamber of Deputies and the Senate, wiped his eyes, and hurried from the hall to spend the afternoon alone, walking in his garden outside his apartment.

Three men of a younger generation, already well known in their countries, also savored the news. Assistant Secretary of the Navy Franklin D. Roosevelt, with his wife, Eleanor, mingled with the throngs on Washington's streets, cheering and throwing confetti. The Minister of Munitions, Winston Churchill, stood at his office window looking toward Trafalgar Square, where Londoners were busy building bonfires at the foot of Nelson's Column; then, accompanied by his wife, Clemmie, he went to pay his respects to Prime Minister Lloyd George. In Milan the editor of the daily *Il Popolo d'Italia,* Benito Mussolini, veteran of a short and undistinguished tour on the Italian front against the Germans' chief allies, the Austrians, held court for some admirers, who were dressed in swaggering black uniforms.

In Russia, the day passed virtually without notice. Having made a separate peace with Germany eight months earlier, the country was now in the throes of civil war between rightist White forces and Red armies committed to the Bolshevik cause of Vladimir Ilyich Ulyanov, better known as Lenin. The "dictatorship of the proletariat" proclaimed by Lenin was still shaky; helping him tighten his grip was a shoemaker's son, Iosif Dzhugashvili, alias Stalin, recently returned from Siberian exile to serve as Lenin's commissar in charge of keeping an eye on Russia's disparate and sometimes rebellious nationalities.

Nowhere in Europe did word of the Armistice prove more shattering than at a military hospital in the small German town of Pasewalk. Among the soldiers who learned the news from a sobbing pastor was an obscure corporal, Adolf Hitler, still half blinded as a result of a British gas attack on the Belgian Front the month before. As he later described his reaction: "I tottered and groped my way back to the ward, threw myself on my bunk, and dug my burning head into my blanket and pillow. . . . So it had all been in vain. In vain all the sacrifices and privations." The Armistice, he raged, was "the greatest villainy of the century."

War had bled Europe for more than four agonizing years. France counted 1.4 million dead, Germany 1.8 million, the British Empire 900,000, and Italy 650,000. In still-bleeding Russia, it was impossible even to make an estimate of the number of lives that had been lost. Old dynasties had been brought down—the Hohenzollerns of Prussia, the Habsburgs of Austria, the Romanovs of Russia; the last remnants of the ancient Ottoman Empire lay collapsed.

For the first time in history, men had fought one another not only on land and sea but in the air. They had employed implements whose ferocity few had foreseen: planes bearing bombs, submarines bearing torpedoes, giant cannon hurling tons of steel, poison gas spreading its noxious fumes. Soldiers had endured intolerable conditions dictated by a new military concept, trench warfare. Those conditions had been well summed up in a German propaganda leaflet vainly aimed at keeping the Americans out of the War. To get an idea of life in the trenches, it suggested, "Dig a trench shoulder high in your garden, fill it half full of water and get into it. Remain there for two or three days on an empty stomach. Furthermore, hire a lunatic to shoot at you with revolvers and machine guns at close range." In the years of trench warfare, neither side had moved the other more than 10 miles, until the last battles of 1918.

By Armistice Day the treasuries of most of the combatants were depleted. An epidemic of influenza was taking a

Among the convalescents in the German Army hospital at Beelitz, near Berlin, in October 1916 was Corporal Adolf Hitler (rear row, second from right). As a fearless runner shuttling messages between the front and the headquarters of his Bavarian regiment, he had dodged death for two years. But after volunteering for a particularly dangerous mission during the Battle of the Somme he was felled by a shell fragment in the thigh. Returning to the front the next spring, he fought until October 1918, when he was gassed out of action for good, winning high praise from his officers, and the Iron Cross First Class—seldom awarded enlisted men.

heavy toll. Although hostilities were over, the Allies were continuing their wartime blockade of food ships bound for German ports. Malnutrition was widespread in Germany; people there were subsisting on pine cones, nettles, flour made from chestnuts, and ersatz coffee made from acorns. Populations in lands farther east faced more acute famine.

In the wake of personal misery and of economic and political chaos, a legacy of bitterness and hatred was inevitable. But any idea that these emotions would linger and fester, that they would help to bring on another terrible war only two decades later, was unthinkable; statesmen of the time who felt otherwise were disinclined to air their troubles in public. For despite the carnage and grief, there was, on Armistice Day, a great surge of hope and an expectation that mankind was on the threshold of a new era, one that would make another such holocaust forever impossible.

The hope and expectation, shared by both sides, fed on two messianic visions. One came out of Russia, where Lenin was calling for a world revolution that, under Communism, would sweep away old notions of private property and class distinctions, and unite the human race. The other came from the United States, whose President had captured the imagination of people everywhere in the world by proclaiming the principles that he believed to be essential for the establishment of a just and lasting peace.

Wilson's aims, which he enumerated in 14 points to Congress in January 1918 and amplified in subsequent speeches, included some ideas that were still reverberating in the corridors of diplomacy more than half a century later. In place of secret agreements, there would be "open covenants of peace, openly arrived at." Armaments would be reduced "to the lowest point consistent with domestic safety." All barriers to trade would be removed. People would not be callously "bartered about" as if they were "mere chattels and pawns in a game." They would have the right of "self-determination," with rulers of their own choosing and frontiers that would correspond as closely as possible to their national groupings. In colonies, the interests of the indigenous populations would have "equal weight" with those of the colonial powers. There would be no annexations, and no "punitive damages."

One proposal above all engrossed Wilson: a league of nations was to be formed, charged with keeping the peace and guaranteeing the independence and security of "great and small states alike."

It was on the basis of these declarations that the Germans had turned to Wilson, not to the leader of Britain or of France, when, in early October, they had at last decided to seek an armistice. It was from Wilson, after a series of rigidly polite exchanges by transatlantic wireless, that they had learned that Marshal Foch would receive them.

Of all the world's leaders in November 1918, none seemingly held a stronger hand than the American President. As the one man who had been able somehow to crystallize the aspirations of the masses, among victors and vanquished alike, he had established a moral authority beyond compare. The United States, which had not entered the War until April 1917, almost three years after it began, was now the most powerful nation on earth. The arrival in France of 1.7 million fresh American troops had turned the tide against Germany in the summer of 1918; their total losses in battle, 50,510, had been small by comparison to those of the other

BLUEPRINT FOR A NEW WAR

The victors of World War I redrew the map of Europe. Some of the new borders were unabashedly designed to settle old scores, e.g., Germany lost Alsace and Lorraine to France as well as a chunk of Prussia to a revivified Poland. Other fresh boundaries—particularly within the former Russian Empire and the Austro-Hungarian Empire *(see key)*—were laid down in keeping with Woodrow Wilson's idealistic aim of regrouping Europeans by language, ethnic background and historical association. For example, the new Baltic republics of Estonia, Lithuania and Latvia were roughly homogeneous. But the two new countries that split off from Austria-Hungary were awkward mélanges of minorities: Ruthenians, Germans, Slovaks and Czechs shared a new nation called Czechoslovakia; and a mix of Croats, Serbs, Bosnians, Macedonians, Magyars and Slavs made up Yugoslavia.

Several of the changes were downright payoffs. During the war, Britain and France had secretly enticed some countries to support the Allies with promises of territorial gains. Seldom were the beneficiaries satisfied by the actual redemption of these pledges. Italy, for example, got a bite of southern Austria but saw a coveted area in Dalmatia go to Yugoslavia. Rumania, in contrast, took no chances with her wartime promises and simply grabbed Bessarabia from Russia and Transylvania from Hungary.

The geographical resolution of all these maneuvers and promises left Europe more bitterly divided than ever. Some 30 million Europeans endured as restive minorities under alien rule, and the nations that had lost land and people as a result of the peace burned to reverse the verdict of the victors. The failure was not total—some of the new nations still survive. But within 15 years of the peace talks at Paris, the redrawn map would clearly be seen as a blueprint for another war.

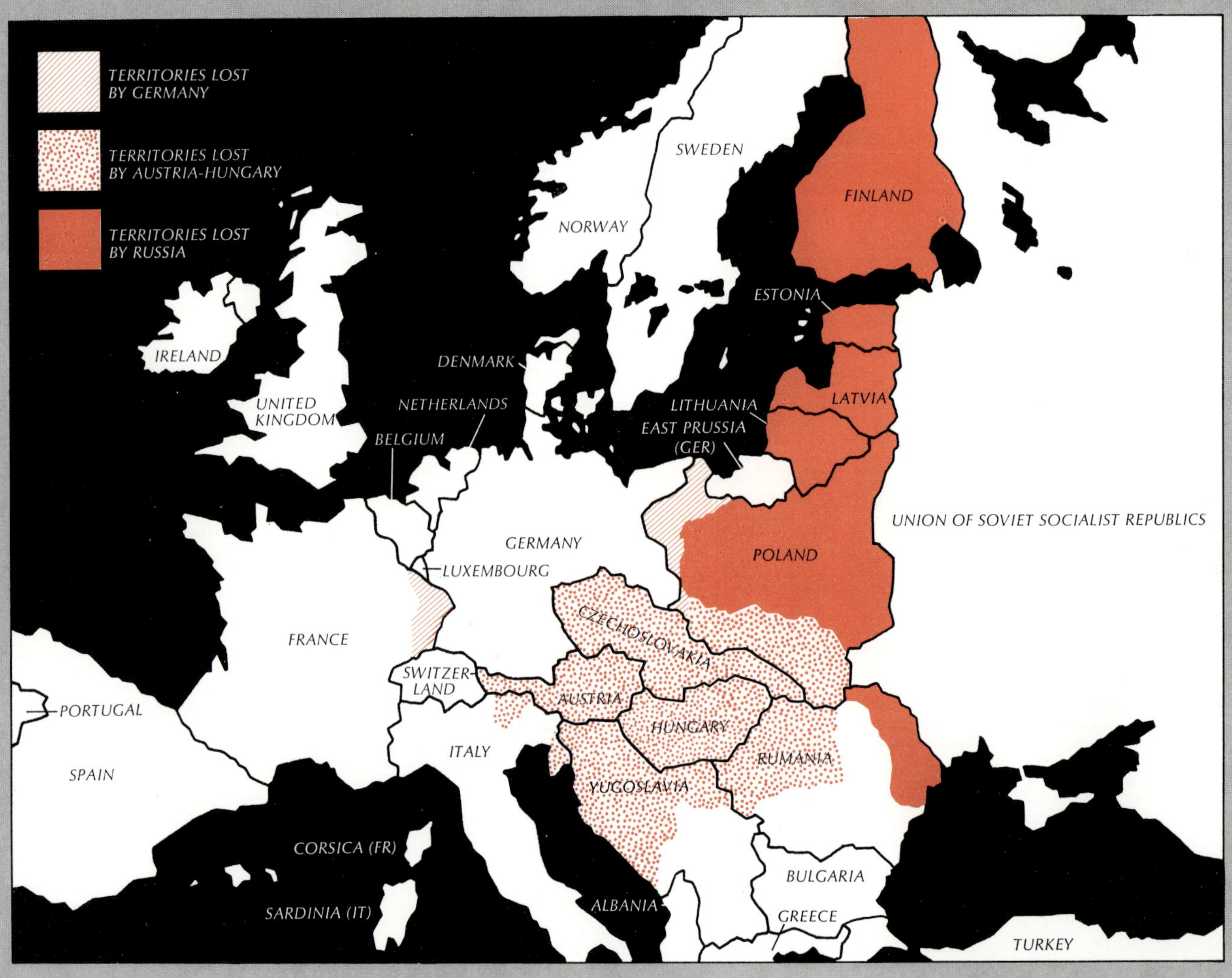

combatants. Shielded by the broad Atlantic, the United States itself had been spared physical destruction of any sort. Its great economic strength, undiminished, was Wilson's to command for purposes of postwar healing.

But even as Wilson's world prestige reached its apogee, his political base at home was crumbling. Against the advice of friends, he had appealed to voters in the Congressional elections—held just six days before the Armistice—to return his fellow Democrats to both houses to help him make the peace. At a time when the nation was still at war, this partisan appeal jarred many people who had supported the President without regard to their political persuasions. The voters returned Republican majorities to both houses. Wilson made no effort to conciliate his opposition. When the time came to select the five official members of his delegation to the peace conference, scheduled to open in Paris in January 1919, he chose only one Republican.

Today Wilson's place as a man of vision and high ideals remains secure; such politically diverse successors to the Presidency as Herbert Hoover, Franklin Roosevelt, Harry Truman and Richard Nixon all professed themselves believers in the Wilsonian doctrine. But he was an extraordinarily complicated personality. A scholar turned politician, he intimidated many by the force of his intellect. His glacial formality kept associates at a distance; yet in his academic career as a professor and later president of Princeton University he had been popular with undergraduates (he had even coached football) and he was a warm, humorous and loving father.

Wilson was determined to head the American delegation to Paris—not only against counsel, but also against precedent. No previous President had ever left the country while in office; his immediate predecessor, William Howard Taft, had even forgone vacations at his Canadian summer retreat. Still more cogent than precedent was the argument that by going to Paris in person Wilson risked surrendering his influential role of calm arbiter. He rejected these arguments out of hand. It was his duty to go, he said; he had sent young men overseas to die and he must see that "others shall not be called upon to make that sacrifice again."

In early December 1918 the President and his entourage sailed from New York for France aboard the *George Washington,* a former German liner that the American government had seized and used as a wartime troop transport. (Wilson was somewhat embarrassed to find that the famed chef of New York's Hotel Belmont had been recruited for the voyage to prepare meals for Mrs. Wilson and himself.) Also on board were some 150 geographers, ethnologists, historians, economists and international lawyers, collectively known as The Inquiry; they had been enlisted to provide the President with background expertise.

Off the Azores, Wilson assembled The Inquiry—not to hear their views but to offer them his. The Americans, he told them, would be the only disinterested delegates at the conference; those they would meet from other countries did not really represent the people of their respective countries. Thus the opinions of mankind would be expressed by the Americans. What was needed was a cleansing process to regenerate the world, for "the poison of Bolshevism was being accepted as a protest against the way the world has worked." Therefore, the United States must fight for a new order, "agreeably if we can, disagreeably if we must."

The *George Washington* steamed into the harbor of Brest on Friday the 13th of December. Some of the crew thought this a bad omen, but Wilson considered 13 his lucky number. He was given a reception never before or since accorded a visiting statesman. As he stood on the liner's bridge, the French Fleet passed in review, batteries booming salutes, bands blaring *The Star-Spangled Banner.* On shore, thousands cheered: dignitaries in gold braid alongside women of Brittany in their traditional white coifs. The trip by rail to Paris proved no less a triumph for the President. "We heard that here and there along the way peasant families were seen kneeling beside the track to pray for him and his mission," wrote the American journalist Lincoln Steffens.

An almost religious fervor also greeted Wilson on visits he made to England and Italy before the peace conference opened. Children strewed flowers in his path; immense crowds shouted themselves hoarse. Watching them, Herbert Hoover, chosen by Wilson to set up the machinery for postwar relief and reconstruction, later observed that to these people "no such evangel of peace had appeared since Christ preached the Sermon on the Mount."

Wilson's residence in Paris was the Palais Murat, an edifice so splendid that King Victor Emmanuel III of Italy, calling to pay his respects, remarked: "I could not live in a place like this." The King himself practiced spartan military virtues; he habitually slept on a simple cot in an uncarpeted bedroom. Wilson's political foes back home were soon making capital out of the Murat's 30-foot-square marble bathrooms and its collection of 3,000 glasses, citing them as examples of undemocratic extravagance.

Paris, chosen as the site of the peace conference in deference to France's key role in the War, overflowed with people from all corners of the earth. Some of the official delegations needed more than one hotel to house them; in the tow of the diplomats were legislators and civil servants, military and financial and juridical experts, representatives of industry and labor, journalists and press agents, secretaries and typists. There were also hosts of the uninvited —pleaders of special causes, armed with petitions, philosophical tracts, propaganda leaflets and ethnographic maps.

Many of the arrivals, official and unofficial, sought a meeting with the President. Their adulation, and the ovations that greeted his every appearance in public, fortified Wilson's conviction that he had become the tribune of all mankind. He was unaware that the attention focused on him did not sit well with his fellow statesmen.

The Paris Peace Conference opened on January 18, 1919, in the massive stone pile of the French Ministry of Foreign Affairs on the Quai d'Orsay, on the left bank of the Seine. The horseshoe-shaped table, covered with green baize, was huge; the damask draperies and the gilt chairs made an oddly ornate setting for the somber and deliberative process that lay ahead. The sheer immensity of the task was appalling. The conference was charged with settling the future of 400 million Europeans, of 10 million former subjects of the Ottoman Turks in the Middle East, and of some 12 million more people in the colonies that Germany had held in Africa and in the Pacific.

Russia was not represented at the peace conference. The outcome of its civil war was still in doubt, and the Western powers refused to recognize the Bolshevik government as long as a final White victory appeared possible. Germany and its wartime allies—now the states of Austria, Hungary, Bulgaria and Turkey—were barred from a place at the peace table. The peace terms were to be hammered out by 32 nations, large and small, that had either been at war with or had severed relations with Germany.

From the start it was clear that the conference was too big, too sprawling, too complicated for Wilson's cherished dream of "open covenants . . . openly arrived at." Soon such prickly problems as territorial boundaries were passed to special commissions; eventually there were 58 of them. A Council of Ten, with two members from each of the principal Allied powers—Britain, France, the United States, Italy and Japan—was set up as the ruling body of the conference. But in the end the crucial decisions fell to the so-called Big Four: Clemenceau, Lloyd George, Wilson and Premier Vittorio Orlando of Italy, with the chief Japanese delegate, the Marquis Saionji, sitting in for Far Eastern questions. They met privately, often without keeping minutes.

The Big Four could not have been more unlike in background, temperament and their views of what the peace should mean for their own countries. Apart from his ability as a political infighter, almost the only bond that Clemenceau had in common with Wilson and Lloyd George was his fluency in English; not just schoolbook fluency—Clemenceau had covered post-Civil War America as a correspondent for the Paris *Temps,* he had taught at a girls' school in Connecticut, he had roamed the streets of New York's Greenwich Village. In contrast, Premier Orlando's knowledge of English was, by his own account, limited to three phrases—"eleven o'clock"; "I don't agree"; "good-bye." The language barrier was to prove but one of his difficulties in dealing with his more influential colleagues.

As chief delegate of the host nation, the septuagenarian Clemenceau was chairman of the conference. Fondly called the Tiger by his countrymen for his ferocity, he was formidable across any table. He habitually wore a skullcap, gloves to hide the eczema on his hands, and a sardonic air. A radical in his youth, long since grown cynical, he had remarked when he first heard of Wilson's Fourteen Points: "God gave us Ten Commandments and we broke them. Wilson gave his Fourteen Points and we shall see." He was willing to indulge the President's lofty generalities so long as he got what he wanted—a Germany that would never again be in a position to invade France, as it had twice in the past 50 years. Clemenceau wanted France's tricolor planted on the Rhine or, failing that, he wanted a separate Rhineland as a buffer state between France and its old nemesis.

Lloyd George, youngest of the Big Four at the age of 56, was a Welshman with a shock of white hair, a quick tongue, and a cheerful mien that masked a flair for adroit political maneuvering. His foes at home had dubbed him the Goat because of his proclivities as a womanizer, but they respected his mettle in the public arena. He had battled his way to the top by denouncing the aristocratic establishment and fighting for such radical social reforms as old-age pensions. He was now a thorough pragmatist. Whatever his own pacific instincts, he and his Liberal Party had just won a new vote of confidence in a post-Armistice election based on pugnacious campaign pledges to "Hang the Kaiser" and to "Squeeze the German orange until the pips squeak." In Paris, Lloyd George intended to preserve Britain's supremacy of the seas and restore its prewar trading advantages.

Orlando was a gentle soul, learned and exquisitely courteous. He also tended to flowery discourses on *sacro egoismo*—the sacred obligation to protect the interests of one's country: he was in Paris to see that Italy received the territories it had been secretly promised in 1915 by Britain and France as a reward for joining the War on the Allied side.

Unlike Orlando, the others of the Big Four could be caustic about one another. Lloyd George saw in Wilson a "noble visionary" but also "an implacable and unscrupulous partisan" and "a man of rather petty, personal rancours." Nor did he care for Wilson's presumed role "as a missionary whose function it was to rescue the poor European heathen from their age-long worship of false and fiery gods." Clemenceau, Lloyd George noted, followed Wilson's movements "like an old watchdog keeping an eye on a strange and unwelcome dog who has visited the farmyard and of whose intentions he is more than doubtful."

In a curiously similar image, Wilson said of Clemenceau: "He is like an old dog trying to find a place to rest. He turns around slowly following his tail until he gets down to it." Clemenceau deftly barbed both colleagues when he said of Wilson: "I never knew anyone to talk more like Jesus Christ—and act more like Lloyd George."

At Wilson's insistence the conference dealt first with the Covenant—the constitution of the League of Nations. The word "covenant" was Wilson's choice, an echo of his Presbyterian boyhood. He devoutly believed that the League would be the cornerstone of peace, the instrument by which future world wars would be prevented.

The idea of the League was not original with the President; it had surfaced even before the War in many countries, including Germany. But the specifics posed complications. To placate critics back home who were fearful of yielding up United States sovereignty, Wilson had to insist that the Covenant incorporate a phrase stating that the League did not supersede "regional understandings like the Monroe Doctrine." The Japanese raised an embarrassing point when they urged that the Covenant affirm the principle of racial equality. This was traded off by an amendment requiring that all decisions made at any meeting of the League be unanimously approved by the members present—thus giving any one of them veto power.

The President compromised on other issues, in the hope that the League would later put things right. Two cases in point arose with regard to Italy and Japan. By the secret Treaty of London of 1915, Italy had been promised, among other new territories, the South Tyrol and the region of Trieste—both then belonging to Austria-Hungary—and a slice of the Dalmatian coast, now part of the new kingdom of Yugoslavia. Wilson went along with the Tyrolean deal, though it meant putting a quarter million Austrians under Italian rule, but he balked at other demands. When he went over Orlando's head and issued a manifesto to the people of

A 1921 cartoon in the postwar German humor magazine Simplicissimus reflects the bitterness most Germans felt over the peace terms imposed by the Allies. The naked, nightcapped figure on the ground is "Michael," then a conventional representation of Germany, like America's Uncle Sam. The U.S., Britain, France, Italy and Japan are combined in the five-headed monster, which is greedily consuming Michael's entrails.

Italy urging them to place world peace above national interest, Orlando quit the conference and left for home. On his departure, punctilious as always, he sent the President assurances of his high esteem. More sincere perhaps was his assertion that "the Italians must choose between Wilson and me." He was later to return to sign the peace treaty.

Japan claimed what it had been promised in a secret pact with the Allied powers in 1917: a takeover of Germany's concessions—in effect, control over important industries in Shantung Province, China. Though China, too, was an ally, with 175,000 men serving as behind-the-lines laborers in Europe, Africa and the Middle East at the War's end, Wilson acquiesced in Japan's demand. When his press secretary protested that this went counter to both American and world opinion, Wilson said wearily: "I know that, but if the Italians remain away and the Japanese go home, what becomes of the League of Nations?"

The almost casual way that the fate of territories was sealed has been recorded by Harold Nicolson, who was at that time a young diplomatic aide to Prime Minister Lloyd George. In this excerpt, Ll.G. is Lloyd George; P.W., President Wilson; and H.N., Nicolson himself:

"A heavily furnished study with my huge map on the carpet. Bending over it (bubble, bubble, toil and trouble) are Clemenceau, Ll.G. and P.W. Ll.G. says—genial as always —'Now, Nicolson, listen with all your ears.' He then proceeds to expound the agreement which they have reached. I make certain minor suggestions. P.W. says, 'And what about the Islands?' 'They are,' I answer firmly, 'Greek islands, Mr. President.' 'Then they should go to Greece?' H.N. 'Rather!' P.W. 'Rather!' Clemenceau says nothing during all this. He sits at the edge of his chair and leans his two blue-gloved hands down upon the map. More than ever does he look like a gorilla of yellow ivory."

Thus did the men of Paris redraw the map of Europe.

One question on which they could reach no agreement was what to do about Lenin and his Bolshevik government. The specter of world revolution haunted the conference. For a time it was touch and go whether Germany would go Communist; a Communist dictator, Béla Kun, was ruling Hungary; Communists were believed to be behind a wave of strikes plaguing Western Europe.

After the signing of the Treaty of Brest-Litovsk in March 1918, by which Lenin had agreed to a separate peace between Russia and Germany, a small Allied force had landed at Russia's northern ports of Archangel and Murmansk, and at Vladivostok in the east; the Allies had sent pre-Bolshevik Russia huge amounts of war materials, including valuable and scarce metals, and wanted to prevent their falling into German hands. The Japanese, along with small British and American contingents, had occupied stretches of the strategically vital Trans-Siberian Railroad. Allied munitions and money were helping to support some of the White armies in the civil war now raging.

Lloyd George and Wilson hoped to effect a truce between the combatants. But Clemenceau feared the Communists would infect Germany with their doctrines, and threatened to resign if any Bolsheviks were allowed to set foot in Paris.

WILSON LLOYD GEORGE ORLANDO CLEMENCEAU

The Big Four at the 1919 Paris Peace Conference, the United States's Woodrow Wilson, Britain's David Lloyd George, Italy's Vittorio Orlando and France's Georges Clemenceau, comprised a quartet of discordant personalities. Lloyd George derided Wilson as a combination of "the unscrupulous partisan, the exalted idealist and the man of rather petty and personal rancors." Ironically, although each leader achieved some of his aims, within two years all four had been politically repudiated on their own home grounds by countrymen who felt that their nations had been duped or shortchanged in the peace settlement.

Instead, both warring factions were invited to meet with Allied representatives on the island of Prinkipo in the Sea of Marmara off Istanbul. Lenin's reply was evasive, but more conclusive was the fact that the Whites flatly refused to sit anywhere, at any table, with their foes.

This ploy failing, another was suggested—by Winston Churchill, one of the younger firebrands in the British Cabinet. Hurrying over from London, Churchill proposed that the Bolsheviks be given an ultimatum: either they end hostilities against the Whites within 10 days, or Allied armies would move in to overthrow the Communist government by force. Wilson disposed of the idea by saying that the Allied troops already in Russia were doing no good, and that the sooner they left the better.

A third notion was the dispatch of a secret mission to Moscow, led by a liberal junior American diplomat, William C. Bullitt, to sound out the Communists as to their terms for a cease-fire. After being warmly welcomed by the Bolsheviks, put up at a palace and amply supplied with caviar, Bullitt had a long talk with Lenin. He returned to Paris to report the results: if the Allies agreed to withdraw their troops from Russian soil, and to end their food blockade—which affected Russian as well as German ports—the Bolsheviks would assent to a cease-fire in their war with the Whites. Moreover, they would agree that all *de facto* governments that had been set up in various parts of the former Russian Empire would remain in control of the areas they were holding when the cease-fire took effect.

Since, at the time of Bullitt's report, such areas included Poland, Finland, the Baltic states, the Crimea, more than half the Ukraine and all of Siberia, Lenin's proposal would have left Russia virtually a shadow of its former self. Historians ever since have wondered what course history would have taken had the Allies reacted affirmatively. But Bullitt's report of his mission came at a time when Wilson, Lloyd George and Clemenceau were deeply immersed in threshing out the problem of Germany. The deadline the Bolsheviks had set for Allied acceptance of their terms—April 10—passed without any action and thus the Communist offer expired. Bullitt resigned in disgust and headed for the Riviera, telling newspapermen he intended "to lie on the sand and watch the world go to hell."

By April the tempers of the Big Three were beginning to fray. The ceremonial air of January was long since gone. There had been unavoidable interruptions. Parliamentary matters had required Lloyd George's presence in London. Wilson had taken an entire month, from mid-February to mid-March, to attend to Presidential duties in Washington. Clemenceau, on his own home ground, had been briefly put out of action by the bullet of a would-be assassin, a French anarchist. The bullet, lodged close to Clemenceau's spine, could never be extracted, but the old Tiger was indomitable. After only 10 days he was back at the conference, energetic as ever.

Even after the three leaders resumed their meetings, it sometimes seemed that their collaboration was doomed. At one point or another each man threatened to quit the conference. During one argument, Wilson bluntly asked Clemenceau if he wanted him to go home. "No, I don't want *you* to go home," snarled the Tiger, "but *I* am going home right now." And so he did—for a few days. Early in April, Wilson created a worldwide sensation by cabling instructions for the *George Washington* to return for him. But he thought better of it and stayed.

The most bitter disputes came over the case of Germany. Clemenceau wanted it permanently weakened. Wilson and Lloyd George were more lenient. Britain did not relish the prospect of a too-powerful France in postwar Europe: moreover, a revived Germany would serve Britain well as a trading partner. At one snappish session Clemenceau accused Lloyd George of being an enemy of France. "Surely," was the cool reply. "That is our traditional policy."

Against Clemenceau's demand for a separate Rhineland as a buffer state, his colleagues stood adamant, but they did agree that the region should be demilitarized. There were other satisfactions for Clemenceau. Alsace and Lorraine were to be returned to France. Germany's Army was to number no more than 100,000 men. There was to be no German air force at all. The production of planes and submarines was to be forbidden, the manufacture of war materials strictly limited. All German colonies were to be surrendered. Large areas of Germany itself, to the east, were to go to the newly independent Poland.

The issue of the reparations to be paid by Germany proved an unchewable bone. The word "reparations" did not sound as harsh as "indemnities" or as bald as "punitive damages" —which Wilson's stated peace aims had specifically precluded—but the distinctions were semantic.

Collecting restitution from a vanquished foe was not new. Britain had done so after Waterloo in 1815; so had Germany after defeating France in 1871. As recently as the Treaty of Brest-Litovsk of 1918, Germany had exacted a staggering price for concluding the peace with the Bolsheviks—among other compensations, a third of Russia's agricultural land, more than half its industries, and six billion marks. By the Armistice that the Germans signed in the forest of Compiègne the Brest-Litovsk treaty had been nullified, but its provisions had shed light on the Germans' own views of how much a victor was entitled to.

As initially discussed at the peace conference, the reparations by Germany were to pay for the damages its forces had inflicted on Allied civilians and their property. Then Britain and France had a bigger idea. They proposed that Germany pay all the costs incurred by the Allies in waging the War. Both countries had borrowed huge sums through bond issues; moreover, France owed a large debt to Britain and both owed large debts to the United States.

Wilson beat back the proposal, agreeing to German payment of all war costs only in the case of prostrate Belgium, which the Germans had almost totally overrun. A compromise followed: the "damages" to be assessed on Germany were more broadly defined. Damage, Lloyd George argued, could mean the destruction of a house near the front lines, but it could also mean the loss suffered by a family behind the front when a soldier son was wounded or blinded or killed. The argument prevailed; the Germans were to be required to foot the cost of the allowances given to Allied soldiers on their separation from the service, and the cost of war pensions for their families.

No total was fixed for the reparations. Both Clemenceau and Lloyd George were afraid that whatever the sum decided upon, their countrymen would say that it was not enough. This problem was deferred by passing it on to a special reparations commission. Meanwhile, Germany was to pay five billion dollars in gold, or its equivalent, beginning in May 1921—by which time the commission would have decided on the full amount of the bill.

One other obligation was to be required of Germany. Later incorporated into the peace treaty as Article 231, it was destined to infuriate the Germans beyond all else, and rankle long and dangerously. Germany, on behalf of itself and its cobelligerents, was to accept "the responsibility . . . for causing all the loss and damage" sustained by the Allies as a consequence of the War—a war "imposed" upon them by the "aggression" of Germany and its partners. As the Germans read it, Article 231 was a verdict of war guilt.

The closing weeks of the peace conference, Harold Nicolson wrote in his journal, "flew past us in a hysterical nightmare." Among other things that were left undone was the convening of a congress—intended as a follow-up to the conference—to which Germany was to have been invited to discuss the Allied peace terms. Some of these terms, such as German disarmament and territorial concessions, were to be nonnegotiable, but others, including economic matters, were to be open to argument and possible change.

The failure to convene the congress was compounded by another failure. The various decisions of the conference had been embodied in what was to have been only a preliminary draft of a peace treaty; contained in it, Nicolson noted, were a number of "maximum statements" that their authors fully expected would be "modified" after the parley with the Germans. Instead, the preliminary draft became the final draft of the treaty.

A dictated rather than a negotiated peace lay in store for the Germans.

Herbert Hoover, as a member of Wilson's committee of economic advisers, received one of the first printed copies of the treaty. It arrived at his Paris flat by messenger at dawn on a day in early May. He read it with growing dismay; troubled, he went out to walk the deserted streets. Almost "by some sort of telepathy" he ran into General Jan Christiaan Smuts, the highly respected chief of the South African delegation, and John Maynard Keynes, a young British economist. The three, Hoover recalled, were of one mind: "We agreed that the consequences of many parts of the proposed treaty would ultimately bring destruction." That morning Keynes wrote to his mother: "This is a rotten peace." He thereupon resigned from the British delegation and dashed off a polemic, *The Economic Consequences of the Peace,*

Military aides of the Allied peacemakers climb up on tables, footstools and sofas for a peek into the main conference room in the Trianon Palace at Versailles on the fateful day of May 7, 1919. At the moment this picture was taken, the humiliating peace terms on which the Allies had agreed were being handed to a stunned, deeply angry German delegation.

which was to have a powerful influence in aligning informed opinion in the United States and Great Britain against the Treaty of Versailles.

That same morning, May 7, a German delegation, summoned by the Allies, prepared to receive the peace terms. En route through northern France, their train—which had been deliberately slowed down, one delegate thought—had taken them through "desolate fields, once rich with fruit, now torn apart by bombs, past the ruins of former villages . . . until we had seen all that we could stand." A special irony had awaited them at journey's end. The meeting place with the Allies was not at Paris but at nearby Versailles, the place where, after the French had been defeated in the Franco-Prussian War, a triumphant German Chancellor, Otto von Bismarck, had proclaimed a new German Empire.

In the six months since the Armistice of November 1918, the German people had suffered the trauma of defeat in a war their leaders had told them they were winning. Many, especially the urban poor, had known actual starvation; the Allied blockade—not lifted until April 1919—had closed off food from abroad, and German farmers either hoarded their homegrown produce or bootlegged it to those who could pay. Revolutionary uprisings in a number of cities had ousted local officials and replaced them with Soviet-style councils of soldiers and workers. In once-orderly Germany, savage street fighting between factions of the Left and Right became a common occurrence.

Yet in the face of turmoil, a republic had been proclaimed and a representative assembly elected. The seat of government had been moved from the shambles of Berlin to the town of Weimar, associated with the best traditions of German culture. Guiding the new Weimar Republic, first as its Chancellor, soon as its President, was Friedrich Ebert. In early years a saddler by trade, Ebert had risen to prominence as a leader of the Social Democrats, the party of the trade unionists and middle-class liberals.

One fateful incident had made it possible to fend off utter chaos in Germany. On November 9, 1918, while his colleague Matthias Erzberger was at Compiègne pleading for some mitigation of the Armistice terms, Ebert was sitting alone in an office of the old Imperial Chancellery in Berlin. He could hear the shouts of members of the Spartacist League, Germany's Communist party, as they marched down the broad avenue Unter den Linden. At that moment Ebert, as head of a government without a constitution, was uncertain how he would maintain himself against the Spartacist leader, Karl Liebknecht, who was imminently planning to proclaim a Soviet republic. Suddenly a phone on the desk

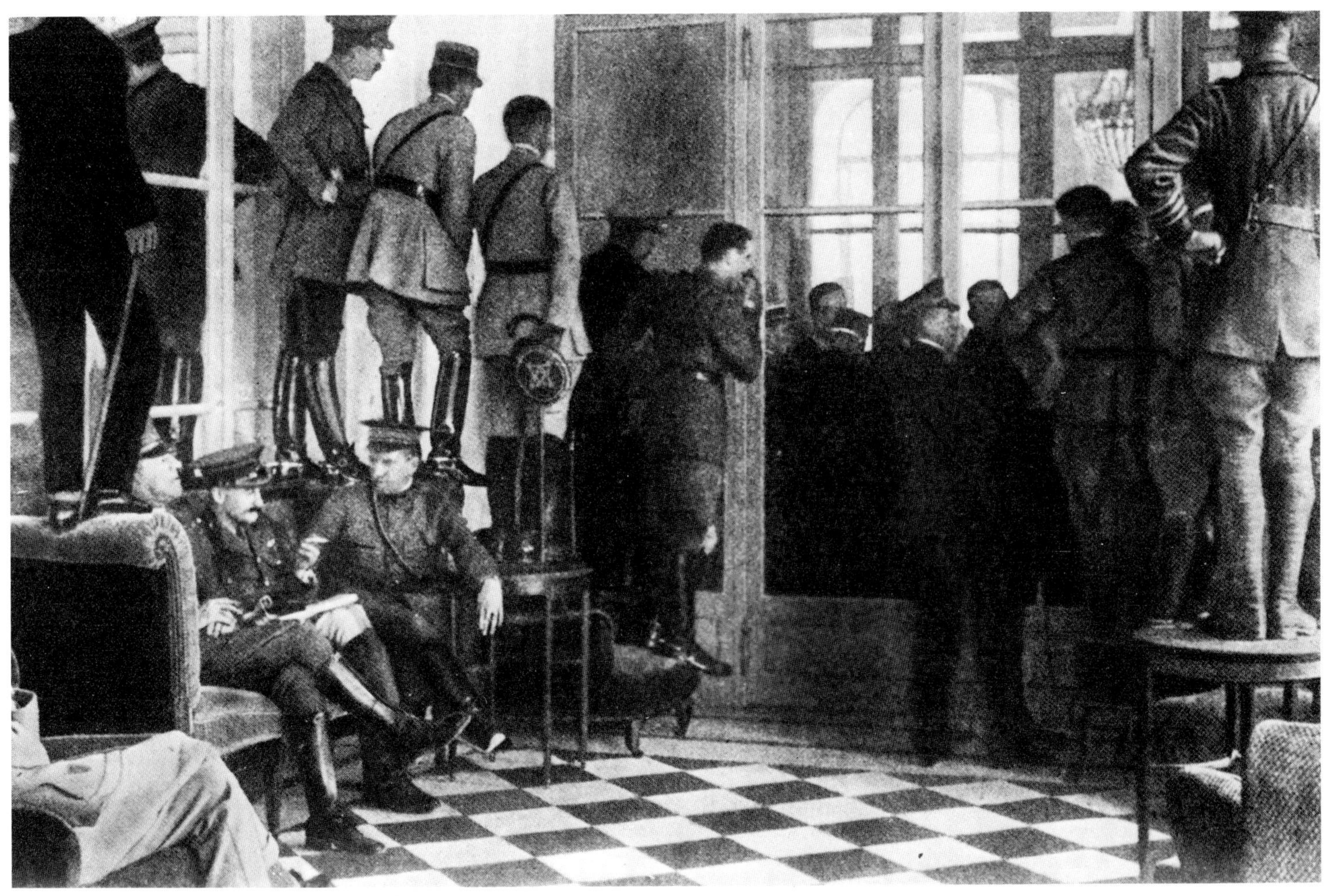

rang; it was the private line between the Chancellery and German Army Headquarters in Belgium.

"Gröner speaking," said a voice. General Wilhelm Gröner, who recently had been appointed Chief Staff Officer under Field Marshal von Hindenburg, had questions for the new Chancellor. Was the government determined to maintain order? It was. Was it determined to fight off Bolshevik-style revolution? The government was. In that case, said Gröner, the German Army was prepared to maintain discipline, to bring the troops back home in good order and to support the government.

In that telephone call, a link was forged between the German officer class and the new government—a link that ensured to post-Armistice Germany a sense of historical continuity. A month later, when the returning German Army marched through the Brandenburg Gate in Berlin, Ebert greeted it with the words, "I salute you who return unvanquished from the field of battle."

Ebert thought he was simply paying the soldiers a compliment. But unwittingly he had contributed to a myth that the German Army would sedulously cultivate—that it had not been defeated on the field of battle but had been "stabbed in the back" by craven civilians on the home front.

The Germans had managed to survive as a nation, but they had also been living on rash expectations as to the world outside. They did not sense the hatred they had engendered, and they had little feeling of war guilt. Having sued for the Armistice on the basis of Wilson's Fourteen Points and his subsequently stated peace aims, they were not prepared for the rigidity and severity of the terms presented to them at Versailles.

Count Ulrich von Brockdorff-Rantzau, Germany's new Foreign Minister, headed the delegation. He personified the continuity between the new Germany and the old, coming from a noble family that numbered among its ancestors a onetime Marshal of France reputed to have been the real father of Louis XIV.

This proud man was shocked to be received like a criminal before the bar of justice. Clemenceau stiffly presented the treaty and said no discussion of its terms was permitted. German objections must be presented in writing.

Clemenceau had risen to make his remarks. The Count replied sitting down. Later he was to say that he feared he might break down if he got to his feet, but others at the scene saw the gesture as calculated insolence. Clemenceau purpled. Lloyd George vented his feelings by snapping a letter opener in two. Wilson turned to him and murmured: "Isn't it just like them?"

The Count did not hide his anger in his response. Bitterly he said: "It is demanded that we confess ourselves guilty. Such a confession in my mouth would be a lie." Hundreds of thousands of noncombatants, he asserted, had perished because of the Allied food blockade. "Think of that when you speak of guilt and punishment," he said. "The peace that may not be defended in the name of right before the world calls forth new resistance against it."

So far different were the terms from Wilson's Fourteen Points that the Germans back home reacted with outrage and a sense of betrayal. President Ebert called the terms "unrealizable and unbearable." Mass protests were held throughout the country. There was furious talk of resuming the War. Brockdorff-Rantzau resigned rather than sign the treaty. But when Ebert turned to Gröner and Hindenburg, they told him that resistance was futile. The Germans filed 443 pages of objections to the treaty—itself 230 pages long—and won only slight mitigation of the terms. The issue hung in doubt until the last. An hour and 20 minutes before the time limit set by the victors for final acceptance of the treaty, the Germans yielded.

The formal signing ceremony took place at the great Palace of Versailles in the Hall of Mirrors, the same resplendent room where the German Empire had been proclaimed a half century earlier. The date was June 28, exactly five years from the day the Austrian Archduke Ferdinand had been assassinated at Sarajevo—the spark that ignited the War. The book of the treaty lay on a table of gleaming rosewood and sandalwood. At Clemenceau's invitation, the Germans signed first. Even as the ceremony proceeded, guns began to boom outside and the sumptuous fountains of Versailles played for the first time since the War began.

The separate treaties with Austria, Hungary, Bulgaria and Turkey were yet to be drawn up. But the treaty with the Germans was the keystone, and on Wilson's return to Washington in July he went at once before the Senate to urge its ratification. When he entered the chamber, two Senators refused to rise. Woodrow Wilson was worn, pale and tense, fully aware of the mounting opposition to himself and to his proposed League of Nations. The Senatorial opposition was compounded of many elements, among them resentment of Wilson's partisan appeal in the 1918 Congressional elections. There also was anger that Japan had been awarded Shantung Province: China was America's friend by tradition and sentiment.

Above all was a distrust of the provisions of the Covenant of the League of Nations, which had been incorporated in the treaty. Among the more extreme objections was that the whole idea of the League threatened America's precious sovereignty and thus "repealed the Declaration of Independence." Many Americans focused their fears on Article X of the Covenant, which provided for preserving the territorial integrity and political independence of League members —and would thus, it was argued, suck the United States into all sorts of little wars in Europe.

Yet the Senate might have voted for American entry into the League had Wilson been willing to accept some reservations: that the League was not to arbitrate any matters concerning the Monroe Doctrine, that no American troops could be employed without Congressional authorization, that the United States could withdraw from the League if Congress so resolved.

Determined that the Senate should accept or reject the treaty in its entirety, Wilson decided to make a direct appeal to his countrymen. Though exhausted by the long ordeal in Paris, and suffering the aftereffects of a severe infection, he undertook a cross-country speaking tour in midsummer. His wife pleaded against it in vain. When his personal physician warned him to conserve his strength, Wilson brusquely cut him off: "I cannot put my personal safety, my health in balance against my duty."

There were then no Presidential jets, no air conditioning or electrical voice amplification to ease the way. Wilson planned some 26 major speeches and many whistle stops. In Pueblo, Colorado, the trip came to an abrupt end. Wilson suffered a stroke. The Presidential train roared back to Washington, with the tracks cleared and blinds drawn. For two months Wilson remained in critical condition, helpless and out of communication. In the Senate, meanwhile, the opposition—led by Senator Henry Cabot Lodge of Massachusetts—maneuvered to kill passage of the treaty.

When the President was able again to face affairs of state, his wife, among others, urged him to consider a compromise that might save the League. "Little girl, don't you desert me; that I cannot stand," he replied. "Better to go down fighting than to dip your colors to dishonorable compromise." To the end, with Wilson, it was all or nothing. The United States did not ratify the treaty; it signed a separate peace with Germany in 1921.

The Treaty of Versailles brought no peace; rather it prolonged the truce that began with the Armistice and led to 20 years of recurring crises that culminated in World War II. The map of Europe, which had been remade on the principle of self-determination, provided boundaries for the new states of Poland, Czechoslovakia, Rumania and Yugoslavia. Yet those new boundaries placed in close proximity ethnic minorities that ranged across the Middle European spectrum from Germans to Slavs—many of whom were mutually and traditionally antagonistic. People in other parts of the world exchanged the rule of one foreign power for the rule of another. In the tinderbox Middle East, Britain and France divided the territories of the old Ottoman Empire under League of Nations "mandates"—a softer term than annexation. And on the Chinese mainland Japan now had a strong physical presence.

Instead of reconciliation, the Peace of Paris left a legacy of frustration and hatred. The French felt deprived of the full fruits of victory, and proceeded to build a new system of military alliances to hedge in Germany. The Italians felt cheated, and began to see merit in Benito Mussolini's new chauvinistic doctrine of Fascism. The Germans felt betrayed, and would be increasingly swayed by Adolf Hitler's expansionist National Socialist movement.

The Russians, having had no voice at the peace conference, felt no need to abide by any of the decisions made there. The United States, having kept itself apart from the League, retreated into isolationism.

Woodrow Wilson had made a bleak prophecy in January 1917. A punitive peace, he had warned, would "leave a sting, a resentment, a bitter memory upon which the terms of peace would rest, not permanently, but only as upon quicksand." By 1919 the prophecy was beginning to come true.

KILLING GROUND IN RUSSIA

Battle-ready soldiers of the post-Czarist parliamentary government guard public buildings in Petrograd against Bolsheviks.

THE MADNESS OF A SAVAGE CIVIL WAR

Mutinous machine gunners roll through Petrograd in June 1917 to protest sending more men to the front in the final days of the war with Germany.

In the five years following the first rattle of gunfire in the Bolshevik uprising in 1917, life became Russia's cheapest commodity. Czarist troops mutinied, murdering their officers. Cities seethed with mobs of rampaging soldiers and sailors, whose numbers swelled when a quickly concluded peace with Germany released millions of men from the front. This was a golden chance to settle grudges, political or personal. Thousands did; but soon this random killing grew into the more methodical death dance of a civil war.

The Red armies of the Bolsheviks battled the White forces of the counter-revolutionaries all around the edges of the former Russian Empire. Guerrillas harried both sides, and few opportunities for slaughter were missed, on the battlefield or elsewhere. At Stavrapol in southern Russia, White General Peter Wrangel captured 3,000 Red soldiers and—to induce the rank and file to join his forces—shot all 370 of their officers and noncoms. At Nikolaevsk, one Siberian partisan band massacred 6,000 Russian men, women and children, along with a Japanese garrison. Red sailors at Sevastopol slaughtered hundreds of men, women and children. Siberian forces under the White commander Alexander Kolchak executed 1,500 captives at Omsk. White Cossacks dragged in prisoners at the ends of lariats; Reds nailed the epaulettes of captured White officers to their shoulders. A troublesome Red guerrilla who fell into White hands was roasted alive in the firebox of a locomotive.

Horrifying though these military killings were, what happened to civilians was, if anything, worse. White pogroms in southern Russia alone killed some 100,000 Jews. The Cheka, or Red secret police, executed scores of thousands—including 500 luckless victims in Petrograd slain in retaliation for the assassination of the local Cheka boss. Disease and hunger, sweeping the land in the wake of national chaos, took 3.5 million Russians from typhus and another two million or more from starvation. Altogether, those five ghastly years of civil war, accompanied by the famine and pestilence, killed up to 15 million Russians—6.5 million more than the total deaths on all fronts during World War I.

Student militiamen flourish bayoneted rifles in front of the entrance of Moscow's Metropole Hotel during the spate of fighting that overthrew the Czar.

Confused fighting raged through Petrograd in mid-July of 1917 as the Bolshevik takeover momentarily faltered. Here, the survivors of a crowd being fired upon by machine gunners flee along the Nevsky Prospekt.

Early in 1917, dissident students fire across Petrograd's Moika Canal at police—hated holdovers from the years of Czarist oppression and favorite targets of revolutionaries.

Reds in Petrograd assume proud postures around an armored car that was captured from government forces in October 1917.

Soldiers of one of the many White Armies that fought in Russia's three-year civil war survey a heap of Bolshevik corpses. At first the White Armies easily routed the undisciplined Reds. But from 1918 on, War Commissar Leon Trotsky, rushing from one battlefront to another in his armored train, reorganized the Red Armies and went on the offensive. Among Trotsky's conducive disciplinary measures were firing squads for laggards and turncoats.

Troops of the 339th U.S. Infantry Regiment guard the Vologda railroad south of Archangel in northern Russia. Ostensibly sent to protect Allied war supplies, the Americans became part of an ill-fated plan to encircle and crush the Bolsheviks. But the Reds, under their new leaders, grew ever stronger, the weather grew colder—down to 50° below zero during the winter of 1919—and American soldiers joined the legions of war dead in Russia.

Beneath an ornate welcoming arch, fresh British troops march into Archangel to relieve departing United States forces in May 1919. The British themselves withdrew, bag and baggage, in August of the same year, leaving behind only an ill-trained and unenthusiastic White Russian Army, which melted away when its general fled to Norway on an icebreaker. The Reds then moved into Archangel at their leisure and took it over without firing a shot.

THE FARCE OF INTERVENTION

To Allied leaders, Russia's civil war seemed a heaven-sent chance to destroy the Bolsheviks, who had deserted from the war with Germany and were now menacing civilization with world revolution. In mid-1918, the Reds controlled only about a tenth of Russia's vast expanse. To bolster the White Armies—and to gain political advantage and perhaps a chunk or two of Russian territory for themselves—the various Allies sent in large amounts of money, supplies and men.

Among the 100,000 troops of 14 nations that invaded Russia from every side were 5,500 United States soldiers, who were diverted in August 1918 from the Western Front to the bleak port of Archangel on the White Sea. Untrained and badly equipped for arctic combat, they nevertheless pitched in and became the core of a joint United States-British-Canadian-French expeditionary force. This jerry-built army almost immediately launched an attack that eventually carried 450 miles south through bogs, blizzards, mosquitoes, trackless forests and gradually stiffening Red armies. Along the way U.S. Army Engineers strengthened their base camps with stout log forts from which the Yanks beat off Red attacks like frontiersmen repelling Indians.

After nine months the Americans were withdrawn and sent home, having lost 244 men in the ill-conceived venture. The field of battle was left largely to the Reds, the Whites—and to the one alien force *(overleaf)* in all of Russia that achieved anything at all worthwhile.

An American soldier ladling out soup to Red Army prisoners inArchangel clutches the basic weapon of the 339th Infantry—a Russian rifle. To their dismay, the United States soldiers were issued these long, clumsy weapons in lieu of their familiar Lee-Enfields since supplies already in Archangel included much small-arms ammunition that could be used only in Russian guns, and to planners in London, a rifle was a rifle.

A TOUGH LEGION'S OUTLANDISH ODYSSEY

Of all the foreign units in Russia, none fought longer, more effectively or with half so good a purpose as a force that was drawn into the conflict by accident. This was a legion of 42,000 Czechs, all former prisoners and deserters from the Austro-Hungarian army. Sponsored and paid by France, they had battled Germany alongside Russian armies on the Eastern Front. When Russia left the War, the Allies persuaded the Bolsheviks to help ship the Czechs home. The Czechs were glad to go, but there was one problem. Since the hostile Central Powers barred the route west, the Czechs would have to cross 5,000 miles of Siberia, then sail from Vladivostok back around to Western Europe.

The Czechs shrugged and shouldered arms, but even as they set off, the Bolsheviks nervously tried to disarm them. That was a big mistake. The Czechs brushed aside the local Red force, seized a section of the Trans-Siberian railroad, complete with rolling stock, and headed down the track for Vladivostok.

En route, the Legion entertained a few proposals—one from Winston Churchill—to support White offensives. For a while, the Czechs even fought under a White commander, Admiral Alexander Kolchak. But they never abandoned their real goal of getting home. As the Legion steamed along, capturing weapons and armoring its trains, it grew in firepower and prosperity. The soldiers—and the women many of them had picked up—lived in remodeled boxcars, which were nostalgically painted with Czech landscapes. Aboard the various commandeered trains were a rolling bank, a post office, the presses that printed a daily Czech newspaper, and a looted Czarist treasure trove: 29 carloads of gold, silver, platinum and gems.

Near the end of their journey, confronted by a formidable Red force, the Czechs offered up the treasure train and delivered Kolchak to a Red firing squad in return for a clear track to Vladivostok. They got it, and late in 1920, after two years and more than 15,000 miles, the Legionnaires arrived home to the brand new, sovereign nation of Czechoslovakia.

Men of the Czech Legion start their long trek across Siberia aboard a commandeered Russian freight train fortified with sandbags. "The pages of history," wrote an admiring Winston Churchill of the Czech odyssey, "recall scarcely any parallel episode at once so romantic in character and so extensive in scale."

2

The Petrograd tea party
Massacre at the Winter Palace
Parliament challenges the Czar
The mortal wound of Tannenberg
Abdication of a stubborn autocrat
Safe passage for an explosive package
A vast army disintegrates
The punishing peace of Brest-Litovsk
Russians against Russians
Violent end for the Imperial family
A surprising dose of capitalism
All power to Stalin

THE SOVIET SPECTRE

On an autumn evening in her apartment in Petrograd, Galina Sukhanova was awaiting guests. She had not told her husband that she would be entertaining; that morning, as he left for his newspaper office, she had suggested that he sleep there overnight. Unsuspecting, he had readily agreed; at this time of upheaval, with the new Provisional Government that had replaced the Czar still shaky, the streets were dangerous after dark. The Sukhanovs were a devoted couple, faithful to each other in everything but politics. He belonged to the Mensheviks, she to the Bolsheviks—two parties that were once one but were now irreparably split.

As she gathered the glasses for tea and prepared sausage sandwiches, Madame Sukhanova felt pleasantly conspiratorial and more than a little flattered at having been asked to lend her apartment for a secret meeting of the Central Committee of the Bolshevik Party. But she had no way of knowing that on this night of October 23, 1917, she would witness history in the making: a decision that would transform Russia into the world's first Communist state, turn it against its allies in the War then still raging, and unsettle the international scene for years to come—up to the start of a second world war and, indeed, beyond it.

At nightfall Madame Sukhanova's guests began arriving, 12 men in all. Three of them were destined to shape Russia's future: Lev Davydovich Bronstein, better known to his companions as Trotsky; Iosif Vissarionovich Dzhugashvili, now operating under his sixth alias, Stalin; and the man who had summoned the meeting, Vladimir Ilyich Ulyanov, alias Lenin. On the run from the police, indicted for treason by his political foes, Lenin arrived disguised by tinted glasses and a thick wig on his bald head.

He wasted no time in coming to the point: the party must at once launch an insurrection against the Provisional Government. There was no need to go into its failings; every Bolshevik agreed that it was inept, vacillating, too concerned with democratic procedures. Worse, it persisted in pressing the war against Germany, honoring the deposed Czar's commitment to his capitalist allies in the West. The masses, Lenin declared, were weary of war, desperate for peace. History would not forgive any further delay.

Lenin was 47. In 17 years away from his homeland he had been preaching and plotting revolution, and now the hour for action was at hand.

He aroused little enthusiasm at first. "The debate was stormy, chaotic," Trotsky later remembered, "the discussion spread to fundamentals, the basic goals of the party." Time and again Lenin brought the talk back to the point—insurrection now—and fiercely he turned on those who counseled caution. Of the dozen men, Stalin alone was silent, impassively smoking his pipe. As dawn neared, Lenin seized a stub of a pencil and on a page torn from a child's school notebook wrote out a resolution: "The party calls for the organization of an armed insurrection." The vote was 10 to 2 in favor, Trotsky and Stalin among those voting aye.

Just 13 days later, after an almost bloodless coup, Lenin stood before the All-Russian Congress of Soviets as head of a new Russian government. He appeared seedy, a short, plump figure in a suit that looked as if he had slept in it. But his air of triumph was unmistakable as he told his mesmerized audience: "Comrades, the workers' and peasants' revolution has come to pass." At that moment, he had perhaps 200,000 followers in all of Russia, an infinitesimal fraction of its 150 million inhabitants. Yet with this tiny minority Lenin was to hold the reins of power in an iron grip.

Revolution was far from a new idea to the Russians, though few had expected it to take such drastic shape. What most critics of the repressive Romanov dynasty had meant when they talked of revolution was reform. They wanted the right to assemble and speak and write freely, an end to constant police spying, a popular voice in the government. They opposed a military system that conscripted soldiers for virtually half a lifetime—25 years. Above all, the reformers—men and women of deep social conscience, drawn largely from the intelligentsia and concerned nobles—yearned to lighten the abysmal lot of the lower classes. Though serfdom had been abolished, peasants were still forced to make yearly "redemption payments" to compensate their former masters for the loss of their labor. Flight from rural misery solved nothing. Workers had the alternative of a 15-hour day in a factory or an 18-hour day in a mine.

The man who was fated to be the last of the Czars, Nicholas II, had been determined to keep his autocracy intact. On acceding to the throne in 1894, he had publicly labeled his liberal subjects' aspirations as "senseless dreams." The effect was predictable. Increasingly, those who had sought reform within the established order began to join those who advocated the order's overthrow.

A militant activism replaced the leisured soul-searching that had characterized clandestine "discussion circles." Secrecy was refined to an art. To outwit the censors, letters carried invisible messages in milk between the lines. Code names masked members of party cells. Political literature traveled in false-bottomed trunks. Through disaffected Russians who had emigrated abroad, those at home became more and more familiar with the writings of a German thinker named Karl Marx, who had died only a decade before Nicholas came to power, and who had foreseen a proletarian revolution rising victorious from the ashes of capitalism.

For a time in 1905 the Russian revolutionaries had reason for some hope. A disastrous war with Japan sparked open criticism of the Czarist role in the debacle. The plain speaking spilled over to domestic grievances, and on a Sunday in January striking factory workers and their families massed at the Winter Palace, the imperial residence in Saint Petersburg. Troops fired into the throng, killing hundreds.

Bloody Sunday, as it was soon known, launched more than half a year of wild disorder throughout the Empire: strikes, peasant riots, mutinies by soldiers and sailors, the assassination of several dozens of government officials every week. Counterterror brought pitched battles in city streets and pogroms against two hapless minorities: the Jews in the Ukraine and the Armenians in Azerbaidzhan.

Unrest peaked in October with a general strike and an event of greater augury for the future: the formation in Saint Petersburg of a Soviet of Workers' Deputies. The word soviet, meaning council, had long been in common usage, but never before in this startling context. The Soviet of Workers' Deputies was soon forcibly disbanded; but the mere fact of its formation sent tremors through the regime.

Persuaded at last that he must yield some ground, the Czar agreed to let his people elect a parliament—though no soldier, sailor, student, woman or anyone under 25 was allowed to vote, and those elected were to have no control whatever over the Czar's ministers. The name chosen for this body was Duma (meaning thought) after an ancient Russian conclave at which nobles mulled their problems. But if Nicholas expected the Duma to pass its time in quiet meditation, he was quickly disabused. Loudly its members called for such reforms as amnesty for political prisoners and redistribution of landed estates to the peasants. The Duma lasted only two months before the Czar irately dissolved it.

A second Duma proved even more fractious than the first and met the same fate. But the institution had taken hold; it was invaluable as a forum. A third Duma functioned, then a fourth. It was this body, for all the restraints that hobbled it, that presided at the Czar's undoing.

The Russians' initial reaction to Germany's declaration of war on August 1, 1914, was everything the Czar could have wished. Duma members outdid one another in expressions of loyalty. Workers pledged not to strike. Outside the Winter Palace, where Bloody Sunday had erupted nine years earlier, crowds knelt in homage when the imperial couple appeared. People cheered a decree that changed the 200-year-old name of Saint Petersburg, with its Germanic suffix, to Petrograd (10 years later it would be changed again—to Leningrad). Less cheerfully, the public gave up another tradition when the government, to conserve grain, banned the manufacture of the cherished national drink, vodka.

The flood tide of patriotic feeling ebbed before August had ended. More than 100,000 Russian soldiers died in the Battle of Tannenberg in East Prussia: another 93,000 were taken prisoner. Responding to pleas by its French and British allies to take some German pressure off the Western Front, Russia had mobilized immense forces and sent them slogging across Russian Poland into enemy territory in 17 days. But the troops were ill-trained, supply lines unreliable and communications between sectors nonexistent.

Despite later victories, the Russians never got over the trauma of Tannenberg. That defeat led them to see, for the first time, the extent of the dry rot behind the Romanov façade: a bureaucracy that had shrugged off the need for decent roads and rail transport; a Minister of War who boasted that he had not read a book on military science in 20 years; factories unequipped to turn out the required quantities of boots and medical supplies.

The scandal in armaments was the worst. A million shells a month were being used up, but only 100,000 were being produced. Rifles were so scarce that infantrymen were ordered to advance empty-handed in battle, in the hope that before they made contact with the foe they would find the weapons of comrades fallen in earlier waves. Sheer manpower proved to be Russia's greatest resource. But it was spent so prodigally that of the 15 million soldiers called up in the War, more than four million died in action.

In September 1915 the Czar decided to take personal command of his troops and installed himself at supreme headquarters at Mogilev. Apparently this notion was not his but the Czarina's. German-born, at least as imperious as her husband and of far tougher fiber, Alexandra tried to stiffen Nicholas's spine by bombarding him with letters urging him to be a leader. "Be more autocratic, my very own sweetheart, show your mind," she wrote. "Ah, my love, when at last will you thump with your hand upon the table?" Nicholas, in turn, signed his letters to his wife as "Your poor little weak-willed hubby." In his absence from Petrograd, he was manifestly content to have the Czarina act, in effect, as the regent of Russia.

The War was soon a total catastrophe. By 1917 Russia's Army had lost all plausibility as a threat to the Germans, who occupied part of southwestern Russia and were seizing its rich crops. The people of Russia's cities were short of food, of fuel and of temper. There were long queues for everything and the prices, compared to prewar 1914, were infuriating: almost eight times as much for flour, six times as much for meat, five times as much for common salt.

Antiwar feeling intensified, and so did anger at the monarchy. Browsing in a bookshop, a diplomat noticed a stack of copies of a book about the assassination of Czar Paul I in 1801. "Very popular book right now," the clerk remarked. Increasingly, suspicion was voiced that Russia's reverses in battle, hence its woes on the home front, were the fault of that "German woman"—the Czarina. A joke went around: A general comes upon the little Czarevich, who was crying in a corridor of the Winter Palace. Why the tears? The boy smiles and answers rather impishly: "When the Russians are beaten, Papa cries; when the Germans are beaten, Mama cries. When, then, am I to cry?"

On February 23, 1917, the day after Nicholas left Petrograd to return to his headquarters, the first phase of the Russian revolution began. It was entirely unplanned; as one historian later wrote, "the mass moved of itself." Women textile workers, joined by metallurgical workers who had been locked out after a wage strike, marched on the center of the city, shouting for bigger bread rations and breaking

MURDER OF A MALEVOLENT MYSTIC

Nothing symbolized the corrupt decline of the Romanov dynasty more surely than did the life and death of the unsavory poseur called Rasputin. He was invited to court in 1905 after being introduced to the Czarina as a mystic with unusual powers. Born Grigory Novykh, he was a drunken, semiliterate Siberian peasant who claimed to be a monk, was an unabashed lecher, never bathed and reveled in the nickname Rasputin, "The Debauched One."

Yet women worshipped him. This was particularly true of the Czarina. For Rasputin did have an inexplicable ability to control the lethal bleeding that afflicted Czarevich Alexei, the hemophiliac heir to the Romanov throne. So grateful was the Czarina that by 1916 Rasputin had become her closest adviser—and the most powerful and hated man in Russia.

At last his enemies conspired to remove the monk by assassination—an enterprise that proved to be grotesquely difficult.

On December 29, 1916, Rasputin arrived for a supper at the palace of Prince Felix Yusupov *(right)*, the Czar's nephew by marriage. While a phonograph blared *Yankee Doodle*, and the Czar's cousin Grand Duke Dmitry along with several other conspirators waited nervously upstairs, the guest gobbled cakes laced with cyanide.

Serene in this early portrait, Prince Felix Yusupov became infuriated by Rasputin. A fiercely nationalistic blueblood, Yusupov regarded the fraudulent, brutish mystic not only as a threat to the Imperial Court but also as an insult to the Russian aristocracy.

But the cakes made Rasputin no more than drowsy. He then drained five glasses of poisoned wine—which merely reduced him to a state of glassy-eyed belligerence. At that point the frustrated Yusupov drew a revolver and shot him in the chest. The others rushed downstairs, took a quick look, and with Yusupov hurried off to discuss disposal of the corpse.

After a while, Yusupov returned—and was horrified to see Rasputin lurching toward him. The monk staggered out of the room and into a courtyard, where he was shot twice more, wrapped in a curtain and tossed into the icy Neva River, dead at last.

When the Czarina heard that Yusupov was implicated in the murder, she first ordered the Prince executed, then relented and banished him to his estate near Moscow. Few other Russians shared her anger. Indeed, as the Imperial regime collapsed the following year, there was only a residual feeling of contempt for the botched murder: Bolshevik leader Leon Trotsky dismissed it as an act "carried out in the manner of a moving picture scenario designed for people of bad taste."

A short time before his murder, the bearded Rasputin sat for this picture—probably his final one—at a party given by admiring ladies of the Imperial Court.

into bakeries along the way. A few stones were tossed at police, but the protesters were less interested in defying authority than in filling their stomachs. The next day brought 200,000 workers out on strike and some sharp but still random clashes with the police. On the following day it seemed as if all of Petrograd had taken to the streets, an angry, roaming multitude ready for any action. Shops and private homes were looted and police stations set afire. Cossack horsemen —the Czar's dreaded riot police—arrived to help disperse the mobs. But observers noticed that some Cossacks were actually trading pleasantries with the demonstrators.

That evening the Czar telegraphed the Petrograd garrison's commander: "I order that the disorders be stopped by tomorrow." But most of the 200,000 men in the garrison were resentful new recruits or battle-weary invalids. Sent forth from the barracks to deal with the mobs, one army unit after another shot its officers and deserted to the demonstrators. Five days after the revolution began, the participants recognized it for what it was, and all restraints came off. Police and government officials were overpowered, some slain; the arsenals were seized and the prisons emptied.

The President of the Duma had urged the Czar to return to Petrograd immediately because "the last hour has struck when the fate of the dynasty and the country is being decided." The Czar's reply was: "Dissolve the Duma"—his stock cure in earlier crises. Instead, the Duma elected a dozen of its members to a provisional committee charged with restoring order in Petrograd. Without fanfare, the committee then became the Provisional Government.

But another group also emerged: the Petrograd Soviet of Workers' and Soldiers' Deputies, political heir to the Saint Petersburg Soviet of 1905. A spontaneous outgrowth of the demonstrations, it included representatives of rank-and-file factory workers and of insurgent soldiers, left-wing Duma members and freed political prisoners. The Provisional Government had no choice but to make the raucous soviet its working partner. The soviet took over a wing of the same palace that housed the new government and kept an eye on all its doings. Friction was inevitable. As one observer put it, the government had responsibility without power, the soviet had power without responsibility.

On March 2, on his special train en route from Army Headquarters, the Czar received two envoys from the Provisional Government requesting his abdication. The formalities that ended over a thousand years of Russian monarchy were brief; the Czar's generals had already urged him to take the same step. Nicholas was outwardly tranquil as he signed the act of abdication, though he betrayed some inner turmoil by abdicating first in favor of his son, then suddenly changing his mind and leaving the throne to his younger brother, the Grand Duke Mikhail. But Mikhail refused the throne, calling for a freely elected government.

In this wish, the new provisional regime devoutly concurred. But a month later Lenin arrived back in Russia from exile, bearing his own radically different ideas of the kind of government that would be best for his countrymen.

Like most revolutionaries of his generation, Lenin came from a comfortable background. His father was an inspector of schools who had been honored by the Czarist regime for his services to education. Yet this amiable bureaucrat produced six children all fiercely bent on the regime's destruction. When Lenin was 17, his older brother, a university student, was arrested, convicted and hanged for his part in a plot to assassinate Czar Alexander III.

Within a few years Lenin himself was in trouble, expelled from the University of Kazan for seditious activities. He moved on to Saint Petersburg, studied law, and actually set up practice as a lawyer. But he soon discovered Marxism and a vocation more to his liking—professional agitator.

The Czar's secret police nailed him when he organized a group called the "Union of Struggle for the Liberation of the Working Class," and he was banished to Russia's traditional dumping ground for malcontents, Siberia. There, in 1898, he married Nadezhda Krupskaya, a fellow Marxist who had also run afoul of the police. Under a curiously lenient ruling of the regime, radical couples who claimed to be engaged were permitted to live together in banishment provided they agreed to be married in the rites of the Orthodox Church. Lenin and Krupskaya temporarily forswore their militant atheism to go through the religious ceremony and even consented to wedding rings—which they soon put out of sight (though she secretly clung to hers ever after).

When Lenin's three-year sentence in Siberia ended, he and his wife left at once for Europe. Going abroad was much easier in the days of the Czars than it was later to prove under the Communists, and numbers of politicalized Russians seized the opportunity. Few saw themselves as permanent émigrés; most expected to go home as soon as the Romanovs were toppled. They worked tirelessly to bring about that day, producing a steady barrage of pamphlets and periodicals to be smuggled into Russia.

This was to be Lenin's way of life for 17 years, broken only by a furtive trip home in 1905-1906. He and Krupskaya resided in London, Paris, Geneva, Zurich, Berne and Munich —on the same street where Adolf Hitler was later to lodge. The couple hiked into the Alps from Geneva and cycled to Fontainebleau from Paris, but Lenin's idea of time well spent was a long day holed up in the reading room of the British Museum in London, studying and writing.

Austere in his habits, brusque and even rude in manner, Lenin struck many who met him as a man lacking in warmth. The noted writer Maxim Gorky, who admired him, observed that Lenin's mind had "the cold glitter of steel shavings." He was, in short, a classic fanatic, too unswervingly fixed on his goal to pay heed to normal human relations.

Lenin's first step toward his goal was to publish, with a few kindred spirits, a paper called *Iskra (The Spark).* The choice of the name was clearly explained in a slogan on the front page: "First the spark, then the conflagration."

Iskra served as the voice of the Russia Social Democratic Labor Party, formed inside Russia in 1898 from a number of illegal working-class groups. But Lenin had some ideas that profoundly disturbed most of the party's supporters. As they saw it, the socialist revolution would take an indefinite time; workers would first have to be educated and organized, and a mass labor movement built. Lenin had no patience with this tedious prospect. In 1903 a party congress of 57 delegates met in Brussels to talk things over; after a few days the Belgian police ordered them to leave and they moved on to London. The bombshell Lenin had in store for them was a proposal to restrict party membership to a highly disciplined elite that would prepare for the revolution and lead the proletarian masses to victory.

Lenin was voted down by those who feared placing party control in the hands of a select few. But he took advantage of a walkout by some members over procedural matters to bid for editorial control of *Iskra*. Because he won on this and a number of other organizational points, henceforward his faction was known as the Bolsheviks (majority), his opponents as the Mensheviks (minority)—even though the Mensheviks often held a majority in later party councils.

The rift between the two factions grew steadily. Lenin despised the Mensheviks for patterning themselves after the highly moral Social Democratic parties of Western Europe. The Mensheviks were shocked when Lenin's lieutenants in Russia held up banks—such acts were called "expropriations"—to get the funds needed for their subversive activities; these robberies were committed under the direction of a Bolshevik stalwart named Stalin.

Lenin was in Switzerland at the time of the revolution of February 1917. At first he refused to believe the news. Then he was wild to get home. But he would have to go through Germany, still enemy territory for Russians. He thought of faking a Swedish passport and traveling as a deaf mute. "That won't work," said his wife. "You might dream and curse in your sleep and they would find you were no Swede."

A better idea occurred: why not ask the Germans for safe conduct? In return for passage for a party of exiles, Lenin would, once home, try to persuade the new Russian government to release an equal number of German internees. The Germans agreed, though they had more than internees in mind. Aware that Lenin had repeatedly denounced the War, they foresaw that he would work to exacerbate the antiwar feeling that was growing in Russia.

As Lenin later told the story, he insisted that the train bearing the returnees be "sealed" during its passage through Germany lest he be accused of trafficking with the enemy. In fact, the train was not sealed; the returnees were simply isolated in one car of a regular train, with no one else permitted access. One of the party, traveling companionably with Lenin and his wife, was his mistress, a pretty, auburn-haired Frenchwoman named Inessa Armand.

Lenin was uncertain about his reception in his homeland, wondering aloud if he would be arrested. But when his train pulled into Petrograd's Finland Station, a huge bouquet was thrust into his hands and he was led into the room at the station where the Czar himself used to greet visiting dignitaries. There to extend a welcome was an official party from the Petrograd Soviet Workers' and Soldiers' Deputies, headed by its chairman, a Menshevik named Nikolai Chkheidze.

At this point the Mensheviks were riding high. They had a majority in the soviet and a leading role in the Provisional Government. Despite their ambivalent feelings about their old political enemy, they felt obliged to honor a great name in the revolutionary movement.

Chkheidze was conciliatory. "The principal task is now to defend our revolution," he told Lenin, "and we hope that you will pursue this goal with us." Lenin avoided a direct answer by turning away and addressing the "dear comrades, soldiers, sailors and workers" in the crowded room, calling them "the vanguard of the international proletarian army."

Next Lenin was triumphantly paraded to Bolshevik party headquarters, the former palace of a prima ballerina, where another crowd waited. With this audience Lenin cast off all constraint. From a balcony he shouted: "Capitalist pirates are destroying Europe for the sake of the profits of a handful of exploiters! The defense of the fatherland is the defense of one set of capitalists against another!"

Even in the new revolutionary Russia such words did not sit well with everybody. A soldier in the crowd howled: "You ought to stick a bayonet in a fellow like that! If he'd come down here we'd show him. Must be a German!"

Inside party headquarters Lenin stunned the Bolshevik leaders with his militancy. There must be no support for the Provisional Government, he said, no cooperation with the Mensheviks. The Bolshevik slogan must be "All power to the Soviets." Lenin's strategy was clear; he intended to take over the Petrograd Soviet and the soviets that had been set up in other cities and make them his route to power. Madame Sukhanova's husband, the journalist, reported: "He kept hammering, hammering, hammering. . . . I felt as if I had been beaten about the head with flails."

Next day Lenin summarized his speech in what are now called The April Theses—an outline of which, in his handwriting, is enshrined in a velvet frame in the Central Museum in Moscow. To the theses of the night before, he added a fascinating new one: henceforward the Bolshevik Party would be the Communist Party, because "Social Democratic parties everywhere have betrayed socialism and have deserted to the side of their own national bourgeoisie."

Outside of Russia, Lenin's return was little noted, and even in Petrograd his opponents exulted that he had destroyed himself politically by his extreme statements. One man was not deceived. Alexander Kerensky came from Lenin's home town, Simbirsk, and his father had been Lenin's high school headmaster. Kerensky, a member of both the Duma and the Petrograd Soviet, had risen to become Minister of War in the Provisional Government and was shortly to become Russia's last non-Communist Premier. On Lenin's return, he had warned, "This man will destroy the revolution."

Kerensky and Lenin soon clashed publicly. In June, delegates from the various city soviets met in Petrograd for the first All-Russian Congress of Soviets. When one speaker urged that the Congress support the Provisional Government because there was no single party strong enough to assume power, Lenin interrupted: "There is."

Amid derisive laughter—the Bolsheviks had only 105 out of 822 delegates—he made his way to the rostrum and declared, "We are prepared to assume power at any time." The Bolsheviks, he went on, would publicize the "unheard-of" war profits of capitalists, jail 50 to 100 of them and offer "peace by breaking all ties to the capitalist world." A reporter wrote, "He paced the platform like a caged beast, squinting his eyes as if delighting in the imaginary sight of 50 capitalists being taken through the streets in cages."

Kerensky rose in rebuttal. "You Bolsheviks recommend childish prescriptions," he said. "Arrest! Kill! Destroy! What are you, socialists or police of the old regime?"

In the uproar that followed, observers noted that while Kerensky commanded the applause of a majority on the floor, it was the packed galleries that gave Lenin an ovation.

More immediately important to Lenin, he now had the support of the man who was to prove his most valuable cohort—Trotsky. Though Trotsky had often taken the side of the Mensheviks against the Bolsheviks, his credentials, from Lenin's viewpoint, were excellent. He had contributed to *Iskra,* and he had also served briefly as chairman of the historic Saint Petersburg Soviet of 1905. At the time of the February revolution he was in New York, writing for the Russian émigré paper *Novy Mir (New World).* Arriving back in Russia soon after Lenin, he had listened to the Bolshevik leader's rhetoric and found it persuasive. In Trotsky, Lenin acquired a man who was a rare combination of brilliant theoretician and daring activist. Their partnership was to bring the Communists to power.

From late June to November 1917, Russia teetered on the brink of total anarchy. Under pressure from the Allies, Minister of War Kerensky launched a new offensive against the Austrians in Galicia. This was not merely to honor Russia's old commitments; Kerensky believed that unless the enemy was driven from Russian soil, his country would have no future worth contemplating. But the Germans counterattacked and a new military disaster ensued: a million or more Russians deserted. The Army didn't need this added blow. Its morale was already shattered by an order of the Petrograd Soviet—over the heads of the Provisional Government—requiring the setting up of regimental soviets and the erasure of distinctions between officers and enlisted men.

Meanwhile, the Bolsheviks were hard at work. Their newspapers flooded the country with defeatist propaganda. Their agitators infiltrated the Army urging soldiers to fraternize with the enemy, and fanned out into the countryside inciting peasants to seize the landed estates. Many of the soldiers who deserted did so in order to get back to their villages before the spoils were divided.

In late July the Provisional Government indicted Lenin and several other Bolshevik leaders for treason. They were charged with inciting insurrection among the sailors at Kronstadt—the huge naval base in the Gulf of Finland off Petrograd—and with using German funds to do so. Lenin, forewarned, fled to Finland. Trotsky was seized and jailed. From hiding, Lenin vehemently denied that he was in Germany's pay. Secret German archives opened after World War II confirm that he did indeed have dealings with the Germans, but they do not prove he was a German agent. What they make clear is that in the ruthless pursuit of power Lenin took help wherever he could find it.

Despite the enforced absence of their leaders, lesser Bolsheviks continued their work, since no attempt was made to ban the party or punish its members. Using the increasingly persuasive slogan, "Bread, Land and Peace," they concentrated on increasing their numbers in Petrograd and in the soviets of other cities. By October the Bolsheviks had a majority in the Petrograd Soviet, and Trotsky, who had been released on bail, was elected its Chairman. It was then that Lenin decided to risk a return from Finland for the Central Committee's fateful meeting in the Sukhanov apartment.

Executing the Bolshevik seizure of power was left to Trotsky and selected associates; it was accomplished with astonishing ease. The coup was timed to the convening of the second All-Russian Congress of Soviets which, under Lenin's plan, was to proclaim the demise of the Provisional Government and approve a new Bolshevik government.

On the eve of the congress, the Red Guard—the Bolsheviks' private army, recruited from Petrograd's toughs and unemployed—moved to occupy key positions: bridgeheads, railway stations, power stations, and the central post and telegraph office. Kerensky, now in his third month as Russia's Premier, quickly learned what was happening. He found a car, managed to drive past Red Guard sentries and sped away from the capital in search of loyal troops. He never re-

To music played by a guitar-strumming soldier (left rear), Russian and German infantrymen dance together in the snow moments after learning of the December 15, 1917 armistice that took Russia out of World War I. The weary troops had been fraternizing openly for months, despite attempts by the German High Command to keep its men away from the Russians, who they rightly feared were infiltrated by Bolshevism.

turned; the small force he succeeded in raising eventually disintegrated. Kerensky himself, after eight months of hiding out, was to go into permanent exile abroad.

When the All-Russian Congress of Soviets convened, it cheered news that the Winter Palace, the last bastion of the besieged Provisional Government, had fallen. A final flicker of opposition came from Menshevik delegates at the congress, protesting the illegal usurpation of power. Contemptuously Trotsky turned to them and shouted, "Go where you belong from now on—to the garbage heap of history!"

Next evening the congress, now rid of dissenting voices, delegated its executive authority to a new government, the Soviet of People's Commissars. Lenin was named Chairman; Trotsky, Commissar for Foreign Affairs; and Stalin, Commissar for Nationalities.

In short order, a series of sweeping decrees made plain the new regime's intentions. Private ownership of property was to be abolished and the land distributed to those who worked it. Workers were to control industry. Banks were to be nationalized. Revolutionary tribunals were to replace the courts. In the foreign sphere, a decree called for an immediate armistice and a peace without annexations or indemnities; nations seeking such gains from the War were warned that they faced "the forces of world revolution."

Russia's allies had welcomed the revolution of February 1917; Britain and France had quickly recognized the Provisional Government. In April, in his speech asking Congress for a declaration of war against Germany, President Wilson had hailed the "wonderful and heartening things that have been happening in the last few weeks in Russia," and asserted that in casting off the Czarist yoke the Russians had proved that they were always "democratic at heart."

By contrast, the Bolshevik takeover dismayed the Allied camp. The new men in power seemed altogether an alien breed, scornful of traditional diplomatic niceties, openly predicting the doom of capitalist societies, zealously spreading the inflammatory message of revolution. The mistrust was mutual, and each side nurtured its own illusions. The Communists believed that Europe was on the brink of revolution; the Allies believed that the Communist regime would presently be overthrown. These beliefs were to help abort attempts at reconciliation during the final peace conference at Paris in 1919, and were to color all contacts between the two worlds far into the future.

Less than three weeks after the Communists took over, they confirmed the Allies' worst fears. They opened negotiations with the Germans for an armistice, thus raising the prospect that millions of German troops would be freed for an offensive on the Western front.

The Russo-German Armistice was signed at the bleak Polish frontier town of Brest-Litovsk on December 15, 1917, and further talks to resolve the final peace terms were set for January. It was during this phase of the negotiations that the Communists put on their first spectacular show of contempt for time-tried diplomatic decorum. Trotsky and his delegation arrived not like negotiators but agitators, scandalizing the Germans by passing out revolutionary leaflets to their soldiers. When the head of the German delegation, Foreign Minister Richard von Kühlmann, proposed that the treaty express the desire of the two parties "to live in peace and harmony," Trotsky mockingly dismissed the idea.

"How can you object to so lofty a sentiment?" asked Kühlmann. "Such declarations are merely copied from one diplomatic document to another . . ." Trotsky broke in with

"You—Have you enrolled as a volunteer yet?" demands the glowering Red Army soldier in this 1920 poster, printed during the civil war between Bolsheviks and Whites. The design is oddly reflective of the famous Uncle Sam "I Want YOU!" recruiting poster of World War I, which, in turn, resembled a famous British appeal from the same era, featuring Britain's Army Chief, Lord Kitchener. The vivid Russian version was part of a massive manpower drive that helped build the Red Army from a militia numbering thousands to a victorious force of millions.

cold irony, "and do not represent the true relations between nations." Kühlmann's phrase was deleted.

Then the Germans delivered a shock of their own: unprecedentedly punitive peace terms that, in sum, required Russia to give up a third of its arable land and industry. While the Bolsheviks furiously debated among themselves, some arguing that their war be continued, the Germans resumed their offensive. Lenin then decided that the Soviets would sign a peace treaty at whatever price. Some of his colleagues, horrified, came perilously close to accusing him of treason to the cause. Lenin stood firm. "Yes, I will sign a shameful peace," he told objectors. "But I will save the soldiers of the revolution. I will save the revolution. Comrades, what is your will?" They were silent.

Eight months after the Treaty of Brest-Litovsk was signed on March 3, 1918, its terms were made moot by Germany's surrender to the Allies. But by then the Communists were deep in another war—a savage, no-quarter civil war.

Portents of this struggle had appeared even as the Bolsheviks seized power. In Moscow, their forces had to fight a week's bloody battles against military units opposed to Bolshevik rule before the city capitulated. Southern Russia, less easily accessible to the country's new masters, proved totally recalcitrant; Ukrainian nationalists and other separatist groups set up their own independent regimes.

After only a month in office, Lenin and his associates began to assess the dimensions of the resistance they faced. Right-wing parties and newspapers were banned. For the time being, non-Bolshevik left-wing groups were allowed to go on functioning, but the risks of nonconformity were made clear with the establishment of the All-Russian Extraordinary Commission for Combatting Counterrevolution and Sabotage—Cheka for short. It was, in effect, the reincarnation of the Czarist secret police, and it was destined to become a permanent feature of the Soviet system under a succession of such initials as GPU, NKVD, and MVD.

One of the Cheka's first decrees proclaimed that "all those trying to join counterrevolutionary forces shall be shot on the spot." One early victim was a young woman named Fanny Kaplan, an anti-Bolshevik left-winger who managed to fire point blank at Lenin, wounding him in the neck and lung. She was executed—and so were hundreds of randomly selected hostages.

The new regime also dealt ruthlessly with the Constituent Assembly. This body, as projected by the Provisional Government, was to have drafted a democratic constitution for Russia, and its members were to have been elected by universal secret suffrage. Despite the intervening Bolshevik coup, the balloting had actually taken place on two days in November 1917—the first, and only, free election ever held in Russia. The results spoke volumes about the Bolsheviks' real strength. Of 36,265,560 votes cast, they got 9,023,963—roughly 25 per cent, in contrast to 58 per cent for another left-wing group, the Socialist Revolutionaries—the party of both Alexander Kerensky and Fanny Kaplan.

In January 1918, when the Assembly convened in Petrograd, the Bolshevik delegates—168 out of a total of 707—proposed that the Soviet of People's Commissars be recognized as the present, and future, government. When the resolution was rejected they walked out. The other delegates continued deliberating. But the next morning, when they gathered for a second session, their way was barred by troops. The Soviet of People's Commissars, they were informed, had dissolved the Constituent Assembly.

Six weeks later, for security reasons, the government moved inland from Petrograd to Russia's historic capital, Moscow. No advance notice was given and the train bearing the commissars traveled through the night without lights. Henceforward Lenin and his successors ruled from within the walled fortress of ancient Muscovy, the Kremlin.

Full-scale civil war broke out in May 1918, in the wake of skirmishes between Soviet troops and two divisions of Czech soldiers who had fought as a legion in the Provisional Government's forces against Germany *(page 42)* and who were now en route back to Europe by way of Siberia to avoid risk of capture by the Germans. Somewhere in the Urals, the feisty Czechs clashed with Soviet authorities. In this conflict they were soon joined by anti-Bolshevik Russian forces that had been biding their time underground—so-called Whites, led by ex-Czarist officers. Soon White armies controlled most of the country from the Volga River to the Pacific.

To oppose the White armies, the Bolsheviks had only one understrength division plus the Red Guard, which numbered only 7,000 men. In this emergency, Trotsky assumed the post of War Commissar and began to build the Red Army. At first he recruited only volunteers whose loyalty could be vouched for by party cells or trade unions. But lacking officers, he made an exception for Czarist officers willing to serve the new regime. When party members furiously charged that "Czarist flunkeys" were enlisting only to betray the revolution, Trotsky placed a political commissar beside each officer from company commander on up. No order was valid unless countersigned by both. Moreover, Trotsky decreed, "If any detachment retreats without orders, the first to be shot will be the commissar, next the officer."

The system was cumbersome, it made for suspicion and rivalry, but it worked. By the civil war's end in 1920 Trotsky had built a Red Army of 5,000,000 men—an extraordinary achievement for a man whose name has since been erased from the Communist history books.

The war was an ever-shifting struggle—all across Russia's enormous landspace. At one point the White armies controlled more than nine tenths of the country. What saved the Bolsheviks was the fact they were fighting a divided enemy. The White army attacks, under Admiral Kolchak and Generals Denikin, Yudenich and Wrangel, were never coordinated; the leaders themselves were often rivals.

To complicate the civil war still further, the Allies stepped in—with 100,000 troops and well over $100 million in military aid—on the side of the Whites *(pages 40-41)*. But the intervention, ill-planned and sloppily executed, not only failed to bolster the anti-Bolshevik cause; in the long run it actually worked to the Reds' advantage. They were able to portray themselves as defenders of the homeland against the foreigner, thereby enlisting support from thousands who otherwise would have opposed the Communists.

The war abounded in indescribable cruelty. Both Reds and Whites murdered, pillaged, raped and burned. The Czar and his family were occupying a merchant's house in Ekaterinburg in the Urals. When rumors spread that the Czech Legion was near, the Communists decided to kill the imperial family. They were roused at midnight, taken to the cellar, and shot, bayoneted and clubbed to death. The bodies were then hacked to pieces, soaked with benzine, burned and thrown down a mineshaft. A week later, White troops entering the city could find no traces of them.

News of the execution, telegraphed by the local soviet, reached Moscow as Lenin and his associates were discussing new public health measures. The telegram was read. There was no comment. Then Lenin coolly said, "Let us now proceed to read the draft legislation point by point." Trotsky later felt impelled to offer an explanation of the execution. Among other reasons, he wrote, it had been done to show the Bolsheviks that "there was no turning back, that ahead lay either complete victory or complete ruin."

The price of victory came high. To some 100,000 Russians dead as a direct result of the civil war were added millions who perished of hunger and of typhus. Inessa Armand was one of the plague's victims. The ashes of Lenin's former mistress were buried alongside the Kremlin wall—a high Communist honor even in those early days. Lenin walked in the procession with eyes closed, seemingly on the verge of collapse. It may have been soon afterward that he showed an uncharacteristically despondent side to his friend Maxim Gorky. "Strange, isn't it," he remarked, "that no one has as yet booted us out."

By the end of the civil war in 1921 Russia was prostrate. The government's printing presses had reduced the value of the ruble to zero. To keep the country functioning at the barest level of subsistence, stringent new measures were introduced that hardly jibed with the utopian promises the Bolsheviks had made to the workers and peasants. The peasants, unwilling to sell their produce for worthless money, found their grain requisitioned. Labor was conscripted, and strikes were banned—as it turned out, permanently.

Lenin justified these harsh measures as an emergency program of so-called "war Communism." The program was destined to be short-lived. Strikes erupted in all the major cities. Another warning signal was a rebellion by the sailors at the Kronstadt Naval Base, from the first a Communist stronghold; the Red Army was turned against its own comrades.

Shaken by these destructive consequences of "war Communism," the Bolshevik regime abandoned the program for the New Economic Policy that restored a measure of economic freedom to the peasant and the small trader. In short, private enterprise was permitted—though in carefully limited doses. Political freedom, however, was out of the question; instead the dictatorship was tightened to suppress all dissent. To those who complained that the revolution had gone too far, Lenin had this answer: "Permit us to put you up against the wall for saying that."

By 1922 time was beginning to run out on Lenin; in May of that year he suffered the first of three strokes. In April, just before he was stricken, he entrusted the General Secretaryship of the Central Committee of the Communist Party to Stalin. The appointment caused little comment. It seemed only one more bureaucratic assignment added to the many responsibilities Stalin was then carrying; did not his very name mean Man of Steel?

At the time Stalin seemed to his associates least likely to become Lenin's successor. He had neither Lenin's charisma nor Trotsky's brilliance. He had made his way simply by taking on chores others did not want. A native of Georgia in the Caucasus, he was the son of an emancipated serf turned cobbler, hence, unlike many in the revolutionary hierarchy, a true proletarian. As a youth he had studied for the Orthodox priesthood, but had been expelled from the seminary for "rude and disrespectful behavior." Underground life as a Bolshevik suited him better.

By the time the Bolsheviks seized power Stalin had been a member of the party's Central Committee for five years. But none of his colleagues knew him really well; he was described as "a man not given to confiding his thoughts, in a country where every man talked too much."

Shortly after Lenin's first stroke, it was noted that Stalin, hitherto the leader's faithful lieutenant, was acting more and more like a coadjutor. One of the first signs of Stalin's emerging power was a demonstrated ability to change fundamental party doctrine. Originally, the Communists had thought of the new Russia as a federation of autonomous republics—a concept which clearly recognized the diversity and the independence of the country's numerous ethnic groups. Instead, Stalin wanted to have a Union of Soviet Socialist Republics under the centralized control of Moscow—where he expected soon to rule supreme. In December 1922, at the 10th All-Russian Congress of Soviets, he persuaded the party to adopt his view, even in spite of Lenin's disapproval.

In the same month Lenin, brooding over his own approaching end, dictated a memorandum that recorded his views on the party's "two most able leaders"—Stalin and Trotsky. Of Stalin, Lenin wrote: "He has concentrated enormous power in his hands, and I am not sure that he always knows how to use that power with sufficient caution." This "testament" was never made public in the Soviet Union. After Lenin's death it was secreted in the archives. It came to light after Stalin's death, when Premier Nikita Khrushchev referred to it in his celebrated revelations to the 20th Party Congress in 1956. Even had it been published immediately on Lenin's death it probably would not have mattered, because by then Stalin was solidly entrenched.

Lenin died of arteriosclerosis on January 21, 1924. He was buried under leaden skies on a cold day in the coldest winter of recent memory. At 4 p.m., the hour of interment, every factory whistle, siren and foghorn in all of Russia, as well as artillery batteries and the guns of the fleet, burst forth in a barbaric cacophony that lasted a full three minutes. It fell to Stalin to provide an almost religious invocation at the final ceremonies for a man who had lived and died an atheist. In a curious throwback to his early theological training, Stalin led his fellow Bolsheviks in a series of "vows" pledging that they would carry on Lenin's work.

Soon Stalin moved to eliminate Trotsky from the power structure. He did so by provoking a debate on Communism's future policy, offering the new slogan of "socialism in one country" in opposition to Trotsky's theory of "the permanent revolution." Trotsky had held that revolution could not stop at the Russian border, but must move outward until it eliminated the nation-state and established one world under Communism. Stalin now argued that Russia was strong enough to build a socialist state within its own boundaries. It was an argument with a powerful appeal to Russian pride and chauvinism; it also promised a war-weary people respite from struggle, for the permanent revolution carried with it the intimidating prospect of permanent war as well.

The debate itself was only a screen, of course, for the behind-scenes struggle by which Stalin forced Trotsky from the party and into exile. Even there Stalin would not leave his enemy in peace; in 1940 one of Stalin's assassins was to murder Trotsky in his villa in Mexico.

Trotsky's expulsion began a period in which the inner workings of the Communist Party, and so of the Soviet state, became, in Winston Churchill's famous phrase, "a riddle wrapped in a mystery inside an enigma." It was to be a period in which Russia isolated itself from Europe and turned inward under a man who wielded an authority far more absolute and more brutal than any Czar had ever imagined.

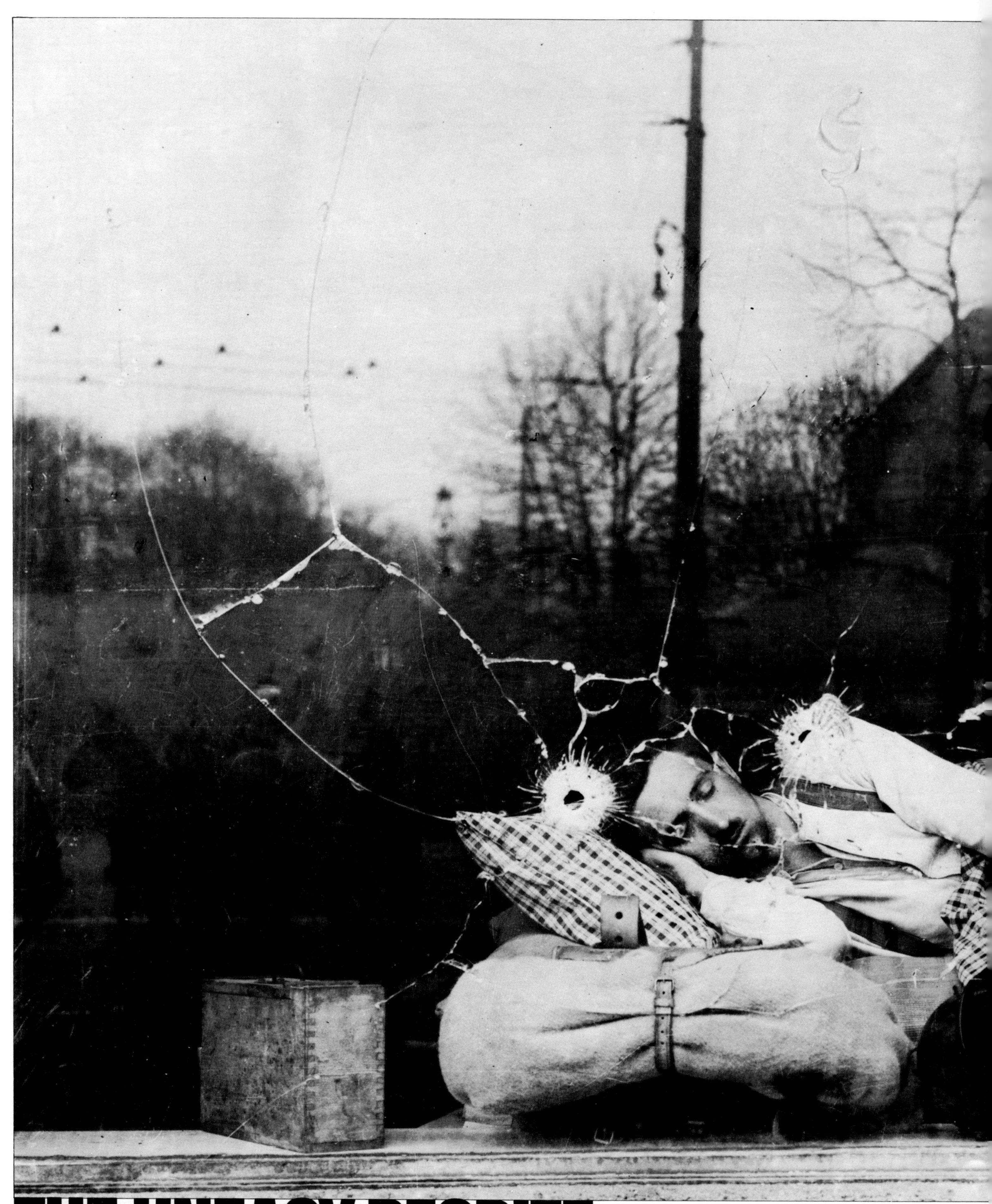

THE UNEASY RESPITE

During a lull in 1919 fighting between Communists and the right-wing Free Corps in Munich, a rightist mercenary naps behind a bullet-pocked cafe window.

THE QUICK DEATH OF "ETERNAL PEACE"

The stable world order envisioned by some signers of the World War I treaties—British diplomat Harold Nicolson predicted an "eternal peace"—perished in frustration and violence almost before the negotiators got home. Starting with Russia, one nation after another exchanged the evils of war for those of revolution and counter-revolution. The counter-revolutionists usually won; Red uprisings in Hungary and in parts of Germany soon folded. In these and other countries where peace alone had proved no cure for misery, people erupted in frantic epidemics of strikes and street fighting.

Underdogs were becoming more militant. Black American soldiers arrived home from combat with a new self-assurance that irked many whites, and the resulting friction exploded into race riots. British miners triggered an unprecedented general strike; using troops and police, the Tories, dominated by the upper class, broke the strike but lost forever a measure of popular confidence.

In the outposts of empire, a new nationalism clashed with stubborn colonial powers clinging to the white man's profitable burden. British authorities jailed, flogged and shot Indians clamoring for more self-determination, but in so doing merely swelled the followings of nationalist leaders like Mohandas K. Gandhi. Elsewhere, nationalists declared open season on the minorities that had been marooned by new treaty boundaries or by rampaging armies. Resurgent Turks, for example, slaughtered hundreds of thousands of Greeks and Armenians who were trapped within expanding Turkish borders, and deported nearly two million more.

Underlying all these disruptive forces was economic disarray. The damage and dislocation of war left millions struggling to survive amid shortages of everything—except, in places, paper money. Successive German governments fell when the economy could not support their flimsy currencies. And as one European regime after another failed to assure its citizens of enough food, clothing, shelter or safety, discouraged and frightened masses hearkened increasingly to demagogues who offered to lead them in a march *(right)* back to some long-lost glory.

Postwar privations reduced many of the Russians, like these young scurvy victims, to a diet of so-called famine bread made of grass, leaves and clay.

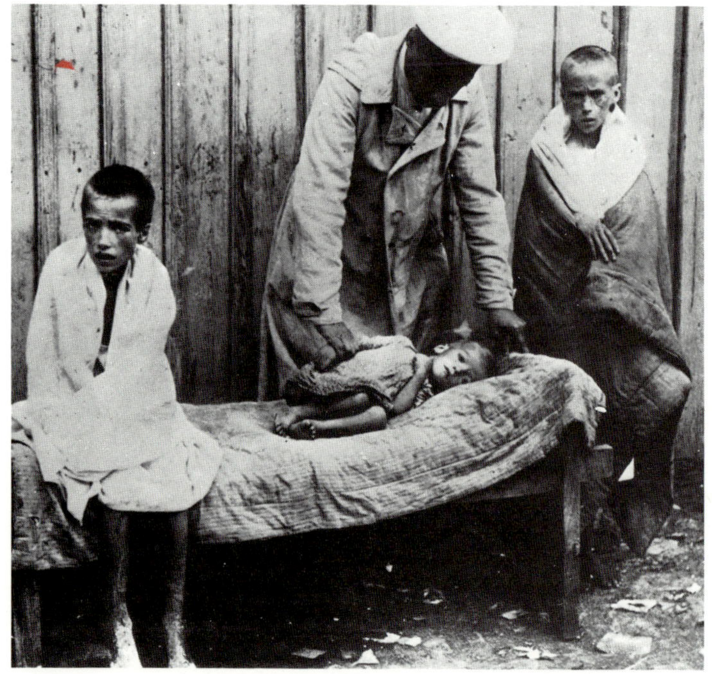

Banner-waving Fascist Black Shirts swagger in Rome after a coup that helped bring to dictatorial power a self-assured newspaper editor named Benito Mussolini.

Red troops guard the Budapest Parliament in 1919 during a short-lived Communist takeover of Hungary.

Armed white Americans herd black captives into a temporary jail in a 1921 Tulsa, Oklahoma, race riot.

Soldiers ride shotgun on food shipments into London as part of the Tory government's effort to break a nine-day general strike that erupted in May 1926.

1463 Cf
1463 Cf

Greek refugees flee from Turkish territory in 1923 after the collapse of a Greek invasion of Turkey. Greece had taken advantage of the postwar dismemberment of the Ottoman Empire to seize two Turkish provinces, Thrace and Smyrna. But the Greek armies were beaten by the Turks under General Mustafa Kemal. The vengeful victors then began a systematic massacre and eviction of Greek residents of Turkey, many of whom had had ancestral homes there since pre-Christian times.

Migrant Chinese (above) huddle in straw shelters alongside a road leading out of the famine-stricken northern province of Shantung. In the early '20s, crop failures forced hundreds of thousands onto the roads, mainly toward more prosperous Manchuria.

Millions of peasants like those at left starved when drought cut Russian harvests in half in 1921. Millions more were subsequently saved when the Bolsheviks, having won the civil war, let foreign relief agencies send in food.

A child lies dead of hunger in Yerevan, capital of a Central Asian republic set up by Armenians who had avoided being massacred by Turks. The forlorn nationalists hoped the United States would help them with food and with firm diplomatic support for their newly hatched land. But U.S. interest waned, and by 1921 Turkey and Russia had divided the republic —and surviving Armenians—between them.

British mounted police in January 1931 charge a Calcutta crowd celebrating the second anniversary of the date on which Indian leaders had defiantly, but futilely, declared independence from Britain. During the Great War, India had contributed a million men and $500 million in cash to the Allied cause in return for British promises of increased autonomy. But when the War was over, instead of autonomy the Indians got tightened British rule—which set off two decades of rallies, hunger strikes and civil discontent in general.

Leftist leader Karl Liebknecht orates at the graves of followers killed by rightist Free Corps fighters in Berlin during January 1919. Liebknecht survived the suppression of an attempted coup by his newly organized Communist party but just a few days after this picture was taken he and a colleague, Rosa Luxemburg, were murdered.

Free Corps troops, in army field gear, man a trench in a Berlin street during the March 1919 Red uprising.

Red Cross nurses tend injured Free Corpsmen at a Frankfurter Allee barricade during the March fighting.

THE POLITICS OF SMASH AND GRAB

At the War's end Germany was exhausted, broke and hungry. The costs of defeat included two million fighting men dead and 800,000 more taken prisoner; millions of widows, orphans and wounded; and more millions of war-hardened ex-soldiers who were turned loose to join in the struggle for scarce jobs and scarcer food.

The War had consumed almost everything that could be eaten, worn or melted down for munitions. The Allied blockade, which was maintained until March 1919 to ensure Germany's submission, made food still more scarce and helped to kill some 800,000 underfed civilians. A humiliating peace treaty quenched hopes for economic recovery by demanding gigantic reparations while impounding most of Germany's coal and iron.

One weak government after the other chipped away at these massive problems, although continually beset by zealots intent on rescuing Germany via a leftist or a rightist dictatorship.

Germany's initial Communist party grew from the ranks of a far-left Socialist group called the Spartacists, led by a bristly little lawyer named Karl Liebknecht. Liebknecht used the pen name Spartacus, after the leader of a Roman slave revolt in 71 B.C. In January 1919, ill-planned Communist uprisings in Berlin and in Munich were crushed by troops of the Free Corps, mercenary bands of exsoldiers who favored a return to monarchy. The next year the Free Corps tried a putsch of its own, which collapsed in the face of a leftist-led Berlin general strike.

Afraid to raise taxes or curtail credit, the government paid its bills by printing more and more marks. An epidemic of paper money infected the economy to the point of collapse: in 1919 the mark was valued at around nine to the U.S. dollar; in 1923 it took four trillion to equal a dollar. The inflation impoverished millions by wiping out their savings, but it created a class of newly rich—entrepreneurs who ballooned their empires on credit and then paid their debts in depreciated marks. Some of their prosperity eventually trickled down to the masses, but the memory of defeat, despair and smash-and-grab politics died hard.

A German housewife of the early 1920s lights her breakfast fire with worthless currency. The wry humor of the Berliners spawned dozens of anecdotes about inflation. One told of the woman shopper who left a basket full of marks outside a store for a moment; when she returned, the money was still there but somebody had made off with the basket.

Steel-helmeted police, who regularly patrolled Berlin's Invalidenstrasse in 1919 (right), crunch through the shattered window glass of a recently ransacked butcher shop. During the postwar years in Germany, any store that was displaying food was a natural target for hungry thieves.

Feine Fleisch-u. Wurstwaren
Ewald Thaleiser
Aufschnitt
Wurst
Schinken
Speck
Engros Endetail

DIZZY, DECADENT BERLIN

Girls of Berlin's Apollo Theater, famed for topless tableaux, create their own 1920s version of the victory sculpture atop the city's Brandenburg Gate.

A MADCAP RETREAT FROM REALITY

While most Berliners in the '20s scrambled just to stay alive amid street fighting and food shortages, a lucky few who had managed to hold onto something—or to cash in on the wild currency fluctuations—found the postwar ferment a seductive invitation to live a little. These adroit survivalists joined with adventurous tourists and a coterie of Bohemian artists to turn Berlin into the hottest pleasure town this side of ancient Rome. In all Europe, Berlin's costume balls were the splashiest, its nighttime entertainment the raciest and its sales of sex and dope the openest.

A lot of the fun was far from wholesome. Thousands of young Berlin girls, many in their mid-teens, worshipped dancer Anita Berber, who performed in the nude at the White Mouse cabaret and who indulged in cocaine, morphine and lovers of both sexes. She roared through Berlin's night life with a gang of pugs, thugs and drunks, and died of tuberculosis at 29.

All over the city, nudity flourished: in nightclubs, on the stage and screen, at private parties where waitresses in filmy panties were paid to be fondled, and even among nature freaks who went ice skating clad only in earmuffs. Prostitutes paraded the streets by the thousands, some of them with boots and whips, some with pigtails and armfuls of schoolbooks. "All the girls registered with the police," reminisced one old Berliner, "and if you caught anything from one of them you could even sue her."

Perversion prospered. "Along the Kurfürstendamm," reported the Austrian biographer Stefan Zweig, "powdered and rouged young men sauntered, and in the dimly lit bars one might see men of the world of finance courting drunken sailors." At transvestite balls, Zweig noted, "hundreds of men costumed as women and hundreds of women as men danced under the benevolent eyes of the police."

Then on January 30, 1933, a killjoy named Adolf Hitler came to power preaching a twisted puritanism. He banned jazz, jailed and shot homosexuals and herded prostitutes into officially sanctioned brothels. Within weeks, Berlin's distinctive music had stopped.

Of these 1926 patrons at a transvestite night spot, The Eldorado, only the one at the far left is a woman. The poster below advertises a lesbian bar.

Chanteuse Claire Waldoff and her partner parody an Apache dance at a ball where costumes imitated those drawn by the popular artist Heinrich Zille.

Celebrants in 1929 ignore the disapproving matron at far left to whoop it up during the festival of

The high-livers of Berlin in the '20s strongly admired things American. The placard at left, advertising a guided tour through alleged criminal haunts in the heart of Berlin, is adorned with likenesses of two "ringleaders of the New York and Chicago underworld"—Al Capone and Jack "Legs" Diamond. Actually, the city had plenty of gangsters of its own, some of them organized so openly and so thoroughly that they had clubhouses and written bylaws.

Faschingszeit, the German version of Mardi Gras.

With the aid of ingenious harnesses, connecting rods and eight identical dummies, dancers Grit and Ina van Elben create the illusion of a full 10-girl chorus line for the patrons of the Kabarett Tingel-Tangel.

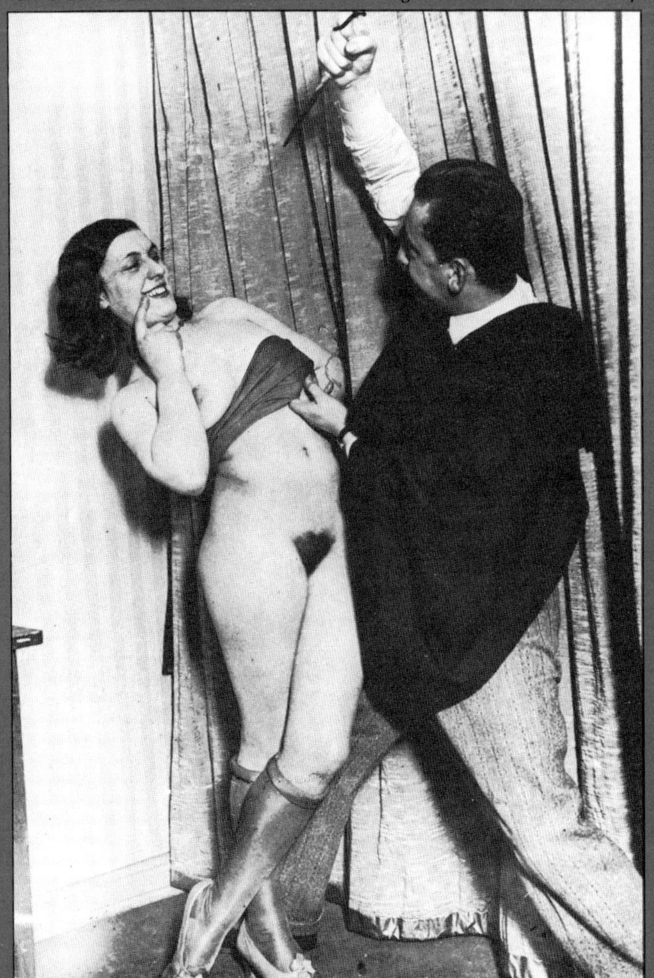

A lightly clad and giggling victim submits to the attack of a slapstick sadist in a nightclub spoof of Berlin's sexual tastes in the '20s.

"So you can't dance the Charleston!" says an ad of the '20s. The solution: a course of dance lessons offered through that marvelous new Jazz Age medium—the radio.

The flapper look, dramatized here by singer Trude Hesterberg in a revue titled On and Off, was the ideal of Berlin girls of the 1920s. As played by Trude, who was much imitated, the Berlin flapper was a free-living, free-loving female who could dish out a wisecrack with the same "Schnauze," or big mouth, for which the trendiest men of the day were noted.

Dance bands like Max de Groof's, here playing a Berlin date in the early '30s, copied the makeup of American combos—down to the banjo and girl singer.

Two Chocolate Kiddies flank an ad for their all-black revue, which wowed Berliners in 1925 with its dance, snappy patter and jazz.

The Ziegfeld-style precision of the all-blonde chorus called the Tiller Girls ensured full houses for the Haller Revue at the Scala Theater.

New Year's revelers in Berlin's Adlon Hotel, one of the world's most luxurious, hail the incoming year, 1931.

Erst Richard Tauber

dann . . .

FONTÄNEN-ZAUBER

IM RESI

Blumenstr. 10

Die größte Wasser-Feerie der Welt.

KAPELLE ROHRBECK

„Das Ballhaus der Technik"

"First Richard Tauber," says a poster, "then the magic fountains of Resi." And many a Berliner indeed went on from an operetta performance by the famed tenor to dine and to dance at the lush Residenz-Kasino night club; the spot was also billed in ads as the Technical Ballroom because of its floodlit water jets and its inter-table telephones for flirting.

Richard Tauber himself (far right) shares

a table with sleek singer Gitta Alper (foreground) and other regulars in the city's cabaret society at the Press Ball, an annual blowout staged by Berlin journalists.

3

The hatching of two tyrannies
A hellion, handy with a knife
A drifter hooked on vegetables and Wagner
A spying job for Corporal Hitler
Castor oil for dissenters
Mock funeral for a landslide loser
Violent resurrection of a political corpse
The surrender of Rome to a Caesar in spats
Blueprint for conquest from a Bavarian jail
The Duce's lusty regimen
The Führer's 50,000 voices

A NEW BREED OF CAESARS

As Communism entrenched itself in Russia, a rival ideology arose to challenge it in Europe. It first appeared as Fascism in Italy, then took on a more demonic form as Nazism in Germany. This new totalitarianism, which was not so much planned as improvised, was largely the creation of two men who, playing upon the fears and frustrations of their time, exploited the mystique of national pride and the spirit of violence that had been unloosed by World War I to further their own pursuit of power. They succeeded beyond all imagining. Benito Mussolini ruled as Italy's dictator, the Duce, for 21 years; Adolf Hitler was Germany's undisputed master, the Führer, for 12 years.

Though Italy had fought on the winning side of the war and Germany had come out the loser, the plight of both countries in the postwar era made them equally easy prey to a totalitarian takeover. The trouble was in part psychological. Italians and Germans alike felt angry at the world —in the one case for having been denied some of the spoils of victory, in the other for having been saddled with the burden of war guilt. Domestically, in each country, the old institutions and leaders had proved wanting, the stability of former years deceptive. A host of converts awaited any man who pledged to restore law and order, redeem the nation's honor and reclaim its place in the sun.

Mussolini and Hitler promised all this and more. Each was a master demagogue, with a hypnotic public presence, a talent for flaming oratory and an utter lack of scruple. They wooed the masses in the language of revolution: they promised to take from the rich to give to the poor; at the same time they were assuring men of means that their wealth would be protected.

Yet certain articles of the Fascist and Nazi faiths remained fixed. Mussolini and Hitler were not only anti-Communist but antidemocratic, despising the multiparty system as ineffectual. Hitler, in addition, was virulently anti-Semitic and obsessively certain that Germans of pure Aryan stock constituted a "master race" (though he did not personally qualify). Mussolini, who was bred in the melting-pot Mediterranean tradition, at first gave these views mere lip service.

On one point—indispensable to both ideologies—the two men saw eye to eye. Every individual, whatever his status, was a creature of the State, obliged to serve it, even to do violence on its behalf. Intellect was suspect, blind obedience was essential. Gradually Benito Mussolini and Adolf Hitler came to symbolize the State—all-knowing and all-powerful—in their own persons.

In time the paths of the dictators were to converge. As they commandeered the energies of their people and embarked on new adventures of conquest beyond their borders, they were to become allies in a second world war—and, ultimately, partners in catastrophe.

The story is told that sometime in the late 1920s, after Mussolini had seized power and while Hitler was still seeking it, the Italian embassy in Berlin received a letter from Hitler respectfully asking for an autographed picture of the Duce. The request elicited this snub from Rome: "Please thank the above-mentioned gentleman for his sentiment and tell him in whatever form you consider best that the Duce does not think fit to accede to the request."

In less than a decade Mussolini would be publicly fawning on Hitler and moving into his shadow. Yet the condescension reflected in the message from Rome died hard. Meeting Hitler for the first time in 1934, by then on an equal footing, Mussolini privately pronounced him a "mad little clown"—a verdict later upgraded to "dangerous fool."

By contrast, the Italian leader saw himself as a savior who had rescued his country from chaos. Those compatriots who dissented from this view were either in exile, in jail or dead—some by lethal doses of castor oil forced down the throat. But millions of Italians, churchmen and bankers as well as clerks and laborers, acclaimed Mussolini; so did many visitors from abroad, reporting home that among the Duce's miracles he had "made the trains run on time." Though destiny was already preparing his downfall, Mussolini then stood on a pinnacle few men had ever reached.

His early years had given little hint of how far he would go. He was born in north-central Italy in the Romagna, a rugged region of chronic discontent. His mother was a village schoolteacher and a Catholic, his father a blacksmith, an atheist and an anarchist who went about smashing ballot boxes at election time. He named his firstborn Benito in honor of the Mexican revolutionary, Benito Juárez. Later he soured on his son; when Benito was wooing Rachele Guidi, his future wife, Alessandro Mussolini advised her to throw herself under a train rather than take such a mate.

As Benito himself once archly recalled: "I was, I believe, unruly." He was, in fact, a hellion. To tame him, his mother sent him to a school run by the religious order of the Salesian Fathers; he was expelled for knifing a classmate. He got away with a second knifing at a state training school for teachers. On graduating, he went off to a village where he took both his first teaching job and—at 18—his first mistress, a young matron whose husband was away in the Army. In a jealous moment Mussolini stabbed her too.

After a year village life palled; worse, compulsory military duty impended. Mussolini decamped for Switzerland, long a haven for disaffected Italians. Sometimes he worked as a mason, sometimes he was reduced to begging. Then he met Angelica Balabanoff, a Russian expatriate who was spreading the Marxist gospel among the Italian exiles.

Their association was to last for 12 years and transform his life. She became his mentor in Marxism and encouraged his ambitions as a writer. He began contributing articles to Socialist newspapers. Mussolini's literary leanings went beyond the polemical, however; he was later to publish a mildly scandalous romance entitled *The Cardinal's Mistress*.

In 1904, under an amnesty for deserters, he returned to Italy, fulfilled his 19-month military service, then took up teaching again. But his newfound appetite for politics and print had been whetted. He combined both in a weekly, *La Lotta di Classe* (The Class Struggle), written entirely by himself. Mussolini's extremist views—he even extolled assassination—alarmed moderate Socialists and irked authorities.

A chance to deal with this noisy upstart came in 1911, when Italy declared war on Turkey and moved across the Mediterranean to annex Turkish-ruled Libya. Mussolini led antiwar riots and publicly asserted that "the national flag is a rag to be planted on a dunghill." He was tried for subversion and sent to prison for five months.

But a large political dividend awaited him on his release. The Socialists hailed him as a coming leader, and soon named him editor of their national daily, *Avanti!* (Forward!).

When the World War broke out in 1914, the Socialists declared for neutrality, *Avanti's* editor sounding the keynote: "Down with arms, up with humanity!" Then, suddenly, Mussolini about-faced. Without bothering to consult Socialist party chiefs, he wrote an article in *Avanti* urging Italy to get into the War on the Allied side. A stormy meeting ensued.

Amid angry cries of "Traitor!" and "Who paid you?" Mussolini was fired as editor and expelled from the party.

This 180-degree turn by Mussolini seems to have been executed for cash—secret funds from the French government, which was seeking to draw Italy into the Allied camp. Mussolini now had the wherewithal to start his own newspaper. Though *Il Popolo d'Italia* (The People of Italy) proclaimed itself "The Socialist Daily," it denounced the pacifism of the Socialists and summoned Italians to their country's service. After Italy joined the Allies in 1915, *Il Popolo's* editor himself saw Army service, a stint on the Alpine front, though he never rose above the rank of sergeant.

Peace found Mussolini with a newspaper but without a party. A new cause, however, was hatching out of Italy's sorry state. The war had cost 138 billion lire—double the government's total expenditures between 1861, when Italy became a unified nation, and 1913. Amid inflation, strikes and the pillaging of food shops, millions of demobilized soldiers were jobless. Some talked of violent redress against an ungrateful country.

From his office in Milan, Mussolini watched events and planned his strategy. Early in March 1919 *Il Popolo* ran a series of notices about a group forming to fight "against the forces dissolving victory and the nation." A meeting was set for the 23rd of the month in a hall, off the Piazza San Sepolcro, owned by the Milan Association of Merchants and Shopkeepers, who were willing to lend Mussolini their quarters even though *Il Popolo's* headlines were screaming "Make the Rich Pay!" He was becoming more and more adept at playing both sides of the street.

About 145 men attended the meeting, disgruntled veterans mostly, some former *Arditi,* the cocky, black-clad shock troops of the Italian Army. Mussolini outlined his plan to organize what he called a *fascio di combattimento*—a "combat group." The word *fascio* came from the Latin *fasces,* the tight bundle of rods carried in ancient Rome as a symbol of authority.

The Milan *fascio,* Mussolini said, was to be the first of many throughout the land, with a threefold mission for members: First, to uphold "the material and moral claims" of veterans. Second, to oppose "the imperialism of any countries damaging to Italy." Third—and most urgent in view of the oncoming election—"to fight with all their means the candidates that were milk-and-water Italians."

By Mussolini's own estimate, only a third of the men at the meeting signed a pledge to support the program. But from this meager start Fascism was to emerge and flourish.

In 1919 Adolf Hitler was a 30-year-old nonentity living in Munich in the barracks of his wartime regiment's reserve battalion. He had no other home and wanted none. His service in Germany's armed forces had proved the happiest period of a hitherto aimless life. Other veterans were stalking the streets ripping off the medals and epaulets of any officers they met. To Hitler such acts were heresy. He revered the military and anything else that summoned up Germany's former glory. His passion for Germany was all the odder because it was not his native land. He was Austrian; some of his peasant forebears may have been Czech. His father was a minor customs official, his mother a servant.

HITLER — PRINCE WILHELM — ERNST RÖHM — HERMANN GÖRING — WINIFRED WAGNER

Early in his career, Adolf Hitler enjoyed the backing of some of Germany's most influential citizens, whom he cultivated both for their standing and for their connections. Thus, being seen with the Crown Prince identified Hitler in the public mind with the Prince's father, Kaiser Wilhelm II, exiled, but still revered by many Germans. Hitler encouraged a professional soldier named Ernst Röhm to build a private Nazi army, but valued Röhm more for his old regular Army contacts, which helped draw ex-servicemen into the party orbit. World War I ace Hermann Göring added heroic glamor to Hitler's enterprise; a wealthy landowner, Göring also loaned Hitler and his struggling party considerable sums of money. And friendship with the late composer Richard Wagner's daughter-in-law Winifred gained Hitler entrée to a cultural world where he reveled in the reflected glory of his own favorite composer.

In the tales Hitler later told of his boyhood—though he furiously forbade others to pry into it—he described a time of struggle and poverty. In fact, his father's salary sufficed for a comfortable life and good schooling for his family.

Hitler detested school; it interfered with his favorite pastime, daydreaming. One of his few "satisfactory" grades was for drawing—and so a dream took shape. Not for him his father's humdrum life as a bureaucrat; he would become an artist or architect. He spent hours sketching grandiose, imaginary monuments and mansions.

At 16, Hitler left the provincial town of Linz and headed for glittering Vienna—and a bad blow to his ego. He applied for admission to the prestigious Academy of Fine Arts, but he was rejected, his trial sketches judged "without sufficient merit." He lived on funds from his now-widowed mother and, after she died, on a stipend the government granted to orphans of civil servants. This benefit ended when he reached legal adulthood, and he was thrown on his own.

An ordinary man would have sought a job, but Hitler was an idler by nature and, moreover, unwilling to demean himself by joining the drab ranks of the mundanely employed. He subsisted on the sale of an occasional watercolor; he produced posters advertising a soap and an antiperspirant powder. A men's hostel for down-and-outers provided a roof overhead. Living was cheap; Hitler was already a nonsmoker, a nondrinker and a vegetarian.

A fellow drifter who knew him then made the mistake of remembering that time congenially in print after Hitler came to power. Hitler had the man tracked down and murdered. He preferred his own version of Vienna as "the saddest period of my life."

Yet he found much to enjoy in Vienna. He went to hear and thrill to the thunderously Germanic operas of Richard Wagner, managing to afford a ticket to 30 or 40 performances of *Tristan und Isolde* alone. He discovered the riches of the public libraries. Of more direct import to his future, he found another fascinating new fount of information in the inflammatory pamphlets then flooding Vienna.

The cosmopolitan capital had attracted people from all over the Habsburg empire—Czechs, Serbs, Slovenes, Croats, Poles, Hungarians, Rumanians, Ruthenians—threatening the long-time conservative dominance of the so-called German Austrians. The pamphleteers railed against this polyglot influx, spewing a special hatred for those of the immigrants who were Jews. The Germanic strain, they warned, represented a master race that must not be defiled; moreover, its members must be united in a Greater Germany.

Hitler embraced these doctrines completely, and in 1913 moved across the border to Munich. Such was his ardor for his adopted country that when war came the next year he promptly enlisted in a Bavarian infantry regiment, serving on the Western Front in Flanders as a dispatch runner. Soon his bravery was recognized by the awarding of the Iron Cross, Second Class, and in time by the even more coveted Iron Cross, First Class—a rare honor for a corporal.

He was an exemplary soldier, sometimes too much so for some of the men in his company. One recalled him as "this white crow among us that didn't go along when we damned the war to hell." But if his comrades found him peculiar, they also looked upon him as lucky. Except for the gas attack that temporarily blinded him near War's end, his only injury in the entire four years under fire was a leg wound. Hitler came out of the War convinced he had been spared for some special mission in life.

An inkling of the form it would take emerged soon after he returned to Munich in early 1919. The political turmoil in Germany threatened to tear it apart. The new Republic commanded little respect; its middle-of-the-road leaders bore the stigma of having signed the hated Armistice. On the Left, the Socialists and the Communists still hoped for a revolution; Munich itself had a brief taste of a Red regime. On the Right, determined to prevent a recurrence of such episodes, stood the nobility, the upper middle class and the Army. Reservist Hitler was delighted to be given a berth in the district command's political department and assigned to check up on a tiny, possibly subversive, group calling itself the German Workers Party.

Attending a meeting, Hitler had a pleasant surprise. The party turned out to be fervently nationalist and patriotic, but unlike other such groups it aimed to compete with the Socialists and Communists for support among the masses. Intrigued, Hitler accepted an invitation to a meeting of the party's executive committee in the back room of a shabby tavern. He thought the reading of the minutes absurd and the treasurer's report pathetic: the party's funds totaled seven marks, 50 pfennigs (less than two dollars).

Yet when urged to join he promised to think it over. In the barracks that night, he reflected that "I was numbered among the nameless . . ." However small, the German Workers Party seemed to Hitler to offer a way out of obscurity. Two days later he became its 55th member, resolved to mold it to his own ends.

A preview of the tactics that were to become the staples of Fascism took place in September 1919 in the Adriatic port city of Fiume. Formerly under the rule of the Austrian Habsburgs, Fiume had been firmly claimed at the Paris Peace Conference both by Italy, on the ground that the city's population was predominantly Italian, and by the new Yugoslavia, on the ground that the surrounding area was Slavic. The peacemakers got off the horns of this dilemma by declaring Fiume a free city.

Most Italians, Mussolini included, merely blustered about the decision; one superpatriot decided to do something about it. Gabriele D'Annunzio was a national idol, in part because of his florid poetry and novels, in part because, as a wartime flyer, he had lost an eye in his country's service. Although some were dubious about his peacetime penchant for monk's robes and lace underwear, D'Annunzio was a law unto himself—eccentric and flamboyant.

Not deigning to consult his government, he rallied a force of about 1,000 armed men, descended upon Fiume and proclaimed it a regency, with himself as *comandante*. The Italians back home went wild. The sheer audacity of the deed was balm to wounded national pride.

D'Annunzio ruled for 15 months before he was evicted by his own government by agreement with Yugoslavia. But while the regency lasted, it provided a pungent foretaste of government Fascist-style.

Even as the gray façades of Fiume blossomed with gaudy flags, its dazed inhabitants learned that henceforth they were to labor in the employ of one or another of 10 government-run corporations. The death penalty was introduced and the folly of dissent was further stressed by the novel weapons D'Annunzio's men flaunted—a dagger, a truncheon, and a supply of castor oil to be administered to recalcitrants.

Wearing the dramatic all-black uniforms made famous by Italy's elite *Arditi,* D'Annunzio's army paraded daily before the *comandante* in Fiume's piazzas. The climax of the show would be a shouted colloquy that went something like this:

D'Annunzio: "For whom is the future?"

Soldiers: "Italy!"

D'Annunzio: "For whom is the power and glory?"

Soldiers: "For us!"

The dialogue would end with a roar of "Ayah, Ayah, Alalala!", D'Annunzio's version of an ancient Greek war cry.

Before long, the staccato give-and-take between leader and followers, the black shirts, the dagger and truncheon and castor oil, would be appropriated by Mussolini for his own movement, now re-named *fascismo*. Taking over D'Annunzio's idea of a corporative state required more doing, but in time it, too, became part of Mussolini's grand design.

At heart he envied D'Annunzio, though wary of an ego as monumental as his own, but until the Fiume adventure ended in fiasco he was the *comandante's* highly vocal admirer,

using the columns of *Il Popolo* to raise 3,000,000 lire for D'Annunzio's cause. Little of this money reached him, however; it was diverted to support Fascist candidates for Parliament in Italy's first postwar election in November 1919.

Not one Fascist was elected. In Milan Mussolini received 4,000 votes to his Socialist rival's 180,000. Next day his old newspaper *Avanti* exulted: "This morning a dead body in an advanced state of decomposition was fished out of the Naviglio [a canal]. It would seem to be the body of Mussolini."

That night a hand grenade was tossed into a Socialist victory party, wounding many celebrants. Searching Mussolini's office, the police found bombs and explosives everywhere—even in the editor's desk drawers. He was jailed, but released after 24 hours. Fellow journalists had intervened for him, arguing that he was "a relic, a defeated man."

The obsequies were premature. No party in the election was able to enjoy the victory. Not one had a majority. The government was immobilized; no serious steps could be taken to relieve Italy's ills. Strikes—some 1,880 altogether in 1920—flared anew. Workers in Milan and Turin occupied factories. Mobs attacked banks and public buildings. Some Army units mutinied. A number of towns and villages turned Communist, setting up Russian-style soviets.

The Fascists, beaten by the ballot, resorted to force to keep the movement alive. They recruited strong-arm squads of veterans and youths with a thirst for action. In the name of preserving law and order, the *squadristi* engaged Socialists and Communists in street battles; and they beat up union organizers, sometimes adding insult to injury by shaving off half the victim's mustache. Increasingly the *squadristi* had the tacit support of the police and the military, and the applause of Italians fearful for their country's future.

A year after Mussolini had been pronounced a "relic," he was head of a movement that boasted 2,200 local *fasci* and 320,000 enrolled members.

In Germany Hitler was also prospering. In the German Workers Party he revealed an unexpected gift for propaganda and organization. He changed the party's name to National Socialist German Workers Party (Nationalsozialistische Deutsche Arbeiterspartei—Nazi for short) and issued a manifesto demanding abrogation of the Versailles Treaty, denial of German citizenship to Jews, confiscation of war profits, imposition of profit sharing in industry and increased pensions. In February 1920, when he declaimed this manifesto to a mass meeting, a police spy reported a tumultuous reaction in the hall. Hitler had discovered yet another unexpected talent—the ability to work an audience into a pitch of frenzy.

Aware of the power of symbols, he adopted a striking party emblem: the swastika. Since ancient times many peoples had used it as a decorative motif; according to Germanic myth, it was the instrument that had stirred up the primal ooze at earth's creation. In other innovations, Hitler insisted on "Heil" as an obligatory greeting between party members, and had an admission of one mark charged at all public meetings; as word of his rhetorical prowess spread, the fees helped swell the party's coffers.

Political foes often paid just to heckle Hitler, so burly veterans were recruited as bouncers. Uniformed in brown

Four top Fascist aides flank Benito Mussolini in Rome on October 30, 1922, the day he became Premier. Most of the group in the front row eventually had reason to regret the association; luckiest was Michele Bianchi (far left), who died in 1930, still in favor. White-bearded Emilio De Bono was shot in 1944 for voting to oust the Duce; bald Cesare Maria De Vecchi held only minor jobs and was reduced during World War II to relative obscurity. Italo Balbo (far right) won such fame as a flier that the jealous Duce sent him off to govern Libya. He died mysteriously, brought down by Italian antiaircraft fire at Tobruk on June 28, 1940.

shirts, dark trousers and boots, they soon became known as Storm Troopers. Like Mussolini's Black Shirts, they relished brawling in the streets with counterpart toughs employed by the Socialists and Communists.

Physically, Hitler was unprepossessing—sallow-faced and morose-looking, with strangely pale blue eyes. But in Munich's salons he forsook the baleful air he favored on the public platform, affecting a kind of old-fashioned courtesy that could charm and disarm. In the short span of two years, he moved from anonymity to celebrity in Munich.

In 1921 the Fascists' fortunes in Italy took a dramatic upturn. Industrialists and landowners now openly backed them. In an election in May, 35 Fascists, Mussolini among them, won seats in the Chamber of Deputies. Milan gave Mussolini 125,000 votes as opposed to the 4,000 that he had garnered only two years earlier.

He was not as buoyed as might have been expected by his debut as a national figure who had been certified by ballot. He was having trouble with his own people; Fascism had not yet become a one-man show. Much of the power still lay with the fire-eating local Fascist bosses who called themselves *Ras,* after the feudal chieftains of Ethiopia. On their own ground, the *Ras* reigned supreme. Some thought the Duce a weak reed. "The trouble with Mussolini," one said, "is that he wants everybody's blessing and changes his coat 10 times a day to get it."

The charge of political opportunism seemed well justified, especially when he sought a truce with his former arch foes, the Socialists, who were beginning to run out of steam, but who Mussolini, by some mysterious reasoning, thought would help him consolidate his parliamentary base. The *Ras* exploded, and Mussolini actually resigned as head of the Fascist movement. But he quickly thought it over, reclaimed

AN INEPT ASSASSIN SAVED BY A NOSE

One morning in April 1926, Benito Mussolini was briskly departing from opening ceremonies at an International Congress of Surgeons. Suddenly, a band struck up the Fascist anthem and the Duce snapped to attention—which caused a bullet fired from a pistol at point-blank range to graze his nose instead of blowing his head off.

Within minutes, thanks to the surgeons' convention, he reappeared, his wounded proboscis covered by a conspicuous bandage. By that time police had arrested the would-be assassin, a deranged 62-year-old Irish woman named Violet Gibson, who said she had come to Rome with two alternatives: to shoot Mussolini or the Pope. She got to Mussolini first.

Considering his narrow escape, Mussolini reacted with exemplary calm. "Imagine that—a woman," he muttered. Then, with his usual flamboyance, he capitalized on the incident by magnanimously ordering Miss Gibson freed and deported. Four people tried to kill Mussolini during his career. One other assailant got off unscathed in that same year: he escaped when the wrong person was seized. The other two were sentenced to 30 years' imprisonment.

Mussolini sports an adhesive patch covering the gouge in his nose inflicted by Violet Gibson (inset), whose errant shot scarcely deflected the Duce from his duties. Here, the day after the incident, Mussolini greets an officer aboard a battleship bound for the Italian colony of Libya.

his leadership and repudiated the Socialist-Fascist truce.

In May 1922 the *Ras,* on their own, launched a frontal assault on governmental authority. Some 50,000 *squadristi* took over the town hall of Ferrara and demanded that the prefect, or mayor, at once initiate a program of public works for the unemployed. When Rome ordered the prefect to comply, *squadristi* repeated the maneuver in Bologna, Ravenna and Parma. Success moved the *Ras* to plan to take over the central government itself. Mussolini, now back in step with his followers, electrified a party rally at Naples on October 24 by shouting: "Either the government will be given to us or we will seize it by marching on Rome!" The response was a roar: "A Roma! A Roma! A Roma!"

Behind the scenes, however, Mussolini wavered so about the march that the *Ras* had to tell him it would take place whether he approved or not. On October 27, about 14,000 Fascists converged on the three stipulated assembly points, south, north and northwest of Rome. They had no intention of walking the 50 miles or so; the "march" was to be by bus or train. Almost at once the three columns were stalled. Transport proved uncertain and food short. The planners could have used the organizing genius of a D'Annunzio, but the poet was unavailable; he was at his villa in Florence nursing an injury incurred in an unscheduled leap from the window of a lady friend's boudoir.

The marchers could have been easily routed at an order from Rome to the Army. Instead, Rome panicked and tried to dicker with Mussolini. Now back in Milan, nervously waiting to see how the march went, he was offered a Cabinet post by the Premier of the moment, Luigi Facta. Several other politicians, hoping to supplant Facta, made similar bids. Emboldened by all this attention, Mussolini scorned them all. Facta then urged the King to declare a state of siege. He not only refused Facta's request but invited Mussolini to form a government.

An aide relayed the invitation by telephone on October 29. Mussolini demanded written confirmation; it came by telegram. That night he took the train from Milan to Rome.

In the morning Mussolini presented himself to the King at the Quirinal Palace, wearing a black shirt, dark trousers and—presumably as a concession to bourgeois fashion—white spats. Apparently he felt a need to make some statement for the history books. "Your Majesty will excuse my appearance," he said. "I come from a battlefield."

The "march on Rome" materialized only after Mussolini took office as Premier. On October 31 several thousand deflated Fascists arrived in 10 special trains—arranged by Mussolini with the King's approval—and paraded in a dismal rain. It was, as one historian observed, "the token occupation of a citadel which had already fallen."

In an interview with a London *Times* reporter shortly after the Italian coup, Hitler remarked: "If a Mussolini were given to Germany, people would fall on their knees and worship him more than Mussolini has ever been worshipped." There was no doubt about which "him" Hitler had in mind. But a move he made in his eagerness to emulate Mussolini proved distinctly premature.

In January 1923, an event occurred that unified the Germans as they had not been since before the War: French soldiers occupied the Ruhr, Germany's industrial heart. The French government claimed a German default on the reparations required by the Versailles Treaty.

The reparations commission assigned by the Paris peacemakers to determine Germany's obligation had assessed $33 billion, to be paid in yearly installments both in cash and in kind. France was receiving quantities of the Ruhr's richest resources, coal and timber. The specific default it claimed was Germany's failure to meet the delivery deadline on half of a total of 200,000 telephone poles.

Outraged at being subjected to occupation for so trifling an offense, the Berlin government ordered passive resistance in the Ruhr. Workers walked off their jobs; mines, factories and offices shut down. But the resistance exacted a fearful cost. The government undertook to provide financial support for the Ruhr's miners, factory workers, railwaymen and officials ousted by the French. It began printing millions, then billions and finally trillions of marks.

The value of the mark had been in steady decline since Germany's defeat; now it plummeted out of control. In January, when the Ruhr occupation began, the mark was worth 18,000 to the dollar; in July, 160,000; a month later, one million; by November, four billion. Scenes of Germans pushing barrows heaped high with marks to buy a bag of potatoes became terrifyingly common.

Finally a new government in Berlin, headed by the strong-minded Gustav Stresemann, moved to stop the drain on the economy. It called off the resistance and resumed reparations. But it was also forced to place the country under a state of emergency, for the mood of national unity was shattered and political rancors erupted again.

In Bavaria the emergency powers devolved on a triumvirate—Gustav von Kahr, the state commissioner, General Otto von Lossow, commander of the local Reichswehr and Colonel Hans von Seisser, head of the state police. Bavaria had long been separatist in sentiment. Hitler, suspecting that the triumvirs would use the new crisis to break with Berlin, decided to forestall them by compelling their support in a Nazi takeover, or *putsch,* that would rocket him to a position of national power no less commanding than was Mussolini's in Italy.

The occasion presented itself when the triumvirate held a meeting of civil servants at one of Munich's large beer halls, the Bürgerbräukeller. Kahr had just begun to speak when Hitler—in a black tail coat, with his Iron Cross highly visible—burst in, accompanied by Göring and a bodyguard of Storm Troopers. As they set up a machine gun, Hitler leaped onto a table and fired a revolver shot into the ceiling.

"The national revolution has begun," he shouted. "This hall has been surrounded by 600 heavily armed men. The Bavarian and National governments have been removed and a provisional government formed. The army and the police barracks have been occupied; troops and police are marching on the city under the swastika banner."

The astounded audience could not know it, but this was pure bluff. The troops and police were in their barracks. A provisional government existed only in Hitler's imagination. Waving his revolver, he forced the triumvirs into a nearby room while Göring took over to tell the crowd, "You have your beer, keep drinking! You have nothing to worry about."

Meanwhile, an envoy dispatched by Hitler appeared at the home of General Erich Ludendorff, now living in retirement outside Munich. The envoy's task was to persuade the famed First Quartermaster General of Germany's wartime armies to join the *putsch.* Though irate at the abrupt intrusion, Ludendorff—himself a dabbler in racist and nationalist theories—agreed to go to the Bürgerbräukeller.

Kahr, Lossow and Seisser, unintimidated by Hitler's revolver and wild talk, resisted his demand that they join the *putsch.* But Ludendorff's sudden entry gave them pause. They agreed to appear with him and Hitler before the crowd in a show of unity. The crowd cheered and dispersed. The Storm Troopers took some Bavarian state officials as hostages, but the triumvirs were allowed to leave, presumably to order the troops and police to join the uprising. Instead, Lossow ordered radio stations to broadcast word that the Bavarian state government had repudiated the *putsch.*

Hitler was expecting officials, troops and police to flock to his standard. Next morning, with Ludendorff, he stepped out in front of a march through Munich. Some 2,000 Storm Troopers and sympathizers followed, cheering and singing patriotic hymns. Soon the paraders found their way barred by police. It was reopened when Göring threatened to shoot the hostages of the night before.

In the heart of the city a second police cordon halted the march. A shot rang out, followed by an exchange of fire that lasted barely a minute but killed 16 marchers and three policemen. Hitler's wartime luck held. He had been walking arm in arm with one of the victims, the envoy he had sent to Ludendorff. Shot through the head, the man fell and pulled Hitler down with him. Hitler suffered no more than a dislocated shoulder. The Storm Troopers fled in confusion. General Ludendorff, head erect and trembling with rage, passed through the police cordon and stood at attention, waiting to be arrested.

Hitler, too, was arrested, and tried for treason. The trial took 24 days, and all Germany's attention was riveted on it. Hitler later described the failure of the *putsch* as "the greatest stroke of luck in my life." If so, it was because he converted it into a demagogic triumph. Before the *putsch,* he had been leader of a parochial South German movement; after it, he was a national figure.

Though Ludendorff and eight others were on trial with Hitler, he easily dominated the courtroom. He confessed to the *putsch,* but would not concede that it was treason. In a single sentence, he touched a painful chord in German memories, declaring: "There can be no question of treason that aims to undo the betrayal of a country."

The sympathies of the court were manifest. Ludendorff was acquitted. Hitler was found guilty only after the presiding judge assured his associates he would not serve his full five-year sentence.

Two Germans accused of violating Nazi doctrine forbidding sexual intercourse between Jews and Gentiles await an order from their Storm Trooper escort to parade through the streets of Hamburg wearing humiliating placards. Her sign reads: "At this place I am the greatest swine: I take Jews and make them mine!" His declares that "As a Jewish boy I always take German girls up to my room!" From 1935 on, increasingly strict laws not only regulated Jews' sex lives but barred them from occupations ranging from civil service to farming; as early as 1936, at least 50 per cent of German Jews had no way of making a living.

Confined to Landsberg Fortress, west of Munich, Hitler was released after nine months. During his imprisonment he wrote *Mein Kampf* (My Struggle), a strange book, part autobiography, part blueprint for his future plans. It was to serve as his party's bible.

In his early days as Italy's Premier, Mussolini moved with caution, naming only four Fascists to his 14-man cabinet. But he soon dropped his conciliatory air. In his first address to Parliament he made his contempt for that body crystal-clear. Bluntly he told its members: "I could have transformed this gray hall into an armed camp of Black Shirts, a bivouac for corpses. I could have nailed up the doors." The cowed deputies voted him emergency authority to rule without them for the next 12 months.

At 39, Mussolini was the youngest Premier in Italy's history. A leonine head, piercing black eyes and a jutting jaw made up for a height of only 5 feet 6 inches. Fitness was a fetish with him. He broke his official schedule, at least publicly, only for strenuous exercise—riding, boxing and fencing. He boasted that he ate and drank sparingly (he had an ulcer) and he excoriated Italians who overindulged.

One habit he carried over from the past shocked conventional Italians; unaccustomed to shaving every day, he often appeared at official functions with an untidy stubble on his face. Gossip soon disclosed his disregard for other proprieties. He was a tireless woman chaser; attractive women were seldom safe alone with him, even in his office.

Italy at first responded almost magically to Mussolini's leadership. The strikers went back to work and the students to their books. Mussolini tightened his grip. A new election law provided that the party receiving the largest number of votes—so long as it was a quarter of the total—would receive two thirds of the seats in Parliament. In April 1924, in the first election held under the law, the Fascists polled 65 per cent of the votes cast, the largest plurality for any party since the founding of modern Italy.

When the new Parliament assembled in May, Giacomo Matteotti, a moderate Socialist with a background of education and family wealth, challenged the election's validity,

accusing the Fascists of widespread fraud. The Fascist majority in the Chamber turned into a mob howling for his blood. When he finished amid the uproar, he said to a colleague, "Now you may write the eulogy for my funeral." Mussolini turned to a henchman and said: "This man, after this speech, must not be allowed to go around."

Ten days later Matteotti disappeared. Shortly afterward his battered body was found in a shallow grave near Rome. Blazing headlines in the still-free non-Fascist press blamed Mussolini. Overnight, he fell from his peak of popularity, even among Fascists; many threw away their badges of party membership. An outraged opposition withdrew from Parliament, hoping the move would force the King to ask for Mussolini's resignation. The King refused to intervene.

Five men, all former *Arditi,* were eventually tried for the murder. They denied they had intended to kill Matteotti; they had kidnapped him just to beat him up and teach him a lesson. They needed no orders; they were merely anticipating their leader's wishes. They received brief prison terms, later reduced by special amnesty.

Mussolini, once he had recovered his confidence, moved decisively. He had Parliament declare the opposition seats vacant; to the remaining members, now all Fascists, he announced he would henceforward rule as a dictator. "Italy wants peace and quiet, work and calm," he said. "I will give these things with love if possible, with force if necessary."

With these words, spoken on January 3, 1925, civil liberties ceased to exist for the Italians. So did freedom of the press. Thereafter Mussolini considered himself—and conducted himself—as the sole government, subject to the King only nominally.

Eight more years would elapse before Hitler became dictator of Germany. After his parole from prison in December 1924, he set himself two goals: to strengthen his party and to attain power by legal means. No more *putsches;* instead, he said of his opponents: "If outvoting them takes longer than outshooting them, at least the result will be guaranteed by their constitution. Sooner or later we will have a majority—and after that Germany."

Both goals took longer than Hitler expected. Between 1925 and 1929 Germany enjoyed a period of prosperity, thanks in part to the so-called Dawes Plan. In mid-1924, after the Ruhr crisis, an international committee of experts had reviewed the reparations questions. They were headed by a Chicago banker, Charles G. Dawes.

Dawes and his group avoided naming a total figure for future German payments or a date when these should end. But they drastically cut the amount of the annual installments for the next few years and also recommended large loans from foreign banks to help the Germans recover economically. With this vote of confidence Germany stabilized its currency; the loans, chiefly from American banks, proved so generous that they exceeded the reparations obligations.

No less important for the country's stability was Field Marshal Paul von Hindenburg's election as President in March 1925. Now 78, he was an awesome, totemic figure, the man to whom the Kaiser himself had entrusted Germany's armies when he abdicated his throne. Tradition-minded Germans could not look upon the Republic as a betrayal of the nation so long as Hindenburg served as its President.

Against the tide, Hitler bided his time—until an unparalleled opportunity arose for him. In July 1929, yet another reparations agreement was put forward—the Young Plan, again named for an American banker, Owen D. Young. Unlike the Dawes Plan, it specified a date for the end of reparations and fixed a total sum—$9 billion, instead of the $33 billion envisioned by the reparations commission in 1921. But the Germans focused on the date this burden of guilt would finally end—1988, virtually the end of the century.

Hitler savagely attacked the Young Plan as another example of the perfidy of the war victors and the inequity of the Versailles Treaty. He had the powerful support of a diehard nationalist, Alfred Hugenberg, a former director of Krupp, the giant armaments firm, and now the immensely wealthy owner of a nation-wide newspaper chain. Though the Young Plan went through, Hitler's widely publicized efforts paid off in the September 1930 parliamentary election. The National Socialists won 107 seats in the Reichstag, a bloc second only to that of the leading Social Democrats.

Suddenly Hitler was a power to be courted, and confident enough to propose a meeting with Hindenburg himself. "I suppose he wants a free drink," the President's son sneered. But the meeting was arranged. Hindenburg suggested that Hitler support the coalition cabinet headed by Chancellor Heinrich Brüning. To Hindenburg's displeasure,

A BEFUDDLED FALL GUY FOR AN INSIDE JOB

On the chilly, windy evening of February 27, 1933, Nazi Minister of Propaganda Joseph Goebbels was entertaining the Führer at a family dinner when the phone rang, and an agitated Party member announced that the Reichstag, home of Germany's parliament, was on fire. Goebbels thought the report so farfetched that he didn't bother to tell Hitler about it right away.

But the fire was real enough; it gutted the old building. Real enough, too, was evidence brought out later suggesting that none other than Hermann Göring had secretly planned the blaze to generate support for the Nazis—and justify repression of their opponents. The chance to pull off the scheme fell into Nazi hands by luck, in the form of a mentally retarded Dutch Communist, Marinus van der Lübbe.

The week before the fire, and two weeks before the 1933 German elections, van der Lübbe hiked from Holland to Berlin with a muddled purpose of his own. In a bar, he boasted that he intended to burn the Reichstag; Nazi adherents overheard him and told Göring. Nothing was done to discourage van der Lübbe from pursuing his plan. He followed through. When police answered the fire alarm, they found him inside the Reichstag's main hall, naked to the waist, having used his shirt as tinder to start several small fires. But one man could hardly have set the blaze that so quickly destroyed the Reichstag; Storm Troopers may well have helped him. In any case, van der Lübbe was arrested forthwith.

In the midst of this deadly farce Göring arrived on the scene. "This," he cried, "is the beginning of the Communist revolution! Every Communist official must be shot! Every Communist Reichstag member must be strung up this very night."

Thus Göring launched a campaign of terror against Communists and all other anti-Nazis. Meanwhile, van der Lübbe was quickly brought to trial. Alongside him in the dock, on the shakiest of pretexts, were four other Communists—only one a German, the other three visiting Bulgarians.

The court acquitted all but the wretched van der Lübbe. Alternately raging and apathetic, he confessed, and was judged guilty of arson and high treason. Though they condemned him to death, the judges rewarded van der Lübbe's honesty in confessing by sentencing him to the guillotine rather than the hangman's noose that was prescribed by law.

Der Reichstag in Flammen!

Von Kommunisten in Brand gesteckt!

So würde das ganze Land aussehen, wenn der Kommunismus und die mit ihm verbündete Sozialdemokratie auch nur auf ein paar Monate an die Macht kämen!

Brave Bürger als Geiseln an die Wand gestellt!

Den Bauern den roten Hahn aufs Dach gesetzt!

Wie ein Aufschrei muß es durch Deutschland gehen:

Zerstampft den Kommunismus!

Zerschmettert die Sozialdemokratie!

"The Reichstag in flames! Set on fire by the Communists!" A Nazi propaganda poster also bids Germans "stamp out Communism, destroy Social Democracy" and vote for Hitler, whose name, it is helpfully noted, is in "Column 1" on the upcoming election ballots.

At his Supreme Court trial, Dutch Communist Marinus van der Lübbe, wearing prison uniform, sags under questioning about his part in the Reichstag fire.

Hitler refused. The President then let it be known that he had been "prepared at most to appoint this Bohemian corporal Postmaster, certainly not Chancellor."

Hitler's next move was to challenge Hindenburg directly. In 1932, when the venerable President sought reelection, Hitler ran against him. It was a bold step and a bold campaign, devised by Hitler's clever new propaganda chief, Dr. Joseph Goebbels. While the candidate criss-crossed the country by car, Goebbels blanketed the nation with posters, ran films in the movie houses, and gave away more than 50,000 phonograph records of the leader's speeches.

Two weeks before the election Hitler remembered he was not even a German citizen, thus an ineligible candidate. A neat stratagem corrected this: the Interior Minister of the state of Brunswick, himself a Nazi, appointed Hitler an attaché in Brunswick's legation in Berlin. Hitler thereby became a citizen of Brunswick, thus of Germany.

Hindenburg piled up 18.6 million votes to 11.3 million for Hitler, but failed to get the necessary majority. A runoff was required. The innovative Goebbels had his candidate campaign by plane, with the slogan "Hitler over Germany." Though Hindenburg was reelected, Hitler added more than 2 million votes to his earlier total.

For much of the new support, the Nazis could thank the worldwide depression then raging. The United States, still reeling economically from the effects of the stock market crash of late 1929, no longer had bank loans to offer. Germany was hit hard. By 1932 countless small factories and businesses were in ruins, more than 6,000,000 Germans were unemployed, and farmers, devastated by a sharp drop in commodity prices, were losing their lands in forced sales. As social tensions mounted, the Germans were increasingly polarized politically, with the Nazis and the Communists gaining at the expense of the moderate center.

The political situation became worse when, after his reelection, President Hindenburg—possibly in a moment of senility—turned on Chancellor Brüning, his most ardent supporter, and forced him to resign. In a singularly ill-judged move he replaced Brüning with Franz von Papen, who had been expelled from the United States in 1916 for instigating acts of sabotage while military attaché in Washington. Papen had little but his aristocratic Catholic lineage and social graces to recommend him. At a time of deep popular unrest he airily put together a cabinet in which seven of the 10 members were titled. The so-called "cabinet of barons" became a bitter public jest.

In the parliamentary election of November 1932, Hitler scored his greatest electoral victory to date. The National Socialists won 230 seats out of 608—the largest bloc, though not a majority. Papen offered Hitler a post in a coalition cabinet; he refused. Failing to form a government, Papen was then replaced by a political general, Kurt von Schleicher, who also failed to put together a coalition.

Hitler, waiting impatiently on the threshold of power, was —unknown to most Germans—in desperate straits. The cost of his campaigns had all but bankrupted his party. At this juncture, a group of big industrialists, alarmed at the deteriorating political situation, came to Hitler's rescue. They offered to pay the party's debts and meet the payroll for its Storm Troopers in return for Hitler's promise that once in power he would keep hands off industry. Pressure was then put on Hindenburg to make Hitler Chancellor.

Hindenburg's offer to "the Bohemian corporal" was a carefully hedged ploy devised by his wily friend Papen. Hitler had to accept Papen as Vice Chancellor and limit the Nazis to just three cabinet posts. The intent was clear: Hitler was to be tamed by association with the establishment.

Hitler accepted but was not easily fenced in. Unwilling to rule unless backed by a party majority, he demanded and got a new parliamentary election, calculating that with his new prestige as Chancellor his National Socialists would win by a margin that would free him of humiliating conditions.

In February 1933, at the very outset of the new campaign, a spectacular night fire raged through the Reichstag building itself. A feeble-minded, nearly blind young Dutchman named Marinus van der Lübbe was caught at the scene, confessed to arson and was later beheaded. Many people doubted van der Lübbe's guilt. They suspected the Nazis of having set the fire as a pretext for taking Draconian measures against their foes on the Left; strong evidence pointed to Göring as the planner. Whoever set the fire, Hitler exploited it with diabolical brilliance. Claiming it had been intended as a signal for a Communist uprising, he got from Hindenburg an emergency decree annulling all civil rights. Göring, now the Prussian Minister of the Interior, rounded up more than 4,000

Communists, alleged and real, using many Storm Troopers temporarily deputized as auxiliary police.

Despite the recourse to terror and violence, the Nazi still failed to win an absolute majority in the election of March 1933, though they increased the number of seats they held to 288. Normally, Hitler would have had to rely on the Nationalists and other conservatives to form a government. This time he did not intend to abide by precedent. He proclaimed the election a Nazi triumph, had the swastika flag hoisted everywhere, and left no doubt that he meant to rule.

To dramatize "the revolution," as he called it, he staged an elaborate opening ceremony for the new Reichstag in the historic Garrison Church at Potsdam, where Germany's beloved 18th Century monarch, Frederick the Great, lay buried. In the presence of the former Crown Prince of Germany and an array of generals from the imperial past, Hitler greeted Hindenburg at the church door. The new Chancellor was awkward in a formal cutaway, the President resplendent in the full-dress uniform of Field Marshal. After they exchanged handshakes, Hindenburg proceeded up the nave, paused before the empty throne of the exiled Kaiser, and raised his marshal's baton in salute. Hitler spoke briefly and mutedly, acclaiming "the union between old greatness and youthful strength." Next day, reporting the ceremony, one newspaper said "a wave of emotion swept over Germany."

Two days later Hitler rose in the Reichstag to sound the death knell of the Republic. He demanded immediate passage of an act that would enable him, as Chancellor, to rule by decree, without limitation of powers, for four years. It was approved over the dissenting votes of 94 Social Democrats, 24 of whom were subsequently murdered. Three months later their moderate party was formally banned, and its seats in the Reichstag vacated. By the summer of 1933 all other political parties were outlawed and most of Hitler's opponents were in jail, exile or concentration camps.

Most, but not all. Within the Nazi party itself some remained for whom there was to be a bloody epilogue. Ernst Röhm, Hitler's old comrade in Munich and now leader of the Storm Troopers, was dissatisfied about the turn events had taken and incautious about airing his grievance. "Adolf is rotten," he told friends. "He is betraying us all. He goes around only with reactionaries."

Röhm's ambition was to make his Brown Shirts into a people's army that would absorb the regular army, with the whole under his command. The Reichswehr wanted no part of these brawlers; as one of its generals later testified, "Rearmament was too serious and difficult to permit the participation of speculators, drunkards and homosexuals."

Hitler's new businessmen allies were equally distrustful of the Brown Shirts and demanded a curb on their arrogance and violence. What finally sealed Röhm's doom was Hitler's own ambition. Hindenburg was dying and Hitler wanted to succeed him. To do so he had to have the support of the Reichswehr. In return for that support, Hitler secretly promised the high command that the regular Army and the Navy would be the nation's sole bearers of arms.

He then had to deal with Röhm, and as his instrument he used the elite black-coated *Schutzstaffel* (protection squad). The SS was a force apart from the Storm Troopers; its members were bound by a personal oath of loyalty to Hitler himself. He had entrusted the supervision of the SS to a recent Nazi adherent, a mild-faced former chicken farmer named Heinrich Himmler.

At dawn on June 30, 1934, Hitler and an SS detachment surprised Röhm and a party of friends at the resort of Bad Wiessee. According to one version of the encounter, Röhm, roused from sleep, greeted Hitler with "Heil, Mein Führer!" Hitler screamed: "You're under arrest!" and had his old friend hustled off to Munich. There Röhm was handed a revolver; refusing to use it on himself, he was shot by the SS.

All over Germany Hitler paid off other old scores. General von Schleicher, his immediate predecessor as Chancellor, was killed with his young wife in the library of their home.The leader of the strongly anti-Nazi Catholic Action movement was shot down in his office. Gustav von Kahr, whom Hitler had never forgiven for his role in the Munich *putsch,* was another victim. Officially it was announced that 74 enemies of the state had been executed and three of them forced to commit suicide for plotting mutiny and rebellion. Later evidence indicated that the toll of this blood purge was a great deal higher.

The effect was to shock the German people into total obedience. Five weeks later the 87-year-old Hindenburg died. Hitler, now 45, was proclaimed President. In a subsequent plebiscite 38,360,000 Germans voted to ratify his assumption of power. The Nazi reign was under way.

DEADLY GAME OF MAKE BELIEVE

In a dead-earnest military scrimmage in 1932, a German antitank crew defends a soccer field with a wood-barreled gun whose other parts are from a real weapon.

IRON MEN BEHIND THE WOODEN GUNS

A year before Hitler came to power in 1933, the German Army was still frozen by the Treaty of Versailles at a mere 100,000 men. The Treaty terms forbade the Germans to have modern weapons, including tanks, artillery and other heavy equipment. The Treaty also barred the formation of a general staff, which is the brains and nervous system of a 20th Century army. To most outsiders, the Army appeared to be little more than a domestic riot force, even in its name: Reichswehr means state defense. In fact, this all but armless army was being carefully trained as the nucleus of a future war machine. Its leader was General Hans von Seeckt *(opposite)*, a commander who, despite his monocle and Prussian lineage, was anything but the rigid conservative of the stereotype. Rather, he was a canny innovator who slipped around Treaty sanctions with consummate ingenuity to build an expert force of bright, physically rugged young men, who were well paid and who enlisted for 12 years.

To give his men experience in the tactics of tank warfare, Seeckt simulated tanks by draping automobiles with canvas, cardboard or tin armor. Antitank guns and other forbidden artillery were mocked up in wood—except for key mechanisms that were useful for training, such as the breech; these were of metal. Target planes for wooden antiaircraft guns were models whirled on the end of strings, or were toy balloons. In order to camouflage the Reichswehr's combat potential, Seeckt encouraged publicity that gave the impression that the enlistees were being prepared to re-enter civilian life *(page 102)*.

Though a few well-informed people in Britain and elsewhere were aware of what was going on, they tended to ignore or disparage the toy army. After all, Germany was effectively hemmed in by French might on the west and the Polish army with its splendid cavalry on the east. But then came Hitler and, all too soon for the bystanders, the toy Reichswehr disappeared and in its place stood the giant steel façade of the world's most up-to-date army, whose leaders were none other than the iron men who had lately played at war with wooden guns.

Tough tanker trainees like these were delighted to exchange the impoverishment of life in postwar Germany for the pay and security of army life.

General Hans von Seeckt, who was the military genius behind the creation of the Reichswehr, Germany's miniature model army, sits in his Bavarian library.

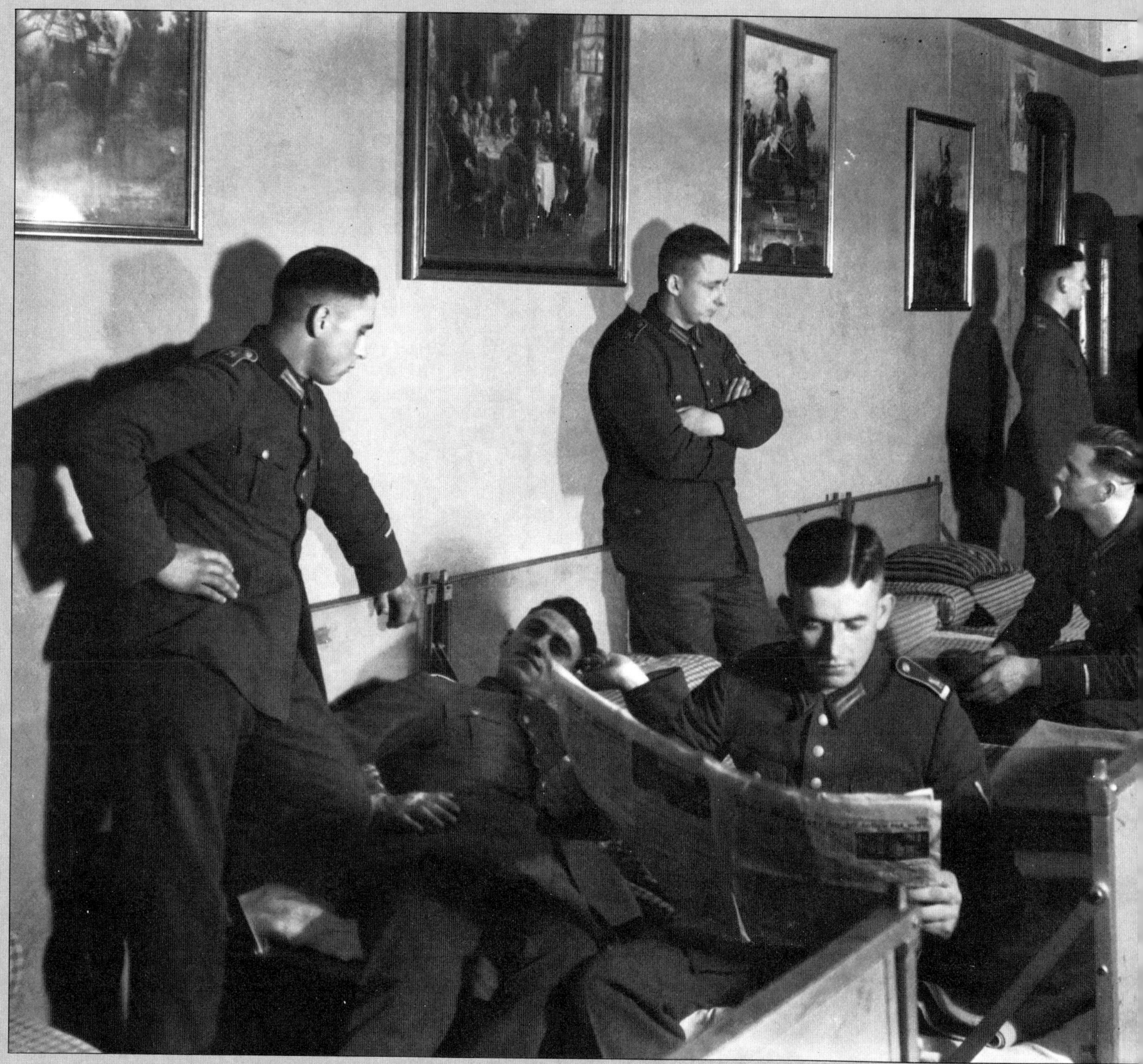

Fresh volunteers at the Berlin Regimental Barracks chat with a noncom, seated at right. The elegant housing and the friendliness of the noncom—the traditional scourge of all enlisted men—were all part of the Reichswehr campaign to make a military career attractive. So was the pay, which was roughly six times that of the French Army.

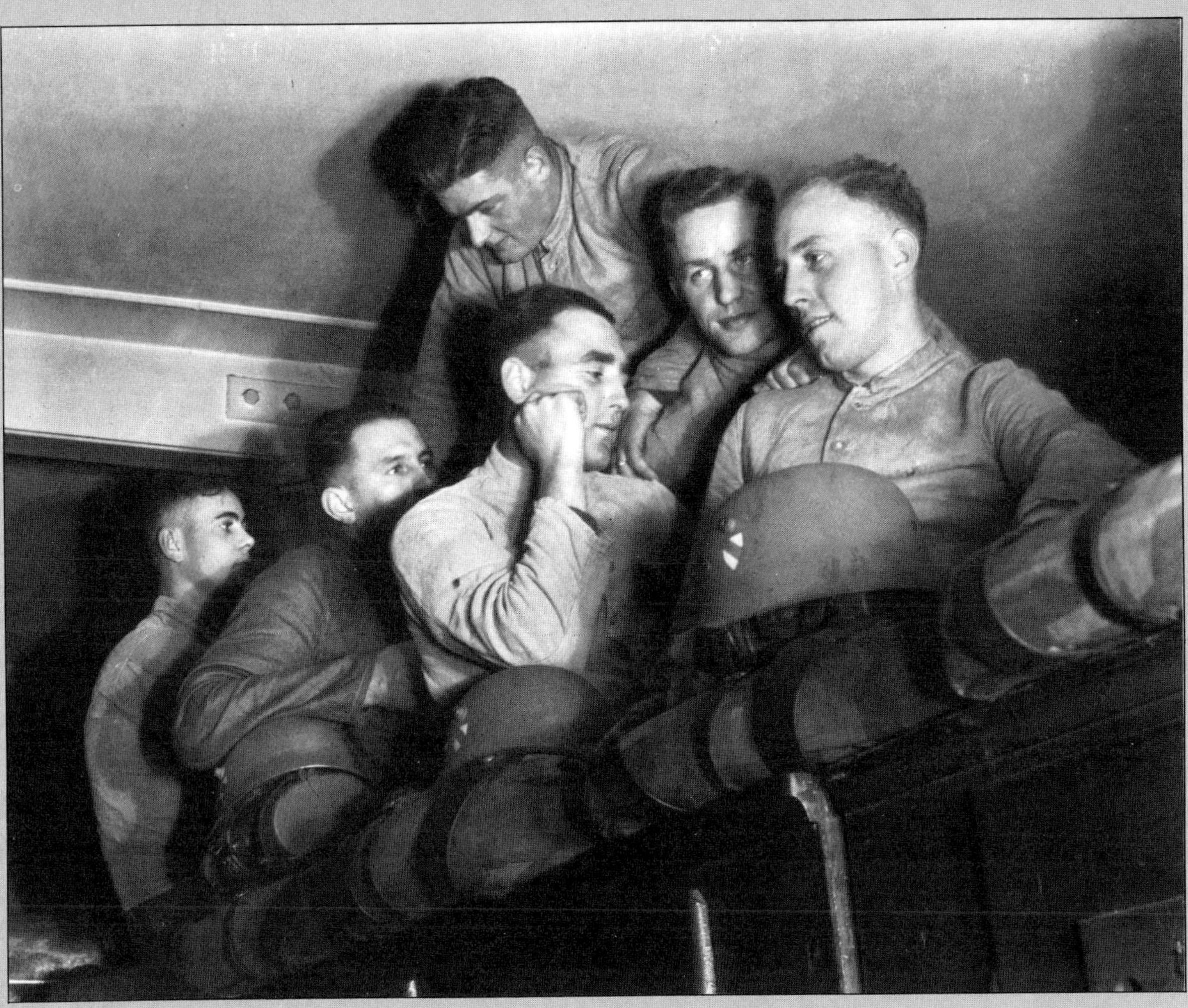

Skylarking recruits crowd a top bunk in the Berlin Barracks. Even punishment in the new Army was tinged with humor, and was infinitely more humane than the beatings common in the old Imperial Army. For talking in formation, a Reichswehr trainee might be ordered to hide under a bed and bellow out the old Lutheran hymn, "From the Depth of My Need I Cry Out to Thee."

Troopers do calisthenics at the Army Sports Academy, a physical training school for officers on the outskirts of Berlin. The physical standards of the Reichswehr were the toughest in the world. In one exercise that was designed to test eyesight, concentration and body control, a man had to balance atop a beam set on a floor where a knapsack, helmet and items of clothing had been scattered. Without stepping off the beam, he had to pick everything up, put it in the knapsack, and toss the sack onto a wall hook. Then, reversing the process, he had to restore each item to its original place on the floor.

An instructor quizzes privates on the anatomy of the horse. Such apparently unwarlike pursuits were publicized to make the world believe that the Reichswehr was preparing soldiers for postservice careers such as, here, animal husbandry. But the instruction also made practical sense. To make the maintenance of the Reichswehr onerously expensive, the Versailles Treaty required a high ratio of cavalry units to infantry—about three mounted outfits for every seven dismounted. Taking care of all those horses put severe strain on the army's expertise as well as its pocketbook.

A soldier student investigates the art of beekeeping—another civilian-life skill imparted to the troops and then, for propaganda effect, elaborately displayed through the press. This one had no military value.

An antitank gun crew sits at rigid attention on the caisson of a wood-barreled dummy weapon. Besides using mock guns, the Germans carried out war games with nonexistent people—a necessity for training commanders to control the large troop units forbidden by the Treaty. One man might carry a sign that said, "I am a platoon," and then be sent to attack a placard in a field bearing the legend, "This is a machine gun nest of eight men."

Tankers buckle an automobile into its cardboard armor at the Lankowitz training installation. Not all the Reichswehr's phony tanks were as substantial as this camouflaged model; some were carts propelled from inside by the leg power of the crewmen.

The real menace of Germany's future army emanates from these Reichswehr soldiers photographed during review. At about the time the first of the superbly trained volunteers —all considered officer material—were completing their hitches, Hitler came to power. Within months, he repudiated the Versailles treaty, turned a revived German war industry to the making of real guns, and began drafting hundreds of thousands of fresh recruits to be led by the nucleus of crack professionals.

THE THEATRICS OF POWER

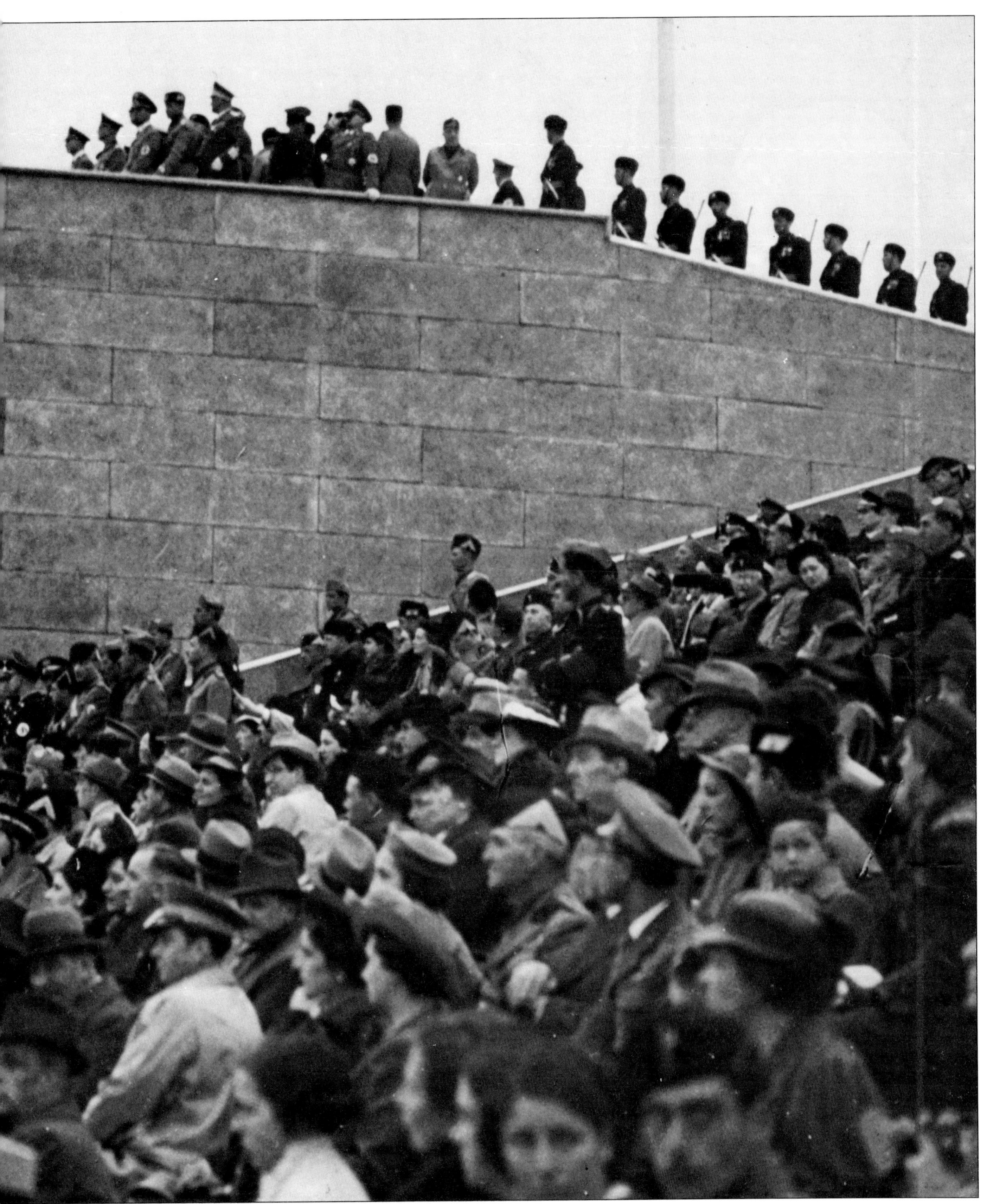

High above the crowd, standing apart even from aides and officials, Adolf Hitler (left) and Benito Mussolini gaze down upon a 1938 Fascist rally in Rome.

A COUPLE OF MASTER PITCHMEN

A diffident Prime Minister, Mussolini bows to Victor Emmanuel III, the king who made legitimate the Duce's Fascist regime in the early 1920s.

Though very different personalities, Adolf Hitler and Benito Mussolini were alike in being two of history's most adept barkers, actors and stage managers in the theatrics of power. Like monarchs of old, they displayed themselves in monumental settings at huge rallies where the audiences became part of the performance, swept away by the carefully orchestrated displays of military might, flamboyant rhetoric and colorful ritual. Yet while the two dictators set themselves above their people like ancient emperors, they also managed to project a more up-to-date image as men of the people, who were dedicated to satisfying the needs and desires of ordinary citizens.

Both men were magnetic leaders, and instinctive politicians. But behind all the pomp and folksiness lay a foundation of masterful contrivance and studied manipulation. Cautious at the outset of their respective careers, Mussolini and Hitler each took pains to cloak his advance to power in a dignified aura of legitimacy, by conspicuously identifying himself with an archetypal figure from the old order. As early as 1922 Mussolini sought and won the support of Italy's King Victor Emmanuel III *(left)* while Hitler courted the friendship—which he quickly exploited—of prestigious Field Marshal Paul von Hindenburg, Germany's President and most celebrated public servant.

However, once the two dictators were securely in office, the old heroes slowly faded away as Hitler and Mussolini grabbed center stage to cultivate loyalty and create an aura of might through stagy speeches *(overleaf)*, radio and film harangues and a score of other devices. Smooth-running propaganda machines, abetted by strong police forces to suppress dissidence, cranked out the material and designed or inspired the props and the sets—from novelty items *(pages 118-119)* to outdoor spectaculars *(pages 122-127)*. Until displaced by the pressures of war, such displays ran as smash hits in Germany and Italy. Indeed, throughout most of both dictators' careers, their skill in the art of totalitarian showmanship made their claims to power seem both natural and inevitable to the nations they ruled.

"The Marshal and the Corporal," proclaims this poster, tacitly implying a soldierly bond between the ex-non-com Hitler and Hindenburg, the old military chieftain.

FIERY VIRTUOSOS OF THE PODIUM

"All great world-shaking events have been brought about not by written matter, but by the spoken word!" Passionate adherence to that Hitler dictum helped sweep both the German dictator and his Italian counterpart to power. And subsequently, to an extent seldom before witnessed, their oratory cemented their hold over millions of diverse people, crossing easily over class lines and appealing to street thugs, solid burghers, wealthy industrialists and old-line aristocrats alike.

Of the two men, the more natural speaker was Mussolini. A former newspaper editor with a gift for choosing evocative words, the Duce enhanced his delivery with highly theatrical gestures and body movements. These instinctive mannerisms, combined with Mussolini's deep baritone voice and insistent, staccato delivery, riveted the attention of his listeners.

Hitler, by contrast, was a shy man and an awkward speaker. Aware of these critical weaknesses, he rehearsed religiously *(right)* to bring impact and the impression of spontaneity to his speeches. Oddly, despite his enormous success, Hitler never lost his nervousness. Even at the crest of his power, he tended to begin speeches in a muted, tentative voice as if he had no assurance of his effect on an audience. Once launched, however, his ever more vehement delivery—abetted by artfully honed gesticulations—imparted such force to his words that they became a raging torrent. To listeners whose frustrations and ambitions Hitler played on with a virtuoso's sure touch, the Führer's voice seemed almost like a knife that opened, in the words of one awed follower, "each wound in the raw, liberating the mass unconscious, expressing its innermost aspirations, telling it what it most wants to hear."

Manipulating his body and face to suit the tempo of his words, a characteristically animated Benito Mussolini delivers a speech from a Neapolitan balcony. The stolid listener to the left of the Duce is Air Minister Italo Balbo, veteran of many similar performances.

Hitler practices gesticulations in a series of studio photographs taken by his personal photographer Heinrich Hoffmann. Afterward the Nazi leader studied each picture, altered movements, and changed each posture until it produced the impact he wanted to impart.

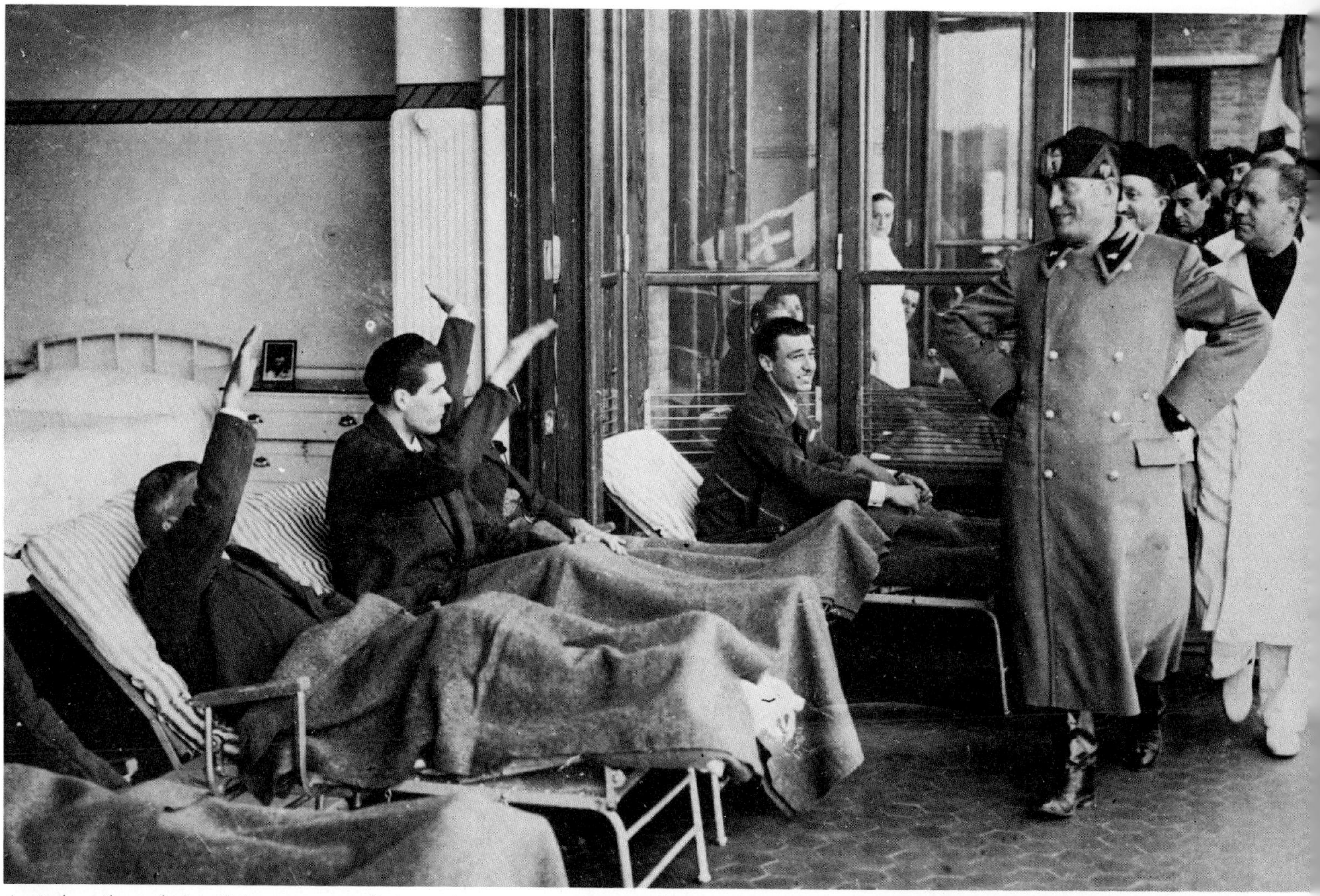

A crisply uniformed Mussolini pays a paternalistic—and stagy—visit to saluting, flag-waving patients at a new hospital built by the Fascist Welfare Organization.

Disdaining to use goggles intended to protect his eyes from chaff, the Duce joins farmers harvesting wheat in the Pontine Marshes, which were reclaimed in the early '30s.

Mussolini pauses for a discreet roughhouse with a lion cub in a Rome zoo. Mussolini staged pictures like this to demonstrate his regal and manly predilection for the king of beasts.

THE OTHER FACES OF THE DICTATORS

Hitler and Mussolini brought the same shrewdly focused energy—but again, different personal styles—to grass-roots politicking that they brought to their elaborate speechmaking. The dictators, both of whom had plebeian backgrounds, were at pains to be photographed mingling with that living symbol of common virtue, the farmer. They projected folksy and paternal concern through visits with housewives, with children and the infirm. Very important for any Continental politician, they showed a proper respect not only for war veterans but also for the elderly.

They were aware in addition that in both Germany and Italy, where inflation and depression had compounded the ravages of World War I, the people expected some evidence of solid material progress to go with the smiles and the speeches. Each of them, therefore, sponsored grandiose public works starting with nationwide transportation systems. Each of the men also launched highway programs. The Führer, who loved machines, lent personal support to a resurgent German automobile industry that boasted a fourfold increase in production between 1933 and 1935. Mussolini rejuvenated the moribund Italian railroads. The Duce also set in motion an effective land reclamation program *(far left)* to increase crop production.

But again, for all their similar ends and means, Hitler and Mussolini remained dramatically different as personalities. Hitler, the more introspective of the two, genuinely seemed to enjoy his sentimental dealings with children and animals. Mussolini, more assertive, used well-publicized encounters with fiery stallions and other symbolic beasts *(left, below)* to reinforce his image of superior male courage.

Mussolini's blatant egotism came across most clearly in a life style of the classic aspirer, with palatial working quarters and a prodigal supply of flashy uniforms in his wardrobe *(pages 114-115)*. For his part, Hitler chose to understate by dressing simply—very often in a plain brown uniform adorned with the Iron Cross awarded him as a common soldier in World War I.

An attentive Hitler learns about a powerful new German-built car at the 1935 Berlin auto show.

Hitler shakes hands with an elderly peasant during an informal trip into the Bavarian countryside.

The Führer prepares to heave a stick for his German shepherd, Muck. Although this photograph was made as propaganda, Hitler once said that dogs were his only friends.

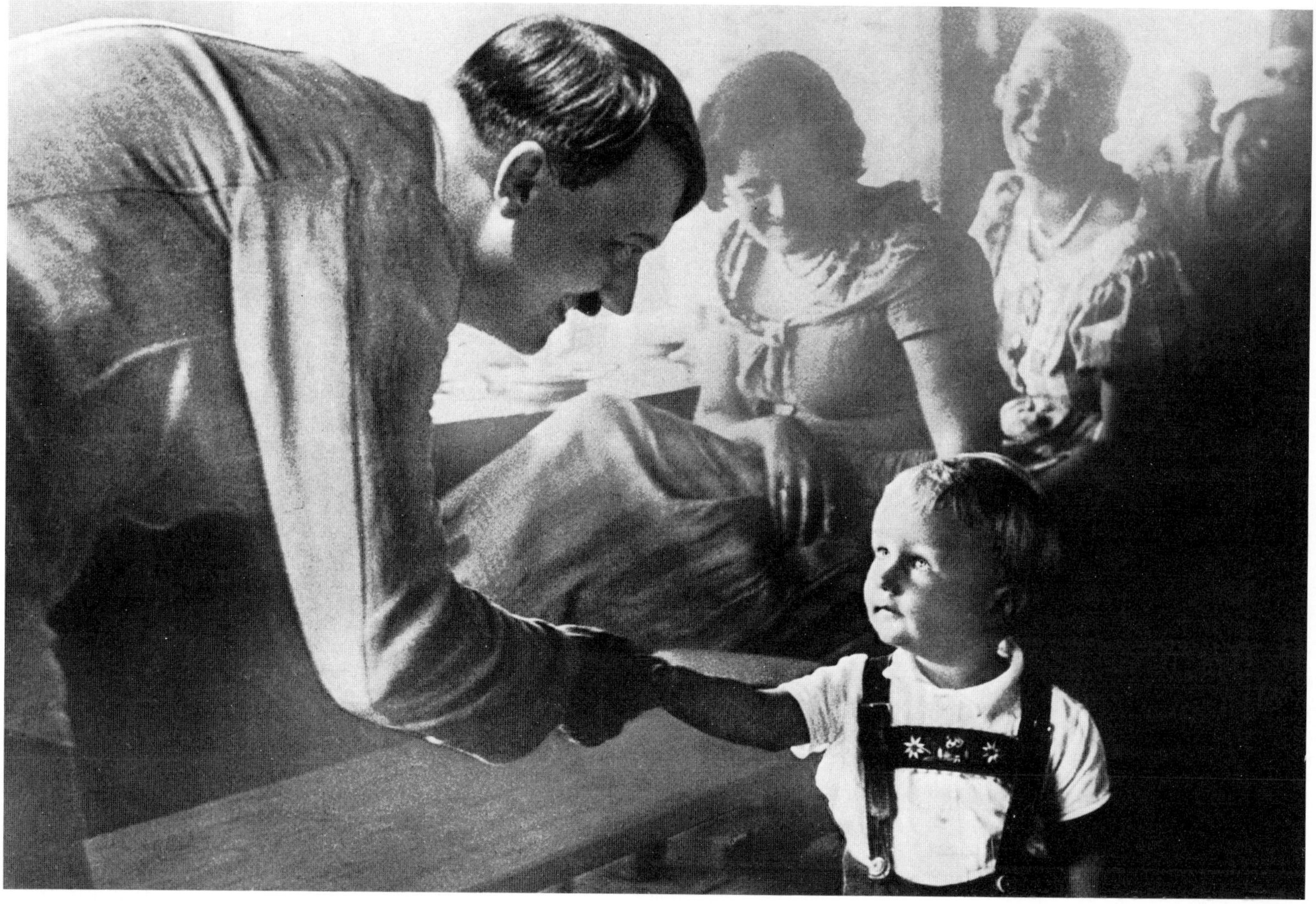

Hitler beams as he is photographed making friends with a little boy in his unceasing effort to be identified as a father to all Germans. The picture was distributed all over Germany as a postcard entitled A Child's Gaze.

Mein Führer!

(Das Kind ſpricht:)

Ich kenne dich wohl und habe dich lieb
wie Vater und Mutter.
Ich will dir immer gehorſam ſein
wie Vater und Mutter.
Und wenn ich groß bin, helfe ich dir
wie Vater und Mutter,
Und freuen ſollſt du dich an mir
wie Vater und Mutter!

Hitler's paternal profile ranged even down into the coloring books used by school children. Here, a neatly dressed girl tells Hitler: "I know you well and love you, like father and mother. I shall always obey you, like father and mother. And when I grow up I shall help you, like father and mother. And you will be proud of me, like father and mother."

Hitler pats the chin of a Hitler Youth—a member of a young people's organization set up in the late '20s to create a generational core of devout Nazis.

A smiling group of SA men and youths crowds in around the Führer at the Braune Haus, the storm troopers' rustic headquarters in the Bavarian city of Munich.

Mussolini liked to refer to this huge, marble-lined chamber in Rome's Palazzo Venezia as his "private office." Visitors to the Duce, shown standing behind his desk, naturally tended to be impressed as they approached him across the ornate 60-by-40-foot room.

Mussolini assumed an array of official and honorary titles—and had an elaborate uniform tailored to go with each. A showman to the last detail, he topped off every costume with the appropriate hat (right).

COMMANDER OF THE FASCIST MILITIA

CHIEF OF THE FRONTIER MILITIA

At a state affair, the Duce wears his Premier's uniform.

In a military parade, Mussolini personifies the archtype of a mounted and helmeted warrior.

MARSHAL OF THE EMPIRE

HEAD OF THE FASCIST PARTY

ICONS FOR SALE: CASHING IN ON THE CULT

As the cult of personality began to envelop first Italy and then Germany, a profitable cottage industry sprang up in each country to exploit the leaders' ideas and images. Some of these products were officially sanctioned; some were even encouraged. Others decidedly were not. For example, in the tobacco shops and the seedy beer cellars of Germany, salesmen hawked an array of junk such as swastikas that lit up, tin Iron Crosses, and hair brushes or cigarette lighters that bore either Hitler's portrait or the swastika. In Italy, millions of enameled likenesses of the Duce appeared on cuff links, hat decorations—and even swimsuited ladies *(left).*

While the Italian Fascists were merely scowling at such tastelessness, their northern allies were taking action. The Nazis felt that the shoddy merchandise—for which the scornful German word is *kitsch* (rubbish)—made them and their Führer appear ridiculous in the eyes of the world. In 1933, Hitler's Ministry of Propaganda under Dr. Joseph Goebbels issued an anti-*kitsch* law that forbade the commercial use of Nazi symbols and personalizations without official permission.

Goebbels' ukase stopped the *kitsch* peddlers cold, but it gave new impetus to the sale of such state-approved iconography as Nazi armbands, pennants and slogan-bearing plaques. The Italians also pushed out millions of state-sanctioned postcards. Above all, regulations in each of the two countries firmly required that all public buildings—offices, hospitals, schools, even opera houses—must display approved portraits of the leaders.

An Italian bathing beauty sports a portrait of Mussolini pinned to the front of her beach outfit and set off with a long string of pearls.

Shoppers at a stationery store in the Saar region purchase officially sanctioned Nazi promotions: swastika flags, banners, slogans and plaques in all shapes.

Postcards like this one were among Fascist-approved methods of promoting Mussolini. The hand-painted scene shows the Duce with sons Vittorio and Bruno, wife Rachele, and daughter Edda.

Das ist nationaler Kitsch!

Wovor uns das Kitsch-Gesetz schützen soll

Eine ganze Industrie ist in den wenigen Monaten seit dem 30. Januar emporgeblüht. Aber ihr Fundament ist ungesund, ihre Fruchtbarkeit schadet dem Volk mehr, als sie der Wirtschaft nützt. Diese „Industrie der Geschmacklosigkeiten" hat das Bedürfnis zu wittern geglaubt, immer und überall die neuen Farben, Symbole und Hoheitszeichen des Reiches, die Bilder der neuen Staatsmänner und historischen Persönlichkeiten zu sehen und zu zeigen — zu Hause, auf der Straße, im Schaufenster, im Gasthaus, an der Kleidung. Sicherlich hat nur eine verschwindende Minderheit dieser Kitschfabrikanten in ehrlicher Ueberzeugung die Fabrikation solcher Gegenstände aufgenommen — in der primitiven Ueberlegung, ihrer eigenen Begeisterung und der des Publikums für den Sieg der nationalen Bewegung in dieser

Zum Kampf des Propagandaministeriums gegen nationalen Kitsch: Einige Beispiele von Erzeugnissen allzu geschäftstüchtiger Fabrikanten, gegen die sich das kommende Kitschgesetz richtet: Eine Kinder-Lärmtrompete.

Künstliche Schneeglöckchen mit Haken-

Allzu große Geschäftstüchtigkeit, gegen die jetzt eingeschritten wird: Herstellung von Papierbechern mit verzerrten Bildern des Reichskanzlers.

"This is the national kitsch!" scolds a 1933 issue of the Berliner Illustrierte Zeitung, which illustrates the kind of bric-a-brac that offended the Nazi hierarchy: a toy horn with Hitler's image printed on it, a glass jar filled with "political candies," swastika-bedecked artificial flowers, and a paper cup that was adorned with the Führer's face.

A formation of Italian boys on a beach spells out a tribute that means: Long Live the Leader.

A customer chooses a portrait of Hitler for a special Christmas gift in a German art shop.

Fascist youth-organization members pack inside a monumental M, erected by party functionaries before a visit by Mussolini to the Italian hamlet of Verres.

MOB ADORATION MADE TO ORDER

All the image-making devices mounted by Hitler and Mussolini were aimed at enticing the citizens toward the great popular rallies, the heart of the dictators' political midway. There, in Hitler's characteristically shrewd words, onlookers would be "swept into the tremendous stream of hypnotic intoxication."

Though a host of ordinary citizens voluntarily showed up at these meetings, attendance for party organization members was far from optional. In Italy, postcards announcing the occasions were sent out by low-level functionaries to all registered Fascists. Refusal to attend a rally could mean a reprimand, or even loss of a job.

Once on hand for such gatherings, the crowd could count on blood-stirring performances. As master of ceremonies, each dictator had his own brilliantly successful act. Mussolini preferred his flock to be herded into a public square like the one in Florence at right. Then, at the precise dramatic moment he would strut out onto a balcony high above what he called "oceanic gatherings." And as he harangued the crowds in a mounting crescendo, blackshirted Fascists pressed toward him chanting "Du-ce, Du-ce, Du-ce!"

Hitler mustered the faithful in a more organized way—and on an even more extravagant scale *(overleaf)*. He preferred his audience in uniform, at attention, standing rank on rank, as he led them in thunderous litanies of response to the glory of Germany and, of course, of its Führer.

Half a million Nazi faithful jam a Zeppelin landing field in 1933 at one of the earliest of a series of awesome party rallies. When Hitler, in the colonnaded reviewing stand, reached the climax of his speeches, the crowds shouted their allegiance in hackle-raising cadences of "Sieg Heil!"

Italians fill every corner of the Piazza della Signoria in Florence to see Mussolini, among the figures on the balcony.

4

CONVULSION IN THE FAR EAST

Toothless in Shensi
Revolt against the ancient order
War with the warlords
Some friends from Russia
Chiang turns on the Communists
Peasant support for a Red poet
The high price of civil war
Japanese sideshow in Manchuria
A Mandarin Marxist in clergyman's garb
The Long March
The primacy of Mao
Hands joined against a common enemy
Shootout on the Marco Polo Bridge
Flood tide for the Japanese invaders

In the rock-strewn mountains of Shensi Province in north central China, the air was bitterly cold at dawn on the morning of December 13, 1936. On a snow-covered hillside a man crouched in a cave, with only a thin robe thrown over his nightshirt against the icy wind. His bare feet and hands were cut and bleeding. He had no teeth—in his sudden flight he had left his dentures behind. He was not only shivering with cold and exhaustion; he was shaking with rage. As his pursuers, a squad of Chinese soldiers, neared his hiding place he rose and screamed, "Shoot me and finish it all!"

The soldiers halted. Their commanding officer stepped forward and saluted, then knelt humbly in the snow. "We will not shoot you," he said. "We are here to protect you. We only ask that you lead us against Japan."

Hours before, Chiang Kai-shek, Generalissimo of all China, had fled these men. Now he was their captive, and was forced to accept an offer from their commander to carry him on his back down the mountainside. In these strange circumstances the stage was set for a dramatic decision in the long and growing conflict between Japan and China. It was a decision that would bring the two nations to open war.

What had brought Chiang to Shensi Province in that bitter winter of 1936 was a showdown with his hitherto loyal subordinate, Marshal Chang Hsueh-liang, the commander of the Chinese army in Shensi. As leader of the Kuomintang, or Nationalist Party, Chiang Kai-shek had long sought to unify his country by suppressing the Chinese Communists who opposed his rule. Some other Chinese leaders, including Marshal Chang, believed that both of the warring factions should put aside their differences and join forces against the greater threat of the Japanese, who had already occupied Manchuria to the north and were making clear their aggressive intentions farther south.

The Marshal, with his eye on the Japanese, had balked at the Generalissimo's orders to launch a new offensive against Chinese Communists who were newly entrenched in his territory. On his arrival in Sian, the capital city of Shensi, the Generalissimo had angrily refused to hear the Marshal's objections, insisting he had a soldier's duty to obey orders. The Marshal and his colleagues, in turn, hit on a bold plan: they would kidnap Chiang, their own commander in chief, in order to reason with him from a position of strength—to "stimulate his awakening," in the words of a later official communiqué. On his orders, the Marshal's fur-hatted Manchurian troops surprised and seized the Generalissimo's staff at their hotel outside Sian. Chiang himself, however, managed to escape from his bedroom. He scaled a 10-foot wall back of the hotel—dropping into a deep moat and severely wrenching his back—then scrambled barefoot up the rocky mountainside and took bleak refuge in the cave where his pursuers finally caught up with him.

The next morning Marshal Chang broadcast to an astonished world the report that he was holding his commander hostage until he would agree to certain conditions, the most important of which was that he call off the civil war against the Communists and lead a united nation in resistance to the Japanese. The report of the "Sian incident," as it soon became known, created an international sensation; the news came, as Madame Chiang Kai-shek later recalled, "like a thunderclap from a clear sky."

What happened next at Sian is still not clear. At first, it seems, the imperious Generalissimo insisted that he either be freed without conditions or shot at once. As the talks dragged on, the negotiators were joined by Nationalist envoys, including Chiang's unofficial political adviser, an Australian ex-journalist named William H. Donald, who had once served the Marshal in the same capacity and who was trusted by both men. Even more important was the arrival of leaders of the Communist party under political commissar Chou En-lai, who argued that if the Generalissimo were put to death all of China would be plunged into an endless civil war, out of which there could be no hope of salvaging a united anti-Japanese front. The Communist argument was undoubtedly dictated by pressure from Stalin, who saw Japan as a threat to the Soviet Union's Far Eastern interests. The arrival of the lovely, iron-willed Madame Chiang, and her skilled negotiating with the Marshal—as well as with her husband—may well have speeded up the Generalissimo's agreement to terms that led to his release.

When, on Christmas day, Chiang Kai-shek, his wife and the other Nationalist negotiators flew back to Nanking they were accompanied by another passenger: Marshal Chang. He had come, he explained, to face charges of mutiny. He was court-martialed, convicted, sentenced—and promptly pardoned, though he was placed under what amounted to indefinite house arrest.

The Sian incident, bizarre as it was, was only one of several crucial turning points in China's history of turbulence in the period leading up to World War II—a history characterized by constant internal strife and external threats. For nearly three centuries, the country of China, whose people called it by the traditional name of the Middle Kingdom, had been ruled by imperial descendants of the Manchus. But beginning about the middle of the 19th Century, China had been exposed to repeated humiliations at the hands of various intruders. As one result, there were so-called foreign concessions in such cities as Shanghai and Canton. The concessions, exacted from China by England, France, Germany, Japan, the United States and other powers, were actual areas within the cities where the Chinese people had become subject to alien laws and creditors. In the first Sino-Japanese War of 1894-1895, the Chinese had been defeated by the Japanese, who had forced them out of the vassal kingdom of Korea and taken other territories including the major island of Formosa, later to be called Taiwan.

These accumulated humiliations helped to breed young revolutionaries. One of their leaders was Sun Yat-sen, who had risen from a peasant background to be educated as a physician in Canton, and yearned to throw off the double yoke of the decrepit Manchu Dynasty and foreign domination. By World War I Sun Yat-sen had succeeded, but the Chinese republic he helped set up was little more than a façade. The real power was divided among dozens of warlords who ruled China like so many medieval barons.

In 1919, the Treaty of Versailles handed over defeated Germany's rights and possessions in Shantung Province, not to China but to her old enemy Japan. To many Chinese this was the final goad to their wounded pride. A student protest starting in Peking swept through the cities, culminating in a general strike at Shanghai. Out of this protest, which became known as the "May Fourth Movement," emerged the beginnings of modern China's two great contending forces, the Nationalists and the Communists.

When Sun Yat-sen, leader of the Kuomintang (Nationalist) revolution, was building his organization from a base in the southern city of Canton, his first encouragement came not from the Western powers, to whom he appealed in vain, but from the Soviets. In 1923 their envoy, Adolf Joffe, offered a hand. Mikhail Grusenberg, also known as Borodin, soon arrived in Canton to help reorganize the government on the disciplined model of the Bolsheviks; General Vasili Blücher, alias Galen, began training a Nationalist Army in the techniques of modern war. To speed the process, Sun sent to Moscow a delegation headed by his trusted protegé, Chiang Kai-shek. Chiang, then 37, had chosen a military career out of patriotic motives, hoping to help free his country by force from the warlords and from foreign dominance. Behind his soldierly bearing was a burning personal ambition and a stubborn tenacity that were later to impress, and at times distress, the world.

After his return from a stay of four months in Moscow, Chiang became commandant of the Whampoa Military Academy, which Blücher had established on an island near Canton to train officers for the Nationalist Army. Sun's first task for his Russian-trained forces was to mount a Northern Expedition that would destroy the power of the warlords and unify the country under the Kuomintang. He did not live to see it—he died of cancer in the spring of 1925—but in July of 1926 the great offensive got under way with Chiang Kai-shek as commander in chief. By early 1927 the Nationalist forces had reached the Yangtze River and captured the major port of Shanghai, where the Chinese part of the city fell with the help of a workers' uprising organized by Chiang's Communist allies. Now Chinese soldiers stood face to face with foreign troops who guarded the international settlements across the line. Following anxious conferences in London, Washington and other capitals, the harbor began to fill with battle-ready warships.

So far Chiang's expedition had been a huge success, but his marriage of convenience with the Communists was already beginning to break up. His supporters were mostly merchants, bankers and landlords interested in halting further foreign encroachment and putting an end to the constant civil strife—not in the sweeping social revolution the Communists seemed to be suggesting as they took over labor unions and roused the peasants with talk of land and tax reform. The Rightists feared, too, that uncontrolled violence against foreigners living in China might provoke a disastrous war with outside nations. Chiang, for his part, was beginning to chafe at his dependence on the Communists and their Russian tutors. Now encamped at Shanghai, where he had friends in both the financial community and the feared secret societies that controlled the underworld, he saw his chance to strike a sudden, crippling blow.

At 4 o'clock on the morning of April 12, 1927, a bugle call broke the silence of the Shanghai dawn, and was followed by a siren blast from a Chinese gunboat in the harbor. They were signals for a carefully planned massacre. Soldiers and undercover agents, members of the notorious Green and Red Circles, moved through the darkened city to close in on key Communist party members—the very men who had organized the workers' uprising that had enabled Chiang's army to take Shanghai. Some of them were shot as they tried to get out of bed. Others were shackled together and led off in groups to be slaughtered by the Generalissimo's firing squads. By nightfall more than 300 had been killed.

The Nationalist government, surprised by the massacre, reacted first with horror and then outrage. Chiang was formally expelled from his party and government; he in turn re-

Flanked by page boys and flower-carrying attendants, China's future Generalissimo Chiang Kai-shek and Mei-Ling Soong pose in 1927 for a wedding picture just after their Western-style marriage in Shanghai's luxurious Majestic Hotel. Mei-Ling, a graduate of Wellesley, was also the sister-in-law of China's "George Washington," Sun Yat-sen, who had died two years earlier after having built a republican government out of the ancient Chinese feudal structure.

treated and set up his own new government in Nanking. The two rival Nationalist governments remained stalemated until it was discovered that the Communists, under secret orders from Stalin, had been plotting all along to take over the Kuomintang themselves, with the help of a workers' and peasants' army. When news of this plot leaked out, the non-Communists, who outnumbered the Communists in the Nationalist government, turned on their foes and the wave of executions Chiang had begun in Shanghai was resumed. Borodin and the other Russian advisers had to flee.

By 1928, Communism in China seemed to have suffered an all but mortal blow; Chiang and the Nationalists appeared in full control. His armies had entered the northern capital city of Peking and forced the warlords' coalition there to disband; his own government had been recognized by all the major world powers. But no one knew better than Chiang himself that he had not yet united China. The warlords' independent armies still totaled more than two million men, carrying with them a crushing economic burden on the Chinese people and the threat of intermittent civil war. Chiang's political leadership, too, was under constant attack from rivals and critics. And in the wings, awaiting their time, were the two ultimate menaces of Communism and the Japanese.

The Red Chinese who survived the savage purges went into hiding with a toughened will to carry on. In April of 1928 two tattered remnants of the Communists' armed bands joined forces in the mountain fastnesses of Kiangsi Province in south central China. In all they numbered only about 10,000 men, but they immediately set about reorganizing as the Fourth Red Army. Their commander was Chu Teh, a professional soldier and longtime Communist. Their political commissar was a man named Mao Tse-tung, at 35 already a hardened revolutionary who had left home and a harsh peasant father at the age of 16, joined Marxist study groups and student protests in Peking and Shanghai, and later worked as a school teacher and peasant organizer in his native province of Hunan. Mao was not only a man of the people but also a visionary with a touch of the poet. He was deeply impressed by the latent power in the disaffection that he saw; in a report to his party superiors he predicted that one day the people would rise with the force of a "tornado or a tempest—a force so extraordinarily swift and violent that no power however great will be able to suppress it."

In the mountains of Kiangsi, Mao tried to put his vision to the test. The army he had helped piece together was wholly dependent on local peasants for support—a fact that dovetailed with Mao's own views about the future of Communism in China. At this stage of his career, Mao was out of favor with top party leaders for his refusal to follow the Moscow line that revolution depended on urban uprisings of industrial workers; to Mao, the key to revolutionary change in a country like China lay in the hands of its swarming and much-abused peasantry. Chu and Mao set about capturing their peasants' allegiance by ruthless and dramatic means. Throughout the countryside they attacked the common people's age-old enemies—the landlords, the bureaucrats, the tax collectors—often murdering them outright in cruel public demonstrations. Gradually they won the confidence of increasing numbers of peasants so that they could move among them freely without fear of betrayal. "The Red Army," said Mao, "lives among the people as the fish dwells in the water."

As the rebel peasant armies grew in numbers, they took the offensive and staged hit-and-run attacks on the cities of Nanchang, Hankow and Changsha. The brazen Communist provocations were more than Chiang Kai-shek could ignore, but three successive "bandit extermination" campaigns totally failed to suppress the Red armies. And before the Generalissimo could mount a fourth offensive, he was confronted by a new crisis far to the north: Manchuria was being invaded and occupied by the Imperial forces of Japan.

The Japanese invasion had been carefully arranged. On the night of September 18, 1931, a small charge of dynamite exploded in the marshaling yards of the Japanese-owned South Manchurian Railroad just outside of Mukden, Manchuria's capital. Ostensibly aimed at damaging a Japanese troop train, the bomb did little harm, for a train was able to pass over the tracks soon afterward. But the explosion, set off by Manchurian agents of the Japanese, served its purpose. It was a prearranged excuse for the Japanese Army that was protecting Imperial interests in Manchuria to go into action and take over the country.

The land of Manchuria, lying between Siberia and Korea, was rich in coal, iron and other resources. The territory had long been coveted by Russia and Japan, and both countries

DISMEMBERMENT OF THE MIDDLE KINGDOM

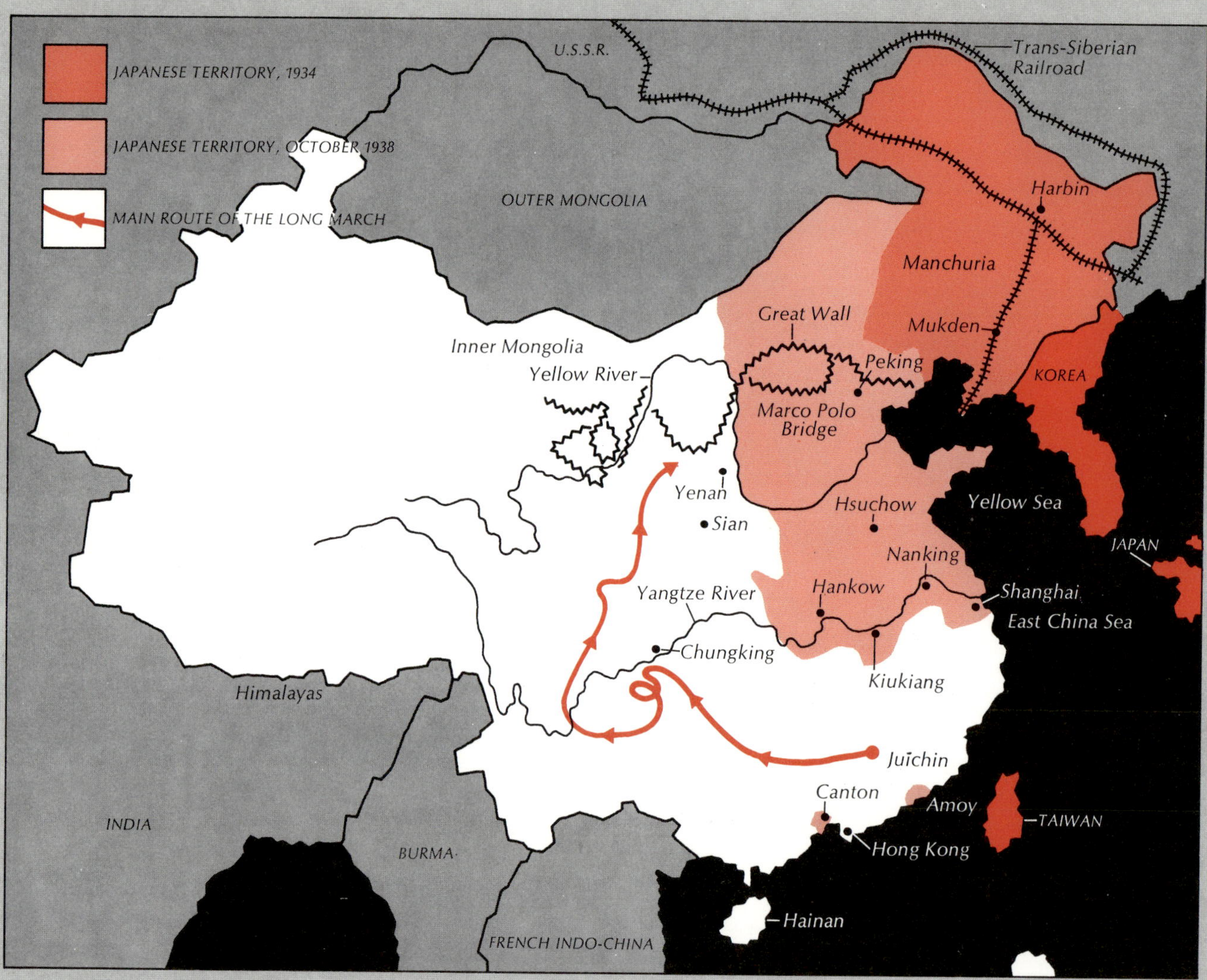

China in the 1930s was a wounded giant, torn by a civil war and a foreign invasion that engulfed the populous central, southern and eastern areas of the country, traditionally called the Middle Kingdom by the Chinese.

When the decade began, Chinese were already fighting Chinese. Communist rebel troops under a young intellectual named Mao Tse-tung had stopped Nationalist government offensives led by Generalissimo Chiang Kai-shek. But in 1934 Chiang's forces trapped a Red Force in the southeastern city of Juichin. The Communists broke out and, to escape annihilation, set off in an epic retreat called the Long March. This desperate journey began in October, and covered a serpentine track of 6,000 miles through central China. The march ended a year later with the establishment of Red strongholds outside Yenan near a section of the Great Wall *(serrated line)*.

Meanwhile, the Japanese, who had ruled Korea and Taiwan *(dark red)* since 1895 and had an army strung out along the rail line running south from Harbin, began to move. In 1931 its army, virtually unopposed by the Chinese, who were busy fighting each other, occupied all of Manchuria. The Japanese moved again in July 1937. This time, the invasion, which started with a firefight at the ancient Marco Polo Bridge near Peking, turned into a full-scale war, a Far Eastern preview of Hitler's blitzkrieg.

In the first six months, Japanese troops pouring across the Great Wall captured Peking and sacked Shanghai and the Nationalist capital at Nanking. The Japanese went on to take the ports of Amoy and Canton and a second Nationalist capital at Hankow. By the decade's end, the Nationalists had retreated up the Yangtze Valley to the city of Chungking, leaving in Japanese hands a swath of newly conquered territory *(light red)* larger than France, Germany, Spain and Italy combined.

held zones of special interest there. The Japanese controlled the previously Russian-held territory in the south as a result of their 1905 victory in the Russo-Japanese War. They also owned the railroad, plus some coal mines belonging to the railroad, and a number of towns along the line. But they wanted more. Overcrowded on their home islands, short of farmland and natural resources, they planned to seize all Manchuria and turn it into a buffer state between Russia and their Korean holdings, at the same time unlocking its riches for themselves.

When the Japanese struck, seizing towns and communications centers throughout southern Manchuria immediately after the Mukden incident, Chiang counseled a policy of no resistance, announcing that China would take its case to the League of Nations. It was a policy that might have restrained the Japanese if any one of the major powers had been prepared to espouse China's rights. Unfortunately, none was. At the League's faraway headquarters in Geneva, the Japanese representatives insisted that they had acted only to restore order, that they had no territorial ambitions and that they would most certainly withdraw once safety of life and property had been assured.

In Washington, Secretary of State Henry L. Stimson received quite different news from the United States Minister to China, Nelson T. Johnson, who reported that what was happening in Manchuria clearly "must fall within any definition of war"—a violation of the 1928 Kellogg-Briand Pact in which the great powers had condemned the use of force. Stimson proposed to act in defense of United States rights in China, but got little encouragement from nations that had signed the pact: the British were cool to his urging, the French did not even reply, and the Japanese answer bordered on outright insolence. The League eventually appointed a commission, which was headed by Britain's Lord Lytton, to investigate the affair.

In February, Manchuria, whose key center of Mukden had been quickly taken over by Japanese army units, was proclaimed a separate nation under the protection of Japan and was given the new name of Manchukuo—"land of the Manchu." At the head of its puppet government, the Japanese installed Henry P'u Yi, the last of the Manchu dynasty, who had been the infant Emperor of China at the time the Republic was set up.

When the League's investigative commission finally reported in 1932, it flatly condemned Japanese aggression. Japan, however, had no intention of apologizing or surrendering what it had gained. When the other nations at Geneva accepted the report, the Japanese walked out and quit the League, then promptly began pushing their Manchurian invasion farther into the interior toward the Chinese provinces of Jehol and Chahar.

Chiang Kai-shek was as stunned as anyone else by the Manchurian conquest, but he knew that neither China's armies nor the underdeveloped heavy industry supplying them were yet the equal of Japan's. Only a China unified under his sole leadership, he believed, could attempt to expel the invaders, and in 1933 he returned to his "antibandit" campaigns to try to bring about that unity by force. Communist-held areas were encircled by fortified lines bristling with pillboxes and machine guns, and a blockade was established to cut off all shipments and communications between the interior and the coast.

Within their tightening perimeter at the city of Juichin, one group of Communists held on under the leadership of Chu Teh and Mao Tse-tung; they were joined there by another senior member of the so-called All-China Soviet, Chou En-lai, who had passed through the Nationalist lines disguised as a clergyman in a flowing black gown and long white beard. Unlike many of his fellow Communists, Chou was no peasant or proletarian; he was the scion of a wealthy Mandarin family, reared in gentle circumstances and educated in France, Germany and Japan. He had not had much contact with the masses; his revolutionary knowledge came principally from books, and from fervent discussions with the fellow members of a Young Communist League he had helped organize while he was studying in France. Chou's keen intelligence and zeal, however, soon propelled him into the party's leading ranks to rival Mao, with whose political strategies and military tactics he often disagreed.

Chiang's full-scale campaign squeezed the Communists harder than ever before—one estimate places the number of soldiers and civilians killed or starved to death in Kiangsi at the astounding total of one million. By mid-1934, they were forced to a painful decision: to try to break out of the Nationalists' fortified ring at the cost of heavy casualties or to remain and face a slower but more certain death. In October of that year some 100,000 men and 35 women, led by Mao, Chou and various Communist generals, packed their belongings and set off on what became known as the Long March—a military exploit that made Hannibal's march over the Alps, as one observer put it, look like a holiday excursion. Their goal was to join with other Communists who had set up their own small soviet in remote Shensi Province in the mountains far to the northwest.

After hard fighting and still more casualties, the main Red column broke through the Kuomintang's lines. The Nationalists had expected them to head north, but instead they moved south and west, then began a long, circuitous journey that would take them within sight of the snow-capped mountains of Tibet and then north across some of China's wildest and most rugged terrain.

As the column wound through the hills during that winter, the Nationalist forces hounded it relentlessly—Chiang himself had the pilot of his private plane follow the struggling line for hours just so he could look down and watch his hated enemy on the run.

At one point in Szechwan Province the Generalissimo was sure he had trapped his quarry, who faced a seemingly insuperable barrier in the mountain gorges of the torrential Tatu River. A successful crossing depended on the capture of a single ancient bridge built in 1701 and supported by 13 massive iron chains. Szechwanese Nationalist troops were already entrenched in positions on the opposite cliff. They might have made the crossing impossible by cutting through the chains—if indeed they had the equipment to sever them. But they were reluctant to destroy their ancient bridge, which was said to have been built with the wealth of many provinces. They removed most of the wooden floorboards, confident that no one could crawl across the chains alone in the face of machine-gun fire.

The Nationalists were wrong. A suicide squad of 30 Communist volunteers armed with automatic pistols and hand grenades stormed the bridge, swinging themselves, arm over arm, hundreds of feet above the raging waters, while their comrades kept up an intense covering fire. Those who made it to the far side, tossing their grenades into the enemy's machine-gun nests, were able to establish and hold a bridgehead long enough for the floorboards to be replaced, after which the full force of the Red Army came up to rout the Nationalists and move the rest of the column through.

After their bold crossing of the Tatu, the marchers pushed on through freezing mountain passes, treacherous, sucking swamps and arid wastes ruled by wild tribesmen who sniped at them. Toward the end of October 1935, a little more than a year after they had left Juichin, the ragged line at last reached the town of Paoan in the mountains of northern Shensi Province south of the Great Wall of China. They had traveled well over 6,000 miles—the equivalent of twice the width of the North American continent—in 368 days on foot, at the astonishing overall rate of 20 miles a day, crossing no less than 18 mountain ranges and 24 rivers, breaking through the enveloping armies sent after them by Chiang. Their success, however, had been bought at a tragic price: of the roughly 100,000 who began the march, fewer than 20,000 finished it—one historian estimated the number at 5,000. The survivors, moreover, found themselves in a new home as remote, as primitive and as poor as any in all China. Here, hopefully awaiting other bands of Communist survivors, they settled down to begin once more the rebuilding of the Chinese Soviet state.

The Communists might not have been able to survive in their new base, remote as it was, except for significant changes that were taking place elsewhere. Each new Japanese advance in the north brought a renewed hatred of Japan. And in 1935 Stalin, seeing Hitler rearming Germany on his west and the Japanese moving ever closer to his eastern flank, laid down a new Communist International line, calling for all enemies of Fascism—in which term he included not only the government of Italy, but also those of Germany and Japan—to form a united front. Encouraged by Moscow, Chinese student demonstrations began to break out once more and a National Salvation Front was organized in Shanghai. Chiang had no patience with this new Communist brand of nationalism; he threw its young leaders in jail. He was, in fact, already planning to attack the survivors of the Long March in Shensi.

This time he proposed to use the Manchurian legions of Marshal Chang Hsueh-liang, who had retreated from his Japanese-occupied homeland and was also encamped in Shensi Province with headquarters at its capital of Sian. Like many of his countrymen, however, Marshal Chang increasingly questioned why Chinese should be killing Chinese while the Imperial emissaries of the Rising Sun were biting into their country and swallowing it piece by piece. He strongly protested his orders to attack the Communists, with whom he had already been in secret contact. It was then that the Generalissimo flew into Sian to berate his subordinate and issue orders for the attack. And it was then that the Marshal decided to kidnap his chief and persuade him to call off the civil purge and join forces against Japan.

The December 1936 agreement at Sian did not produce a signed declaration of war, but the Japanese read its portents quickly and accurately enough. Three days after Chiang's release, the general of Japan's Manchurian army warned that if Nationalist China did not join his country in opposing Communism he would take "all the steps necessary to assure peace." By then, however, the Nationalists and Communists, much as they distrusted each other, had begun negotiations to end the civil war and make preparations for armed resistance against Japan.

These hostilities broke out in a matter of months. On the balmy summer evening of July 7, 1937, a Japanese company on a training exercise near the venerable Marco Polo bridge at the walled town of Wanping outside Peking attempted to search the town for a missing company member. The Chinese garrison refused entry, and the Japanese opened fire. Soon a minor battle was on.

At first the firefight at the Marco Polo bridge seemed a containable scuffle, but hostilities soon blazed into real war. On July 28 the North China Japanese Command launched a punitive expedition against Chinese troops around Peking who, said one Japanese general, had acted in a manner "derogatory to the Empire of Japan." Waves of airplanes bearing the red insignia of the Rising Sun droned in over North China, bombing and strafing everything that moved on the roads. Columns of infantry led by tanks rumbled across the plains, seizing Peking, Tientsin and other railheads and communications centers, breaching the strategic Nankow Pass and the Great Wall of China, fanning out down rail and highway routes toward the Yellow River on the south. Chinese armies, long on manpower but still short on coordination, tactics and modern weapons, were forced to fall back again and again. Within weeks China signed a nonaggression pact with the Soviet Union, complete with secret clauses that promised China airplanes, munitions and other aid.

Japan had early hopes of forcing surrender by a single, overwhelming strike, but they soon vanished as fighting broke out farther south in Shanghai. Following the killing of two Japanese marines in the streets in mid-August, the sizable Japanese fleet in the harbor sent a landing force ashore; before long the fleet was pounding Chinese sections of the city with shells, while planes based in Formosa dropped bombs. Tens of thousands of troops were rushed in by the opposing forces as the international waterfront erupted in blinding explosions and columns of oily smoke.

Neither side distinguished itself by its marksmanship: a Chinese bomb intended for the Japanese battleship *Idzumo* plowed into the lobby of the Palace Hotel, killing among others a visiting Princeton University lecturer named Robert Karl Reischauer and an Australian barmaid known to local admirers as Dodo Dynamite. Another bomb landed in the French Concession right on top of the Great World Amusement Park, killing 450 Chinese refugees and wounding 800 more. Even the U.S.S. *Augusta,* the flagship of the American Asiatic Fleet, which was anchored in Shanghai Harbor, felt the sting of war when a stray 37 mm anti-aircraft shell

The efforts of tiny Japan to chop up dinosaur China with a samurai sword are mocked in this July 1937 Philadelphia Inquirer cartoon, which was published shortly after Japan had invaded North China. Very soon, however, newsreels of a savage Japanese bombing of Shanghai and headlines announcing sweeping victories over the dragon, jolted many Americans into an awareness of Japan's real military strength.

dropped among off-duty seamen who were watching a movie on the well deck, wounding 18 and killing a 20-year-old Louisianan named Freddie John Falgout—who may have been the first uniformed American serviceman to die in what was fast becoming World War II.

A good many tons of explosives, however, found their targets in the massed flesh of Chinese troops brought up to repel the invasion. In the nearly three months of savage fighting that followed, with casualties running into the hundreds of thousands, the Chinese line of resistance broke and fell back in confusion up the Yangtze Valley toward the capital of Nanking 190 miles away. On December 3, some 6,000 Japanese soldiers marched through Shanghai's International Settlement in a victory parade, while Japanese shopkeepers and kimono-clad ladies waved little red and white flags and cheered them on with shouts of *"Banzai!"* At the same moment, another 100,000 troops were joining forces with a Japanese fleet of close to 100 vessels to pursue Chiang's limping armies up the broad Yangtze Valley.

The Nationalist capital was softened up by daily batterings from waves of bombers, opposed only by a relative handful of fighter pilots flying an assortment of obsolete British, German, Italian and American planes, and trained by a former United States Army flyer named Claire Chennault. He had been brought in by Chiang Kai-shek to organize an air force for the Nationalists; Chennault was later to become head of the American "Flying Tiger" volunteers. On December 13, Nanking fell. Each day during the next few weeks the world heard a new and more horrifying report of the orgy that ensued.

For sheer, uncontrolled butchery, the rape of Nanking set a modern historic mark. Panic gripped the ancient walled city even as the Japanese armies approached. Chinese soldiers littered the streets with cast-off arms and uniforms in their haste to flee; thousands of soldiers and civilians fell and died as they tried to scale the walls and let themselves down the other side, or drowned crossing the Yangtze River on overcrowded junks that capsized and sank.

When the victorious Japanese poured in, they brought wholesale carnage. Frightened Chinese who made the mistake of running—or standing still—were bayoneted or shot. Houses were entered repeatedly and their trembling occupants robbed, beaten and raped. One young Chinese girl brought on a stretcher to a missionary hospital more than a month after the city's fall described how she had been carried off from her home and kept in a hovel for 38 days at the pleasure of her Japanese captors, who attacked her as many as 10 times a day. Chinese men suspected of having served as soldiers were tied together in groups and machine-gunned, used for bayonet or hand-grenade practice or simply doused with gasoline and set afire.

According to evidence collected by members of the International Relief Committee, more than 40,000 unarmed Chinese were slaughtered by one means or another during the atrocities at Nanking.

Many foreigners living in the capital counted themselves lucky to escape the bloodlust. Not all did. The United States gunboat *Panay,* stationed in the Yangtze to protect American lives and property and anchored upstream from the city, was deliberately dive-bombed and sunk, despite clear American markings, causing 48 injuries and two deaths. Tokyo hastily assured an outraged Washington that the incident had been a deplorable mistake, agreed to indemnity payments and ordered the senior officer responsible home in disgrace. No amount of talk or money, however, could erase the ominous overtones. Colonel Joseph W. ("Vinegar Joe") Stilwell, then serving as United States military attaché to the Chinese government, summed it up—for Americans, at any rate—in his diary: "The bastards."

Before Nanking's fall, Chiang Kai-shek had prudently removed himself and his government elsewhere: 400 miles up the Yangtze to the major industrial center at Hankow. He was, as one of his military leaders put it, "selling space to buy time." As time passed it became clear that he intended to keep on exchanging space for time, refusing offers of a negotiated settlement, vowing to retreat and defend until the Japanese, overextended and exhausted, defeated themselves —or until the United States, Britain and other powers could be drawn into the war on his side.

Despite the urgent lobbying of Chiang's supporters in the United States, such help was slow in forthcoming. Many individual Americans felt profound sympathy for the handsome and touchingly heroic figures of Chiang Kai-shek and his wife, the devoutly Christian, American-educated beauty Mei-ling Soong. A century of religious missionary efforts in China had also given many Americans a strong sense of responsibility to the Chinese people, and church groups appealed for relief funds. Against this hopeful background, Nationalist envoys lobbied for United States government loans and active intervention. But American fear of involvement in a foreign war proved too strong; the most that could be mustered officially was a token loan of $25 million arranged through the Export-Import Bank.

In the spring of 1938 Chinese morale soared briefly when the Japanese war machine met its first notable defeat. Northwest of Nanking, Chinese divisions set a trap with the city of Taierhchuang as bait, then hit the overconfident, advancing Japanese columns from both flanks with seasoned troops and new Russian-supplied tanks; the Japanese sustained 16,000 casualties. But the setback proved to be only temporary. By autumn the last great port city of Canton had fallen under aerial bombardment; the Japanese now held the important seaports and most of the key eastern cities, the rail lines and the rich agricultural and manufacturing areas deep within the heart of China.

In late October, Hankow, the capital Chiang had chosen after the fall of Nanking, was taken by a Japanese pincer movement. Once more, however, the Generalissimo was a step ahead of his pursuers. He had again moved his government 500 miles still farther west, this time to the ancient, hill-crested city of Chungking, a stronghold built high on the cliffs above the turbulent Yangtze. As the Japanese drove inland, whole factories and universities were dismantled ahead of them and carried west to be set up again in or near Chungking. One of the country's largest textile mills packed up its 8,000 tons of machinery early in 1938, shipped it from central China by railroad to Hankow and then by steamer upriver to the mouth of the Yangtze gorges, where the heavy cargo was repacked again to fit on 380 fragile junks. More than a hundred of the boats sank in the river's rapids, but all but a score were salvaged by monumental labor, and the machinery was carried on to Chungking, where the mill was reconstituted in April 1939, the spindles cleaned of rust and set whirring into action again.

Among the many incredible processions that wound their way along the river's cliffs that year were thousands of coolies pulling rickshas loaded with manhole covers, sewer gratings, old radiators—any scrap metal that could be reclaimed in the furnaces of western China and turned into precious iron and steel. Among the travelers were also thousands of students, carrying their libraries and laboratories on their backs, abandoning their shattered universities in occupied Peking, Canton and other cities to reestablish them in the mountains around Chungking, Chengtu and Kunming.

With a million men now tied down on the mainland and no end in sight, Japan desperately tried once more to persuade China to join its "New Order" for East Asia. It managed to win over only Wang Ching-wei, a former premier and rival of Chiang. Wang's views about the future of Asia —he believed that it should be reserved for Asians only —meshed with official Japanese policy; he saw his chance for glory as the head of a puppet government in Nanking. In Chungking, the Generalissimo hung on with granitic patience and an almost messianic pride. "We hope to lure the enemy farther inland," he announced grandly on his arrival in Chungking. "The farther they come the sooner victory will be ours."

Chiang spoke for posterity—and much too soon. Cut off from the coast, China's western strongholds had to be supported from abroad. War material and supplies were trucked in from Rangoon to Kunming over a rough thoroughfare that was to become a legend during World War II—the Burma Road, built by Chinese coolie labor over 700 miles of rugged mountain terrain. An alternate supply route was the long Silk Road from Russia to Sian, on which 2,000 years before camel caravans had plodded with Oriental silks, lacquerware and jade bound for Samarkand and thence to Byzantium and Rome.

In the north, meanwhile, the Chinese Communists held on in their Shensi mountain headquarters of Yenan, slowly building their armies while their guerrillas harassed the Japanese rear. In Chungking to the south, the Nationalists conserved their strength and crouched in cave shelters in the hillsides as the Japanese Air Force tried in vain to bomb into submission the capital city they could not otherwise reach. Their supply lines stretched to the snapping point. Although frustrated by a costly stalemate in a land of over 400 million people that bent and bled and burned but would not break, the island-born Japanese hung on too. But at last they began to turn their eyes to the easier and more alluring prizes that lay far to the southeast.

SAMURAI SLASH AT CHINA

A mounted officer, traditional Japanese warrior's sword at his side, leads his troops through a shattered village near the Chinese city of Hankow.

A VICTORY TOAST, A SOUR AFTERTASTE

Japanese generals raise cups of the rice wine called sake in celebration of their victory after the fall of Hsuchow, an industrial city in central China.

The Japanese generals who took time out to toast the early success of their China campaign in 1937-1938 drew their jubilation not only from the quick rout of a numerically superior enemy, but from deep cultural roots. By the very act of fighting they were fulfilling the ancient role of the samurai —the medieval warrior whose fate was conquest or death. The Japanese warriors in China found plenty of both.

Within two years after they first swarmed over the Great Wall from attack points in occupied Manchuria, the Japanese had swept south and east some 1,200 miles. On the way their 600,000-man force suffered 60,000 casualties and killed two million Chinese, among them 42,000 civilians, butchered in a distinctly unsamurai-like orgy of murder at Nanking. By autumn 1938 they controlled half of China, all its major cities and most of its antiquated rail system. It was a thunderous victory, one of which any man, general or private, born to the samurai tradition, might well feel proud.

But it was a campaign, too, that tended to breed misery. Even as they rolled ahead, the Japanese soldiers, accustomed to a relatively modernized existence in a tightly organized island empire, were appalled by the limitless expanses of China, and by the flyblown medieval apathy in which it was immured. Alternately frozen and baked by the harsh climate, exhausted by the dust and the distances, the Japanese suffered scarcely more from enemy bullets than from chilblains, insects and sickness. Much disease was caused by filthy drinking water; thirsty soldiers often had to fill their canteens from streams choked with corpses, though they did so only if they could see fish swimming in the water.

But as soldiers so often have, the men made do. They quickly learned to boil water and drink it only in tea. They supplemented army rations with delicacies improvised from local foodstuffs. They stifled camp boredom—and improved their footwear—by fashioning straw sandals in their spare time. But they never got used to China. And despite their enormous initial success, they never really succeeded in beating the Chinese, who finally mired them in a war of attrition that was to last for seven more years.

Launching their campaign against China, Japanese scramble up the Great Wall, built in the Third Century B.C. to ward off marauding northern tribes.

Following the hand signals of a soldier and the lead of a bearded crewman, a medium tank rolls onto the right of way of the Shanghai-Nanking Railway. The Japanese used the roadbeds as an expedient route for moving armor when China's dirt byways were too muddy for the movement of heavy equipment or were flooded out altogether.

At dawn, Japanese infantrymen, some still wearing the white sashes they wrapped around their helmets for identification during the previous night's fighting, rest in front of a ruined Shanghai school. In the background, fresh troops march off to engage the Chinese defenders still holding portions of the city.

A cavalry horse is lowered in a loading harness from a ship that is docked at the Chinese port of Kiukiang. Horses were the main means of transport used by the Japanese Army to traverse the muddy plains and roadless mountains where many of the war's battles were fought.

Sweet cakes called dorayaki, made of flour and sugar, fill the tray of a Japanese Army cook. Such tidbits were a welcome change from the dreary rations of rice, dried fish and canned vegetables that were the standard fare for the Japanese soldiers who were serving in China.

Taking advantage of a lull in the fighting, Japanese infantrymen use their toes to anchor the strands of straw that they twisted into thongs for sandals called waraji. Traditional farm footgear in Japan, the waraji were better adapted for going through China's muddy terrain than were government-issue boots.

On a troop transport bound for Nanking, a Japanese soldier gives his comrades an impromptu shower by splashing them with a bucket of water. For the fastidious Japanese, who were accustomed to regular baths, a chance to clean up was a coveted rarity during the war in China.

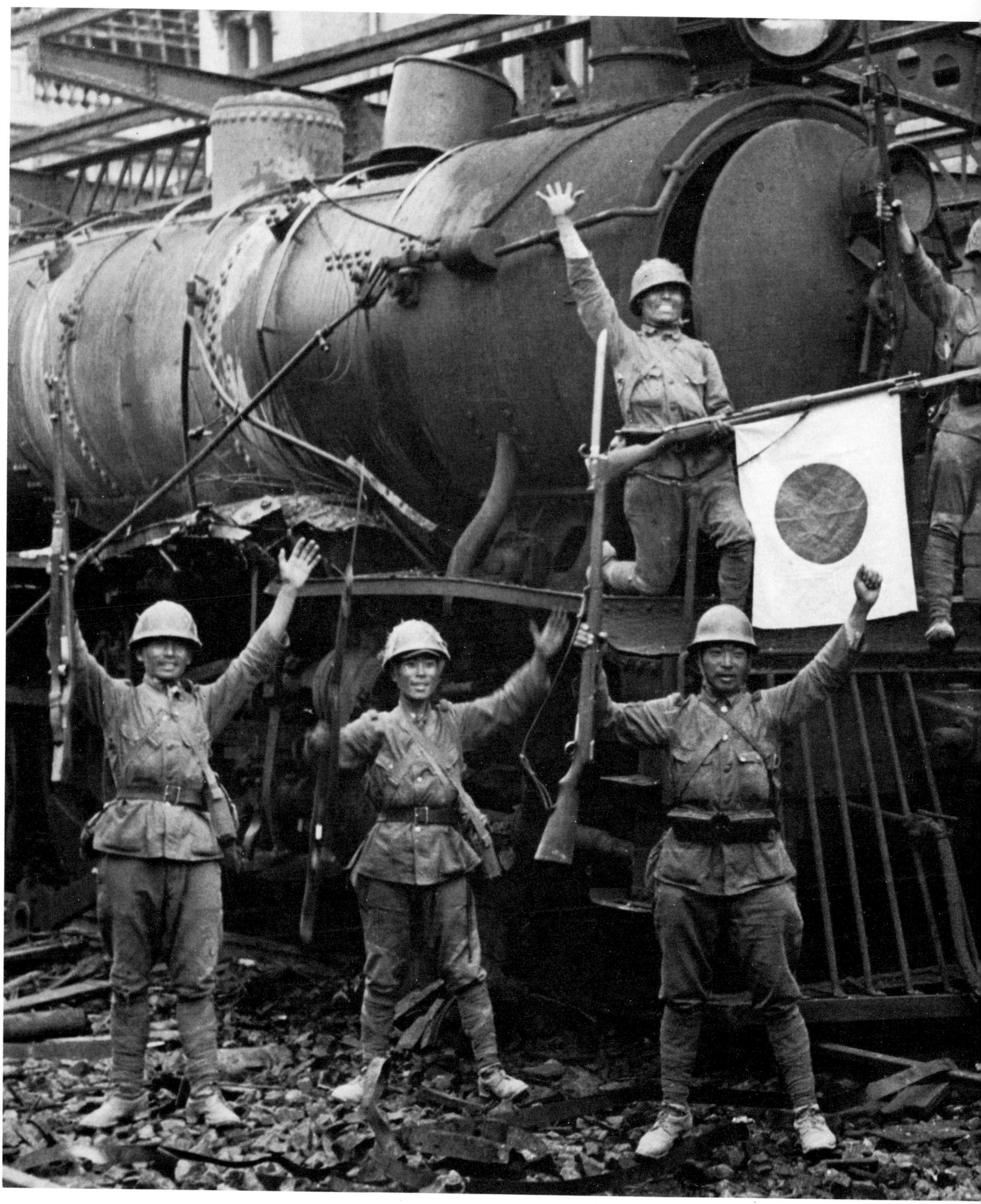

Exultant Japanese soldiers, one holding his country's flag, pose for a victory picture amid the rubble of the Hankow railway station. Hankow, which had served as the temporary Chinese capital for nine months after the fall of Nanking, itself collapsed in October 1938 after an 89-day siege. The capture of that city gave Japan its last victory of any consequence in China; thereafter, the Chinese government, and the bulk of its army, withdrew west to Chungking, a mountain-rimmed city that remained unconquered.

5

A royal visitor snubs the League
Stirring words from an ice-skating diplomat
An ominous silence amid the applause
New Year's gift for an embattled Emperor
Showing the flag in the Mediterranean
Festive send-off for the Italian invaders
The League slaps the Duce on the wrist
Secret maneuvers to placate Mussolini
Comeuppance for high-level plotters
Massacre and poison gas
Fascist salutes in Addis Ababa
A victim's unheeded warning

DOWNFALL OF A FEEBLE LEAGUE

As a rule, celebrities caused little stir in Geneva. Since its selection as the home of the League of Nations, the city had become accustomed to them. But on the morning of September 11, 1935, even the most stolid Swiss burghers were agog. A special train had arrived from the French Riviera bearing the Prince of Wales and his good friend, the American Wallis Simpson. A report spread that the vacationing heir to the British throne would look in on the League. Its 16th annual session was under way, and a visit by His Royal Highness would lend some luster to its tarnishing image as the guardian of world peace.

The Prince had other plans. He went directly from the railroad station to a hotel on Lake Geneva, where he had a bath and a hearty breakfast. Then, after a brief shopping excursion, he and Mrs. Simpson reboarded their train for a livelier destination—Budapest and its gypsy violins. But as it turned out, the day was by no means a total loss for the League or for ordinary Genevans looking for a trace of excitement.

In the afternoon another Englishman appeared on the rostrum of the League Assembly. The visit of Sir Samuel Hoare, Britain's Foreign Secretary, had been expected, but not the tenor of the speech he proceeded to deliver. Many in his audience—representatives of the League's 54 member nations—had begun to doubt that the organization would ever amount to more than a futile debating society and an arena for cynical power plays. When China had protested Japanese seizure of Manchuria in 1931, the League had inertly accepted assurances from the Japanese that they were merely restoring order; and even when Hitler had walked out of the League in 1933 and repudiated the Versailles Treaty, the organization had done nothing to chastise him.

Now, in growing surprise, the delegates to the League listened as Hoare summoned that organization to live up to the role that Woodrow Wilson had envisioned for it—as a group of nations that would act in concert to deter and, if necessary, punish aggression.

Not once did Hoare name the aggressor he had in mind. He did not have to. Benito Mussolini had not bothered to conceal his designs on Africa's sole independent country, Ethiopia. For several years Italy's dictator had been sending laborers to his African colonies of Eritrea and Italian Somaliland, along Ethiopia's northeastern and southern borders, to build the docks and hangars and roads he would need as a backup for invasion. Even as Hoare spoke, 300,000 of the Duce's soldiers stood ready to move into Ethiopia as soon as the June-to-September rainy season ended.

The members of the League were well aware that hostilities impended, yet they drew new hope from the Foreign Secretary's words. Hoare was no orator; what gifts of showmanship he possessed were reserved for the ice rink, where he was an expert skater, and the dance floor, where he had once won a tango championship. But the substance of his speech made up for its somewhat toneless delivery.

With disarming frankness, he conceded that his country's motives were often suspect; that because of its world-wide territorial holdings, it was thought to support the League only to keep "things as they were." Such was far from the case, Hoare insisted. "If these suspicions are still in anyone's mind let him once and for all dispel them," he said. "No selfish or imperialist motives enter into our minds at all."

Hoare then offered a pledge: "On behalf of the British Government, I can say that it will be second to none in its intention to fulfill, within the measure of its capacity, the obligations which the Covenant lays upon it." He brought the flat of his hand down on the podium sharply and repeatedly, asserting: "Britain stands for steady and collective resistance to all acts of unprovoked aggression! Steady and collective resistance to all acts of unprovoked aggression!"

In the thunderous ovation that followed, only Italy's envoy, Baron Pompeo Aloisi, sat silent. One delegate after another, speaking for nations large and small in every part of the globe, rose to affirm that if the Covenant's ban on aggression were flouted his government would meet its obligations as a League member. Even the representative of the Soviet Union—which had joined the League of Nations only the year before, after a long period of isolation—proved less wary than usual. "This Assembly," Maxim Litvinov ventured to predict, "may become a landmark in the new history of the League."

Behind the scenes, a few cautious souls studied Hoare's speech for possible loopholes—for example, a brief passage in which he had said: "If risks for peace are to be run, they must be run by all. The security of the many cannot be ensured solely by the efforts of a few, however powerful they may be." But most delegates agreed with the esteemed Paul Hymans of Belgium that there could be but one interpretation of Hoare's remarks: "The British have decided to stop Mussolini, even if that means using force."

Hymans would have been less sure had he been able to observe a scene in the foreign secretary's hotel suite that night. Hoare sat reading and rereading his speech, trying to figure out why it had evoked so fervent a response. By his own later account, all he had meant to do at the League was to inject enough "new life into its crippled body" to bluff Mussolini into calling off his war.

The bluff was to turn out to be one of diplomacy's more dismal failures. Within three weeks, Mussolini's "new Roman" legions would advance into Ethiopia. By the end of the year Hoare, exposed as co-author of a secret scheme to appease the Duce's imperial ambitions, would be forced out of office by his outraged countrymen.

Turning points in history are seldom recognized except in retrospect. The period between Hoare's jubilant reception at Geneva and his fall from grace at home proved to be such a historical hinge. The decisions taken—or left untaken—in the final months of 1935 so weakened the League that its demise was inevitable. With it was to die, for this era, at least, the hope that the rule of law would prevail in international affairs, the dream that clashing national interests need no longer be resolved by war.

Such an outcome would have seemed unthinkable in the days just after Hoare's speech. The League appeared ready to assert itself at last. In Ethiopia's ramshackle capital, Addis Ababa, word of Britain's stand reached Emperor Haile Selassie and his Empress in the little chapel of their palace. On the calendar of their Coptic Christian faith this was New Year's Day, and they were marking it at a quiet service mingled with prayers for peace. The coincidental arrival of the news from Europe struck the Emperor as an augury. "A wonderful New Year's present," he whispered to his wife.

His spirits remained high despite the receipt of a stern message from Washington, a reminder by Secretary of State Cordell Hull that Ethiopia had been one of the 62 signatories of the Kellogg-Briand Pact of 1928, pledged "to renounce war as an instrument of national policy." Haile Selassie, though ruler of a primitive country, was himself a sophisticated man; in his travels abroad, he had acquired not only a taste for fine wines but also an insight into the intricacies of diplomacy. Hull, he surmised, simply wanted to appear evenhanded; the same stern reminder had been simultaneously sent to Rome—its real target.

The Germans affected indifference to the hubbub at Geneva; no one expected otherwise. Actually, Hitler followed the developments there with rapt interest; he would have to rethink his own expansionist plans, far more sweeping than Mussolini's, if Hoare's call for collective action against aggression bore fruit. So far as the Nazi leader and his cohorts could tell, members of the League were on fire to move against Italy. Early in October, Hermann Göring remarked to a Polish diplomat: "I wouldn't like to be in the Duce's skin at this moment."

What prompted the comment was a massive show of British naval strength in the Mediterranean—more than 100 warships, including the *Renown* and the *Hood,* two battle cruisers; the *Hood* was then the biggest warship anywhere in the world. They had steamed into the Strait of Gibraltar the day after Hoare's speech, creating just as much of a sensation. The few doubts at the League dwindled. Obviously, it was agreed, Britain meant business.

In the excitement, a salient fact went overlooked. The *Hood* and the *Renown* had been en route from England for days; the timing of their arrival was simply fortuitous.

In Rome, Mussolini put on a display of anger, but privately he was calm. Documents stolen from the British Embassy by his military intelligence service had informed him that many of Britain's ships were far from fully equipped for action. He was satisfied that the Admiralty's dispatch of the fleet was an empty threat, no more than the old familiar navy tactic known as showing the flag.

At dawn on October 3 the Duce's forces, striking southward from Eritrea, moved into Ethiopia. The border was the Mareb River, a mere trickle between sandy foothills; it was quickly traversed on a pontoon bridge, but almost at once the going proved less easy. Roads fit for motor vehicles were nonexistent and the soldiers had to get out and walk. Nobody minded. Banners and blaring trumpets gave the expedition the festive air of a parade. Adding to the gala atmosphere were the impromptu songs and dances of the native Eritrean tribesmen who had willingly joined up, eager to do battle with their hated Ethiopian cousins.

On the eve of the invasion, from the balcony outside his office in the heart of Rome, Mussolini had addressed a cheering multitude. As a gesture of contempt for the foe, he had made no formal declaration of war on Ethiopia. He now expressed disdain for his critics at Geneva. "Not only is an army marching," he told the crowd, "but forty million Ital-

BARON POMPEO ALOISI PIERRE LAVAL SIR SAMUEL HOARE

ians are marching in unison with this army, because an attempt is being made to commit against them the blackest of all injustices—to rob them of a place in the sun." Should the League take action against Italy, he was prepared. "To sanctions of an economic nature we will reply with discipline, with sobriety and a spirit of sacrifice," he shouted. "To sanctions of a military nature we will reply with war."

The League's response to Mussolini was uncharacteristically fast and firm. By an overwhelming vote a week later, it branded Italy an aggressor—the first such action in League history. Then came the next step required under the Covenant: to decide on the punitive measures to be taken against the aggressor. The League assigned the task to a committee representing 18 member nations and a few weeks afterward approved the measures it recommended.

The recommendation did not include closing the Suez Canal, which would have stopped the venture cold, since Italy's access to Ethiopia lay through the waterway. And although three of the suggested sanctions seemed tough and effective—League members were to stop all arms exports to Italy, cancel all financial transactions with it, and stop buying Italian goods—the fourth, concerning the materials they were to stop selling to Italy, proved ludicrously weak.

As one cynic observed, the experts who had drawn up the list of items to be denied Italy were "not lacking in a sense of humor." The items included camels, mules, donkeys and aluminum—a metal Italy itself produced in enough quantity to be exported. And though industrially important commodities like nickel, tin and rubber were shut off, no embargo was placed on the sale to Italy of the fundamental raw materials of war: coal, iron, steel and, most notably, oil —without which the Duce's motorized forces in Ethiopia were certain to be stalled.

Behind the closed doors of the committee that had prepared the list, Britain and France had argued that depriving Mussolini of oil might drive him to spread the war to the European continent, perhaps starting with a "mad dog" attack on the British Mediterranean fleet. Such suppliers of oil as Russia, Rumania and the Netherlands had seen no point in stopping their trade with Italy; they knew that Mussolini could count on continued imports from the United States, which was not a party to the sanctions. Though Congress had passed a resolution of neutrality immediately upon Italy's move into Ethiopia and embargoed arms shipments to both sides, it had not banned petroleum sales.

As finally approved by the League, the sanctions represented little more than a slap on the wrist. But Mussolini seized upon them to spur his people to greater effort, including support of a Buy Italian campaign. To ease the financial strain of the war, voluntary contributions of gold were invited, and were soon forthcoming. In nation-wide public ceremonies, more than half a million Italian wives—and their husbands—made a gift to their government of their gold wedding rings, receiving bands of steel in return. Another enthusiastic source of gold was the clergy, the Duce's staunch admirers since his 1929 accord with the Vatican settling a long-standing conflict between papacy and state. The Bishop of Civita Castellana, at the end of a speech in which he thanked "Almighty God for permitting me to see these days of epic grandeur," slipped off his gold pastoral chain and handed it to Mussolini with the Fascist salute.

Mussolini had further cause to be gratified. The opening months of the Ethiopian campaign had gone exceedingly well. Resistance had been nominal; just before the war's outbreak, Emperor Haile Selassie had pulled out all the forces he had near the border zones in hope of avoiding provocative incidents. Italian columns, some moving north from Italian Somaliland along with those moving south from Eritrea, had easily taken one objective after another.

Their names were strange-sounding to European ears —Gerlogubi, Gorahai, Gabredarre, Adigrat, Adowa—and they were little more than collections of mud huts. One, however, held special meaning for the invaders. At Adowa, in 1896, another Ethiopian emperor had inflicted a stunning defeat upon another Italian force bent on conquest. The "shame of Adowa," as it came to be called by smarting Italian patriots, was erased by the Duce's legions only three days after the war began. The town yielded under an onslaught it had no way of stopping—bombing from the air.

By early December of 1935 the Italians were 80 miles inside Ethiopia, and temporarily halted. Their ultimate goal, Addis Ababa, lay 400 miles farther inland over wild and mountainous terrain. To reach it, roads were being built to accommodate the heavy artillery and the mechanized equipment of modern warfare.

The machinations of three men helped weaken the League of Nations, shown here in session. France's Premier Pierre Laval (center) and Britain's Foreign Secretary Sir Samuel Hoare (right) sought to deter the Duce from further aggression by confiding to Italy's League representative Baron Pompeo Aloisi (left) a secret plan for carving up Ethiopia and giving Italy a conquest without added bloodshed. It was an arrangement nobody really liked: Mussolini felt Italy needed a war to gain world respect; and when the scheme leaked, Laval had to step down, as did Hoare. The British cabinet member was widely criticized in England; his countrymen called him, among other things, "Slippery Sam."

Europe's military experts did not doubt that Italy would eventually win the war, but they figured that at least another year would be required to finish the job. To the diplomats, this time estimate seemed to present a golden opportunity. Within a year, the sanctions directed at Italy —even if less potent than they might have been—could do serious damage to its domestic economy. Viewing this prospect, Mussolini might prove to be amenable to ending the war now—provided that the terms of a settlement appeared attractive enough to him.

On Saturday, December 7, Hoare stopped off in Paris on his way from London to an ice-skating holiday in the Swiss Alps. Breaking the journey provided a chance to get together with France's Premier, Pierre Laval. Personally, Hoare did not much like Laval, put off both by the stained white tie he habitually wore and by his wily manner. But in their conversations on that December weekend, full harmony prevailed. By the time they parted on Sunday evening a plan had been devised to persuade Mussolini to cut short his Ethiopian venture. They were confident of success; private talks with Baron Aloisi, the Duce's representative at Geneva, had given them grounds for optimism.

Under the proposal, Italy was to be awarded more Ethiopian territory than it had already seized. Some 60,000 square miles were to be ceded outright. Another 160,000 square miles, virtually the entire southern half of the country, were to be "reserved" as an Italian "zone of economic expansion and settlement." Haile Selassie was to retain his realm in the mountains—the original Kingdom of Ethiopia. In exchange for giving up the more fertile plains below, Ethiopia was to get a long-desired outlet to the Red Sea. Even on this point Hoare and Laval were prepared to placate Mussolini. Should he balk at having this corridor carved out of his new holdings, either Britain or France would let it run through their own neighboring colonies.

The plan concocted by Hoare and Laval was meant to be kept secret until it was approved by their governments, the belligerents and the League. But alert French journalists got wind of it, and by Monday it was making headlines the world over. By Tuesday word of the scandalized reaction reached Hoare in the village of Zuoz in the Swiss Engadine. Gliding around the ice rink, he fell and broke his nose. "Too bad it wasn't his neck," one former admirer remarked.

Britons had more reason than others for feeling shocked. Hoare's stirring speech at the League in mid-September had made him an instant hero at home to people of every political party; some had predicted he would one day be prime minister. Disillusionment and anger swept the country. If the plan's details were being accurately reported, one Labor member of Parliament suggested, a new sign should be erected over the portals of the League: "Abandon half, all ye who enter here—half your territory, half your prestige."

A young Conservative member, who in time would hold the office of prime minister forever barred to Hoare, sent a letter to the London *Times* pointing out the possible fatal damage to the League. Should the government approve the Hoare-Laval plan, wrote Harold Macmillan, it would be helping "to undermine the very structure which a few weeks ago the nation authorized us to underpin." Macmillan then drew an analogy. "I have never attended the funeral of a murdered man," he noted, "but I take it that at such a ceremony some distinction is made between the mourners and the assassins."

For the plan's co-authors, the reckoning came quickly. Both men had to resign their posts. In line with ceremonial tradition, Hoare personally surrendered the seals of his office to King George V—only to receive the unkindest cut of all, in the form of a royal joke. "You know what they're all saying," the King told him. "No more coals to Newcastle, no more Hoares to Paris."

A stinging cartoon by British artist David Low shows obsequious Continental diplomats delivering ironic reassurances to Haile Selassie while British League of Nations delegate Anthony Eden (left) registers embarrassment at the implications of leaving all initiative to Mussolini. In the picture on the mantel, Prime Minister Stanley Baldwin appears with mouth taped; he had reacted to news leaks of British involvement in the scheme to dismember Ethiopia with a never-explained statement: "My lips are not yet unsealed." Low seems to be implying that Baldwin himself was implicated in the giveaway plan.

George V repeated this sally to Hoare's successor, Anthony Eden, at 38 Britain's youngest Foreign Secretary in almost a century. The King expressed bafflement at Hoare's reaction. "The fellow didn't even laugh," he said to Eden.

The Hoare-Laval plan was dead but not soon forgotten. For years it would be cited as a classic example of the gap between the ideals of international cooperation and the realities of national self-interest.

Weighing alternatives, the men then in power in Britain and France thought they had good reason for catering to Mussolini. The British were less concerned over a Mussolini triumph in Ethiopia than over their own future role in Europe should the sanctions work too well. As one of the British delegation at Geneva confided to a Manchester *Guardian* correspondent, "It is of no use to blink the fact that, if sanctions should succeed this time, we shall be morally bound to resort to them in the future in similar cases." The British government did not relish the prospect of being called upon to take action every time a Continental neighbor got into a quarrel; it was tired of war.

The French wanted to keep Mussolini's friendship, at whatever cost, in order not to drive him into the camp of a dictator they considered far more dangerous—Hitler. Almost without exception, every French government since 1919 had been obsessed by the fear of a revitalized Germany. Despite the Versailles Treaty's curbs on the Germans' military strength, they had been secretly rearming for years. With Hitler in power, all pretense had been dropped; rebuilding Germany's armed might was his loudly avowed goal. France's long-range aim was to create and nurture strategic agreements it had made with countries around Germany's periphery, Italy among them. Alienating Mussolini might mean losing a key link in the chain.

As it happened, Mussolini had no intention of aiding Hitler in any way whatsoever. His initial dislike of the Führer, after he had sized him up in person in the spring of 1934, had turned to loathing when Hitler resorted to mass murder in order to purge his enemies and tighten his grip on Germany. On learning the gory details of these assassinations, Mussolini had rushed into his sister Edvige's bedroom crying: "He is an evil and ferocious character!" Lately, loathing had turned to anger; Hitler's manifest designs on Austria were threatening the Duce's own plan to make Italy the dominant power in the Danube basin.

Apart from his aversion to Hitler, Mussolini had other reasons for not wanting a break with Britain and France. Over the years he had basked in the praise of many of their leading citizens. "He is not only a great man, he is a good man," Aristide Briand had said. Winston Churchill had declared that if he were an Italian he would "don the blackshirt." Prominent Americans had joined in the acclaim; Cardinal O'Connell of Boston had pronounced Mussolini "a genius of government."

Even more satisfying to Mussolini's ego was his acceptance as a prime mover in Europe's affairs. He was still relatively untried in office when, in 1925, Italy was made coguarantor with Britain of the Locarno Pact, by which France and Germany agreed not to use force in settling any of their border disputes. As recently as April 1935, at the Italian lakeside resort of Stresa, Mussolini had played self-assured host to the British and French prime ministers and their foreign secretaries—the highest-ranking gathering of political luminaries since the Paris Peace Conference of 1919. Out of Stresa had come an agreement by the three powers to use force, if necessary, to keep Europe's existing political structure intact—a message clearly beamed at Hitler.

Mussolini counted himself the equal of his colleagues in every respect but one: he felt that compared to the overseas empires ruled by the British and French, Italy's holdings were humiliatingly small—mostly a "collection of deserts," as he put it, in North Africa. The subject easily worked him into a fury; he would bristle as he recalled that despite the Italians' sacrifices as Allies in World War I, at the peace table they had been "left only the crumbs from the sumptuous colonial booty of others." The wrong would have to be righted—and Ethiopia, Mussolini decided, would be his test case.

The choice was, in a sense, ironic. It was Italy that had championed Ethiopia's admission to the League in 1923 over British objections that a country where slavery still flourished was unfit to be allowed into the company of civilized nations. The argument had collapsed when it was revealed that one of Ethiopia's largest slave-holders was the butler to the British minister in Addis Ababa, and that the minister was not disposed to deprive the butler of "his life's savings." In 1928 a treaty of friendship had reaffirmed the cordial relations between Italy and Ethiopia. But as time went by Mussolini was no longer content with the role of Ethiopia's patron; nothing would do but owning it outright.

All that was needed was an excuse—which was provided at an obscure desert waterhole called Walwal that lay along the ill-defined border between Ethiopia and Italian Somaliland. At Walwal, in December 1934, a clash between a small Ethiopian force and Somali soldiers under the Italian flag resulted in some 130 casualties to both sides. Although the 1928 treaty required arbitration of such incidents, Mussolini chose instead to flex his muscles. He demanded an indemnity of $100,000 as well as a public apology from the local Ethiopian governor—more than an apology, a humiliation. The governor was to appear in person at Walwal and, in the presence of Italian and Ethiopian troops, salute the Italian flag.

In Addis Ababa, Haile Selassie reacted with a series of telegraphed appeals requesting the League's help in resolving the dispute. The League's initial response, in January 1935, was an omen: it postponed consideration of the problem until its next session, in the vague hope that the two countries would meanwhile patch up their differences.

But despite an offer by Haile Selassie to concede a strip of the region near Walwal, Mussolini was not to be mollified. He had new reason not to be swayed from his course; on a visit to Rome, Premier Laval gave him to understand that so far as France was concerned he had a free hand in Ethiopia. Mussolini remained adamant in the face of a wave of worldwide (and occasionally mindless) public sympathy for the Ethiopians. Residents of New York's Harlem wrecked a number of Italian-owned shops following a knockout victory by a black man, Joe Louis, over the world's former heavyweight boxing champion, the Italian Primo Carnera. (Meanwhile the Duce ordered a ban in the Italian press of all photographs showing Carnera on the ring floor.)

On September 3 a report by an arbitration commission working under the League's auspices concluded that neither side in the Walwal affair was to blame because each had thought it was fighting on its own territory. This in effect negated Mussolini's grounds for grievance against Ethiopia and thus his pretext for waging war. But by now his intensive preparations were near completion, and a month later his forces were on the move.

Victory in Ethiopia was to be his, but at such subsequent cost that he later voiced regret that his stomach ulcer had not killed him at the hour of triumph. For success led him to a fateful error: piqued at the British and French for what he considered only lukewarm support for his enterprise, he began to move toward an alliance with Hitler.

The odds against Ethiopia in a war with a well-equipped foe were evident from the start. To counter Italy's planes, tanks and superior firepower, its major weapon was manpower—mostly untrained and, as Haile Selassie's mobilization order implied, not always dependable. "Every one will now be mobilized," it read, "and all boys old enough to carry a spear will be sent to Addis Ababa. Married men will take their wives to carry food and cook. Those without wives will take any woman without a husband. Women with small babies need not go." A few more exceptions were made—"the blind, those who cannot walk or for any reason cannot carry a spear"—but otherwise the order was all-inclusive, with a dire warning to those who disobeyed it: "Anyone found at home after the receipt of this order will be hanged."

As the Italians learned, the Ethiopian soldier could be a demon in hand-to-hand combat but was untrained in handling modern firearms—and military discipline was beyond his ken. After a spurt of fighting, he was likely to head for home. Even on the march, the food-short soldiers were easily diverted. "When they saw a field of beans, corn or maize," a war correspondent recalled, "it was stripped and eaten raw." A heterogeneous mix, they were prone to intertribal rivalries and plundering one another's possessions.

Nor were the Ethiopians immune to Italian bribes. The savage Azebu Galla tribesmen, long resentful of Haile Selassie and his ruling Amhara tribe, spied on troop movements for the Italians, meanwhile indulging a ghoulish pleasure of their own: the dowry of many a Galla bride included the genitals of a dead Amhara soldier. Some Amharas, too, wavered at the offer of Italian funds; more than one Ras, as Haile Selassie's powerful provincial chieftains were known, rose to the bait. The Emperor viewed the problem without dismay. "It is bribery without corruption," he said. "They pocket Italian money and remain steadfast to Ethiopia."

His optimism was not to be borne out on this or any other score. In mid-January of 1936, after some two months of road-building and relatively minor skirmishing, Italian forces resumed their advance toward Addis Ababa. A new Italian general, Marshal Pietro Badoglio, was in command, replacing 69-year-old General Emilio De Bono, whom Mussolini had found too poky. But like De Bono, Badoglio had to endure dozens of messages a day from the Duce, containing a range of instructions from "I authorize you to drive away the Swedish missionaries" to "I authorize you to use gas, even on a large scale." As one critic put it, Mussolini gloried in the role of armchair Caesar.

At Geneva the League was also busy, deluged by both combatants' complaints of violations of the "rules of war." The Italians accused the Ethiopians of mutilating and decapitating the soldiers they killed, using Red Cross emblems to camouflage military supplies, and firing dum-dums—the kind of bullet, prohibited by international law, that expanded on impact with shattering effect. The Ethiopians accused the Italians of deliberately bombing Red Cross units and using poisonous mustard gas, sprayed over the ground or dropped in bombs.

To bombing itself the Ethiopians seemed resigned. The Italians would in any event defy demands to cease the practice; it was not only vital strategy but "magnificent sport" for Mussolini's 19-year-old son Vittorio and his fellow pilots. In an account entitled *Flying Over Ethiopian Mountain Ranges,* Vittorio later lyrically recalled the effect of a bomb dropped from his plane: "One group of horsemen gave me the impression of a budding rose unfolding as the bomb fell in their midst and blew them up."

For the League of Nations, getting at the truth about the atrocities in Ethiopia loomed as a difficult and amorphous task. For instance, although the Italians' wholesale use of mustard gas was easily documented, the stories of their attacks on Red Cross units had to be measured against the fact that in Ethiopia red crosses were the traditional mark of a brothel. The League took a time-honored way out of its dilemma. It put off the need for any immediate decision by launching a study of all the allegations. The investigative project became moot in early March 1936, when Ethiopian resistance to the Italian invaders suddenly crumbled and the war came to an end—long before Europe's military experts had thought that it would. At about the same time, the Germans reoccupied the Rhineland in defiance of the Treaty of Versailles. This Nazi *fait accompli,* handed to the League for adjudication, fell into a vacuum when the League solemnly declared that the treaty had indeed been broken, but did virtually nothing else.

On May 5, 1936, Marshal Badoglio entered Addis Ababa at the head of his conquering army. Some 50 of his planes roared above him and an awesome procession of tanks and armored cars rumbled in his wake. Many Ethiopians along the triumphal route raised their arms in the Fascist salute. They had nothing to fear from Haile Selassie; he and his family had left the capital three days earlier, aboard a rickety train on a rail line that was Ethiopia's sole link to the outside world. At its terminus, the port of Djibouti in French Somaliland, a British warship waited to take the party to the Holy Land. The Ethiopian monarch wanted to pray at the sacred places in Jerusalem before going on to Europe.

On June 30, Haile Selassie appeared in Geneva at a special session of the League Assembly, convened at his request so that he could state his case against Italy. Small and thin, a somber black cloak around his shoulders, he looked too frail to bear the weight of his array of titles: Conquering Lion of the Tribe of Judah, Elect of God, King of Kings, Emperor of Ethiopia.

He spoke in his native Amharic, while simultaneous translation relayed the speech in English and French. Almost at once, a group of Italian correspondents in the visitors' gallery rose to shout and jeer and whistle him down—as the Duce had instructed them to do. Amid the tasteless furor, the Rumanian delegate demanded, "throw the savages out." Haile Selassie remained silent and motionless while this was done. He then resumed his speech.

It took about 45 minutes, combining a detailed review of the war and an impassioned appeal for justice. It was destined to go unheeded. Two weeks later the League called off the sanctions against Italy.

But Haile Selassie's words remained to haunt League members. What was now essentially at stake, he said, was international morality, the confidence that any nation could place in any treaties, the value that small states, in particular, could attach to promises that their integrity and independence would be respected and ensured.

"It is us today," he said. "It will be you tomorrow."

ROME'S NEW LEGIONARIES

"My command in one word is ENDURE," Mussolini exhorts his men in a placard posted on the deck of a ship filled with troops bound from Naples to Ethiopia.

HIGH ADVENTURE IN THE HILLS OF AFRICA

Among the Italian soldiers who sailed off to conquer Ethiopia in the fall of 1935, the prevailing mood was one of exaltation. To many, the expedition meant a chance for high adventure: the act of conquest would be a vindication of Italy's past and a sure sign of future greatness. "A new cycle has begun for our country," a volunteer reflected. "The Roman legionaries are once more on the march."

Accompanied by combat photographers (one of whom took the pictures that appear on these and the following pages), the legionaries did more marching than fighting in the days after the expedition first crossed into Ethiopia; that October the men of the force felt that they could crush Haile Selassie's wilderness nation within four months. After all, they were 300,000 strong and equipped with the latest weapons, including 150 tanks and 400 aircraft. Selassie's 500,000 ragtag army, by contrast, was poorly armed; many carried only swords. In the early encounters, the Italians captured hundreds of prisoners, and thousands of tribesmen revolted against their Emperor and joined his enemies.

But as Selassie fell back farther and farther into Ethiopia's rugged interior, even the marching got tougher, and the combat heated up. One of the worst—and least expected—features of the highlands was a choking, pervasive dust that seemed to a journalist "the concoction of some devilish pharmacy." Tanks were hampered by the terrain—and by the unconventional tactics of the Ethiopians. In one mountain battle, waves of Ethiopian warriors stopped a unit of tanks by tearing off the drive chains with their bare hands.

Long before the last decisive battle in March 1936 many a legionary had lost the fine edge of enthusiasm that had swept him into the war. But a surprising number retained it; one young officer, fatally wounded, requested that the Duce be told that "I die with his name on my lips." The officer might have felt differently had he lived to hear about a conclusion reached later by his leader: that the figure for Italian soldiers killed in the war, about 1,500, was ingloriously low; too few had died, he felt, to accomplish the stiffening of the country's character demanded by the Fascist ideology.

A fearful greeting is given the invading Italian troops by Ethiopian farmers, one of whom has been canny enough to have got hold of an Italian flag.

Self-assured Italian infantrymen armed with rifles and carrying ammunition, dismounted machine gun barrels and tripods, march up an Ethiopian hill.

"Now I'll fix you!" says a cartoon-character Mickey Mouse as he shoots a bottle of Chianti from a gun at a squealing "Lion of Judah" —Ethiopian Emperor Haile Selassie. Such derisive signs appeared on many Italian troop trucks that were driving toward the front.

Selassie's hold on his primitive country was insecure; thousands of tribesmen like these defected to the Italians.

A proud Italian infantryman guards a bandaged Ethiopian prisoner, one of scores captured after an early battle. Once interrogated, the prisoners were usually freed to save the cost of feeding them; when they were released, most dropped out of the war and went home.

The Azebu Galla warriors were traditional enemies of the tribesmen who were allied with Emperor Selassie, and were recruited in substantial numbers by the Italians. A striking picture of bellicosity with his spear and leopard-skin cloak, this warrior would be given a rifle by the Italians for use in combat.

Crack Alpine troops, originally trained to fight on skis, fire a machine gun at Ethiopians from the concealment of a clump of scrub.

Ethiopian Imperial Army soldiers killed by Italian shelling are barefoot but uniformed and armed with rifles bought in Europe.

Italian officers gallop across an arid, treeless plain in northern Ethiopia. Mussolini's war was fought in a jumble of desert sinks, lofty plateaus and mountain gorges—wild terrain that proved to be as stubborn an obstacle to conquest as Ethiopian armed resistance.

Defiance burns from the eyes of this exhausted Ethiopian prisoner, a member of Haile Selassie's elite Imperial Guard. Marshal Pietro Badoglio, the Italian commander, gave these troops credit for "a remarkable degree of training combined with a superb contempt for danger."

An Italian chaplain prays over an infantryman killed in action. In most of their battles with the Ethiopians, the Italians suffered only one casualty for every 10 men lost by the enemy.

6

A bogus tourist in Morocco
Violence in the bloodstream
Abdication of a reckless king
Cabals against the Republic
Voting by assassination
An angry junta
The grand plan for conquest
Massacres on land and sea
Target practice for some powerful outsiders
The annointing of Franco
On the barricades in Madrid
When the sky fell on Guernica
Death stroke by a German sword
Last days in a doomed capital

DRESS REHEARSAL IN SPAIN

The De Havilland Dragon-Rapide, a light airplane, had been quartered in the Canary Islands for several days, ostensibly under charter to some British tourists on holiday. But at 2 p.m. on July 18, 1936, three Spanish gentlemen boarded and instructed the pilot, Cecil Bebb, to take off. He had been expecting these passengers, and knew he was to fly them to Tetuán, Spanish Morocco. But he had no real grasp of the character of their mission, and he was astonished when, en route, one of the men changed out of his dark suit into the khaki uniform and tasseled sash of a Spanish general.

At Tetuán, Bebb was told to fly low so the general could scrutinize a group standing near the airstrip. Upon recognizing one of the men below, the general ordered the plane to land, then stepped out to a flourish of salutes, and assurances that he was among friends. As part of a military plot against the left-wing government of the five-year-old Republic of Spain, General Francisco Franco had arrived to command 24,000 troops sympathetic to the uprising.

Ultimately this rebellion stretched into a 33-month civil war with a significance well beyond its Spanish battlefields. In the process it offered a preview of World War II, a dress rehearsal not only for new weaponry and tactics, but also for combat itself on the part of some of the major actors in the global catastrophe to come. Nazi Germany and Fascist Italy sent men and matériel to Franco; the Soviets did the same for the Republican government. The United States, France and Britain stood aloof from direct involvement.

The Spanish war engendered something else. It fostered an upwelling of idealism and of a genuine spirit of sacrifice among individuals from the Western democracies. Thousands of young men poured across the Pyrenees to fight for the Republic, not at their countries' behest but acting upon their own convictions. They were ready to die—and many did—in another nation's conflict: partly because it offered them the chance to fight against dictatorship, but mostly because it appeared from afar to be a battle between rich and poor, oppressors and oppressed. It must also be said that among these highly motivated foreigners were tough Communist street fighters who used the Spanish civil war as a finishing school in the arts of violent revolution.

Though the issues and opportunities seemed clear both to pragmatists and idealists from the outside, from inside the torn nation itself, very little was clear. Spain had long been a divided, faction-ridden country, where violence and injustice were facts of life. In the relatively brief period between 1870 and 1921, four prime ministers were assassinated. In the cities, through the late 1920s, laborers rose and fought against suppression of their unions and sweatshop exploitation in the factories. As the 1930s began, 7,000 absentee landlords in one large rural part of the nation controlled 60 per cent of all arable land, while millions of landless peasants barely subsisted. This inequality and unrest all existed under the reign of an ancient Bourbon monarchy and its dictatorial prime ministers, a system so rigid and cumbersome that even the relatively comfortable middle class had begun to press for more voice in their government.

Faced with discontent, an economic depression and a potential armed uprising, King Alfonso XIII's regime agreed to general elections in 1931, with the avowed aim of creating a much more representative government. As a consequence, the so-called Republican government came to power with a mandate to sweep out the monarchy. Alfonso abdicated with the statement: "Sunday's elections have shown me that I no longer enjoy the love of my people." It is little wonder; he had regularly dismissed them as rabble, flaunting his contempt with such acts as closing down their national highway so he could race his sports cars.

Neither factionalism nor violence died with the old regnancy. Upon the advent of the Republic in 1931, the peasantry put manors and churches to the torch, and lynched landlords. Surviving landlords kept score in anticipation of revenge. Roman Catholics, whose church had long been tied to the monarchy, fought Republican efforts to separate church and state, becoming staunch right-wing dissidents.

There were periodic outbreaks of bloody rioting around the factories, and the new Republican Army often used excessive brutality in dealing with the workers' protests. Worse yet, many military leaders, who had kept their Army commands right through the power shift, were even more hostile toward the policies of the Republican government than toward rebellious laborers. When, for example, in 1932 the Republic granted autonomy to the province of Catalonia, the military began to suspect that the Republic was unraveling the very fabric of Spain. When the government considered similar independence for the Basque provinces, the military was convinced that Spain was being betrayed.

By 1936 few of the 200 generals in the Spanish Army were unquestionably loyal to the Republic. Many were conspiring to overthrow the government, a notion that did not displease their conservative political allies, particularly those of a powerful faction called the Falangists, a rightist movement resembling Italian Fascism and named for a formidable ancient Greek military formation called the phalanx. Within four short years, Spain was completely split, Left and Right. On the Left, the Republicans had backing from socialists, Communists, trade-unionists and from varied liberal splinter groups. Arrayed against them on the right wing were Army leaders, diehard monarchists, Falangists, landowners and the Roman Catholic parties. In the Spanish parliament, the Left was in control but faced growing opposition.

Under pressure from the right wing, the government held general elections in February 1936. This time the Left was returned to power. But a round of political assassinations followed, with victims on both sides. On July 13 José Calvo Sotelo, parliamentary leader of the Right, was murdered; his supporters called the murder the final, intolerable act, and urged the military to overthrow the Republic.

The military was just about ready. Three generals had, in fact, taken hold as leaders of a powerful anti-Republican conspiracy. One of them, José Sanjurjo, had already led one abortive revolt against the Republic in 1932. But he had failed—according to at least one report, because he had boasted of his plans while in the arms of a prostitute who passed the information along to the government. Deported, Sanjurjo had helped push forward the plot by lining up promises of German support for the coup from exile in Portugal. Alas for his ambitions, he was a vain man, and his vanity was his undoing. As the hour of the uprising drew near he packed the small plane that was to carry him to a triumphal return to Spain so full of fancy uniforms that it crashed on takeoff from a tiny, tree-lined airstrip, killing him.

The second major conspirator, Emilio Mola, was a more formidable officer—although oddly preoccupied with the notion that Spain was over-industrialized. (During the war to come he would implore German airmen to level "at least half of Bilbao's factories for the future good health of the Spanish nation.") Devious and ruthless, he had been the widely hated director of State Security under King Alfonso. Now Mola was commander of troops in northern Spain.

Meanwhile, the third of the plotters, General Francisco Franco, was preparing for his own airplane flight into the conflict from the Canary Islands. Franco was the most powerful of the trio, with a chilling reputation for lethal action. As commander of the Spanish Foreign Legion in the 1920s, Franco had seemed to his enemies to be a living embodiment of the Legion's motto: "Down with Intelligence! Long live Death!" The story circulated that when an irate legionnaire had thrown food at him, complaining that it was "unfit for human consumption," Franco had improved the menu and then had the man shot.

In becoming a part of the movement to overthrow the government, Franco had moved in a slow and methodical way, trying to pin down the details of preparation so carefully that the hot-headed Sanjurjo once blurted, "With little Frankie-boy or without little Frankie-boy, we shall go ahead and save Spain." It was Franco's opinion, however, that "people are mistaken who think this business will be a brief affair. Far from it. It's going to be difficult, bloody and it'll last a long time." By July of 1936, the cautious Franco judged the moment ripe, and in the developing uproar over the assassination of right-wing leader Calvo Sotelo, he endorsed a call to arms to defend the "Unity of the Motherland."

As soon as the formalities on July 18 at the Tetuán airport in Morocco were over, Franco took formal command of the Army of Africa. It was a fierce mix of the highly professional Spanish Foreign Legion, acerbic officers and raw conscripts from the mainland of Spain, and native Moroccans who had a history of courage, brutality and plunder in combat. The Army of Africa already had an iron grip on all of Spanish Morocco. General Mola's troops stood ready to secure the north for the uprising. Rightist forces had also occupied the Canary Islands and patches of western Spain; key cities in the southwest declared themselves sympathetic to the rebellion. The Republic was in command elsewhere.

The rebels' grand plan called for Franco's troops to cross the western end of the Mediterranean and enter Spain from the south. He and Mola would then converge on the center of the country, with the principal objective of closing from either side on the city of Madrid. General Mola, dispatching his northern force toward Madrid on July 19, made a lasting contribution to the language. When asked which of his four advancing columns might be expected to capture the capital, he replied, "The Fifth Column," meaning undercover rebel supporters within the city.

A densely populated industrial center as well as the capital of the country, Madrid was, at once, a military and a symbolic stronghold. Both sides sensed that if the rebels conquered Madrid early, that act could crush Republican spirit and resistance everywhere, ending the war.

Not that anyone on the Republican side was conceding victory to the rebels. Of the 165,000 men in the Spanish Army, approximately 30 per cent—mostly of lower rank—remained loyal to the government. And when the enlisted men of Spain's Navy were ordered to take up arms against the Republic, they refused, using the edict as an excuse for revenge on the most tyrannical leaders in the Spanish forces. In midocean aboard the battleship *Jaime Primero,* officers and crew fought savagely until all the officers were killed. Two days after the first shots of the war were fired, 98 per cent of the officers on all ships at sea were dead. Except for one holdout squadron at El Ferrol in northern Spain, the Spanish Navy was being commanded by committees of crewmen who clamped a blockade on the Army of Africa. On August 5, Franco managed to slip 1,000 of his men across the Strait of Gibraltar on a tug, a tramp steamer and two

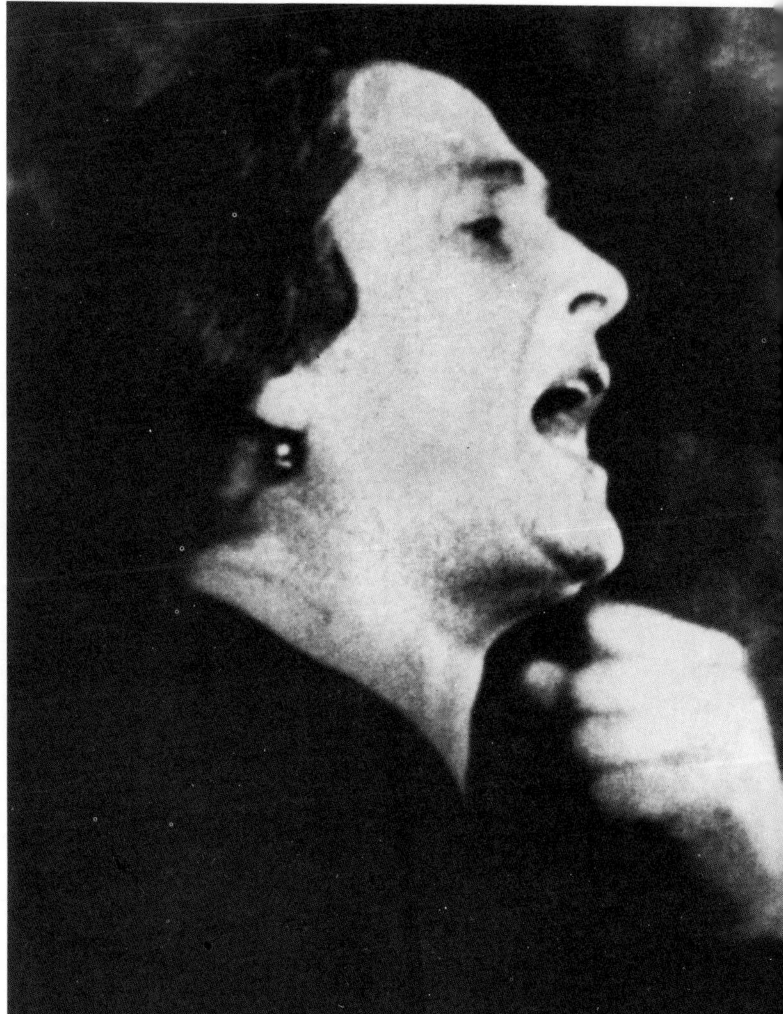

Spanish Communist Dolores Ibarruri exhorts her countrymen to defend the Republic in the dynamic style that earned her the public name of "La Pasionaria"—the compassionate one. In one fiery speech, she urged Spanish women to fight Franco's army with knives and burning oil, and declared, "It is better to die on your feet than to live on your knees."

mail packet boats. Then, for a time, he could move no more.

In the capital city, meanwhile, Manuel Azaña, President of the Republic, could call on the services not only of the Navy, various units of the Army and some Air Force personnel, but also thousands of citizen-soldiers. Numerous Spanish civilians who belonged to labor unions and political parties had formed unofficial militia units, which by and large had little or no military training. Now, with the outbreak of civil war, four of every five militia units were mobilizing in behalf of the Republic. All those who remained loyal to the Republic became known—particularly in the United States and Britain—as Loyalists. The rebels, proclaiming their love of the Spanish nation, referred to themselves as Nationalists.

Azaña, at the beginning, had a combined force of perhaps 250,000 men, as opposed to 150,000 for the Nationalists. The latter, however, were better armed; Azaña's forces lacked artillery and even sufficient small arms for many units. Moreover, Azaña himself had no real passion for the war. Azaña was characterized in right-wing publications as "The Monster," in part because of his homely looks but mostly for his unwavering opposition to the Right. Yet of all the important protagonists, he was now the only one who possessed enough detachment to plead for compromise. Azaña, through his War Minister, General José Miaja, proposed a coalition government that would include General Mola. Mola rejected the compromise as dishonorable. "If we were to seal a bargain," he told Miaja, "we should both deserve to be lynched." With that, Azaña finally understood that he had no alternative but to accept what a Madrid radio commentator called "Fascism's declaration of war."

Throughout Spain, workers demanded arms with which to fight the Nationalists. Azaña refused to supply them. His decision ultimately deprived his side of critical firepower, but at the time it seemed reasonable. The Republican government, a blend of many groups, was loosely held together by a liberal center. On the fringes was a volatile mix of anarchists, Trotskyites and Moscow-line Communists. Azaña feared giving them arms, knowing that they were capable of turning them on one another, or on him and his government.

Yet the workers' desire not to be without weapons was understandable; the first weeks of the war were characterized by a frightfulness from which the unarmed were not immune. Correspondent Jay Allen of the *Chicago Tribune* witnessed one ghastly incident in the bull ring of Badajoz. For five years the surrounding region had exploded with peasant violence, and now landlords—supported by Nationalist troops—took revenge. Allen reported that "Files of men, arms in the air . . . are turned out into the ring through the gate by which the initial parade of bullfighters enter. There, machine guns await them. . . . Eighteen hundred men—there were women too—were mowed down."

Meanwhile, in the center, the southeast and the east of Spain—regions controlled by largely anticlerical Republican forces—stories abounded of devout Catholics who were bound to crucifixes and then had their limbs hacked off. The Loyalists executed 12 bishops, among them two prelates who spent their final hours forced to scrub down the deck of a prison ship.

The city of Toledo fell to Nationalist troops, but was then assaulted by Loyalist militia. Soon the Nationalist garrison, under the command of Colonel José Moscardo, was besieged in the Alcazar, the city's fortress. With little food, but many weapons, Moscardo was determined to hold out. The Republican commander then reached Moscardo on the telephone, and the Nationalist leader was told that if he did not surrender immediately, his son, Luis, who had been captured that morning, would be shot.

Luis was put on the phone. "Papa," he said.

"What is happening, son?" said Moscardo.

"Nothing," said the boy. "They say they will shoot me if the Alcazar does not surrender."

"If it be true," said the Colonel, without pause, "commend your soul to God, shout *Viva España,* and die like a hero. Goodbye my son. A last kiss."

"Goodbye father. A very big kiss."

Colonel Moscardo's final words into the telephone were: "The Alcazar will never surrender." His son was shot. The Alcazar never did surrender; two months later Nationalist forces rescued Moscardo.

There was no real pattern to the early fighting in the war. Instead it was marked by scattered gain and loss. Several times Loyalist leaders in Madrid placed phone calls to authorities in distant Spanish locales and were told, by the person who answered, to go to hell. That was the way they learned that the town was now in Nationalist control.

But gains by the rebels were neither large nor consistent. With Franco's Army of Africa trapped in Morocco the Nationalists could make no significant march through Spain. Franco appealed to Mussolini for 12 transport planes, three fighters and a supply of bombs to help break the naval blockade. Assured that this small donation would settle the conflict, Mussolini dispatched 12 Savoia 81s. They were the first of 763 Italian aircraft ultimately to be shipped to Spain, along with at least 50,000 troops, and matériel that would include 1,930 cannon and 240,747 small arms.

Franco sent requests for additional aid to Berlin. Göring and Hitler readily agreed to send men and munitions. Hitler's hope was to draw Italy into Germany's orbit through alliance in Spain, and to secure a future supply of vital Spanish iron ore. Göring's reasons, as he later explained, were "firstly, to prevent the further spread of Communism; secondly, to test my young Luftwaffe in this or that technical respect."

By August, 30 German transport planes were airborne for Morocco. These planes and their crews, soon followed by six fighter pilots and their craft, composed the nucleus of the so-called Condor Legion, an air and ground force composed entirely of Germans. Soon, large numbers of German technicians and flyers descended upon Spain. They arrived in civilian clothes, carrying regular tourist passports to get them through Loyalist territories and into the areas under Nationalist control. Eventually some 6,000 Germans manned planes, tanks and antiaircraft units, though the Legion's numbers and composition varied from month to month.

The Loyalists also sought foreign aid, but from the Western democracies—initially France, which, in an early burst of support that was later cut off lest it provoke Mussolini and Hitler, supplied some 200 planes and a quantity of ground weapons. But the United States and Britain, wary from the outset of any involvement that might lead to world conflict, sponsored only food and clothing for relief.

Next, the Loyalists turned to the Soviet Union. Originally, Russia also leaned toward nonintervention. But after several months of war, with Italian and German help pouring to Franco, Moscow sent 2,000 or more Russians to support the Loyalists; Soviet assistance also included at least 240 planes, 1,200 guns and 700 tanks. In return Madrid shipped its gold reserve, more than $315 million, to Odessa.

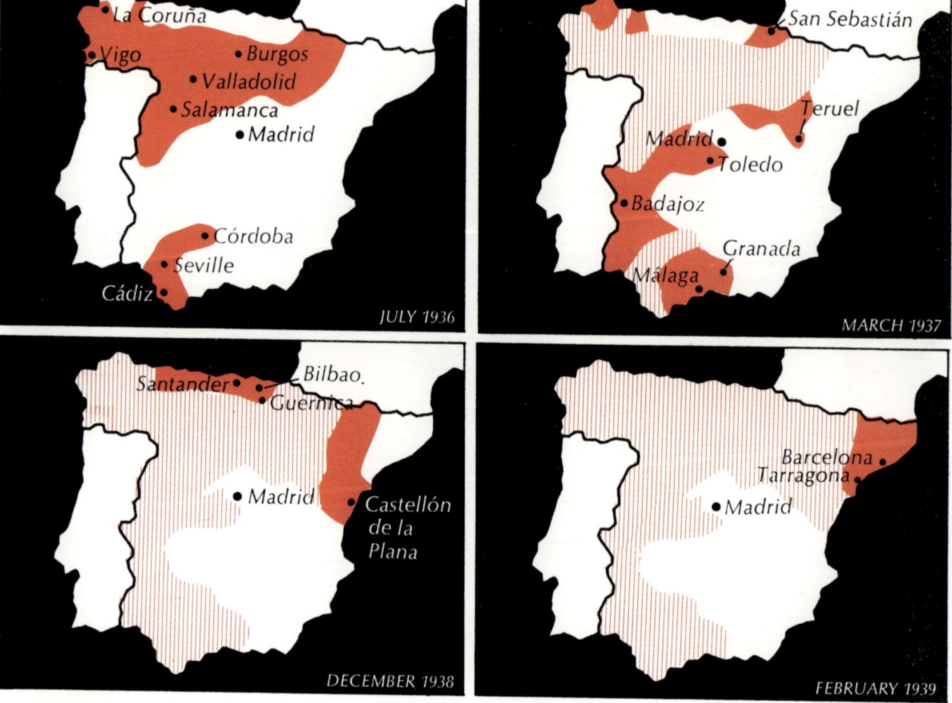

Four critical stages of the Nationalist conquest of Spain are shown at right. Red is territory captured by Franco's forces in the period just before the dates on each map; striped areas represent previously occupied territory. At the start of the civil war (above, left), the Nationalists took much of northern Spain and a chunk of the south. Then (above, right) they consolidated gains by occupying territory on the Portuguese frontier. With German and Italian help they drove to the Mediterranean, dividing the Loyalist holding (below, left). In the final phases, Franco was victorious in Catalonia (below, right), enabling him to absorb the rest of Spain except the area southeast of Madrid. The remainder, including Madrid, fell in March 1939.

Simultaneously, the Republican government began to receive the first of the foreign volunteers. In the initial months of battle, a number of outsiders, most notably the French writer André Malraux, had come to fight for the Madrid government. By the end of the summer, there was a surge of volunteers. They arrived as part of a combined force called the International Brigades. These were made up of men recruited throughout Europe, the United States and Canada, with most of the organization coming from the Communists, who furnished the Brigades with the bulk of their senior officers. Eventually, 40,000 people bore arms in the Brigades, including the 3,000 Americans of the Abraham Lincoln Battalion.

In late September 1936, bolstered by German and Italian airpower, Franco was able to drive off the Loyalist Navy and transport his Army of Africa to the Nationalist-held areas in the south of Spain, landing in Algeciras. Then, on September 29, he took temporary leave of his troops to attend a meeting of Nationalist leaders near the city of Salamanca. He was greeted there by a General Alfredo Kindelan, representing a group of generals who strongly felt the Nationalists needed a single political and military leader. This junta, Kindelan said, had chosen Franco to be their man. Franco assented, and on October 1, he was sworn in at Burgos as the Nationalist head of state. Immediately signs appeared at Nationalist outposts: "One state. One country. One Chief."

Firmly in power, Franco began moving the Army of Africa toward Madrid. Outside the city, workers' militia units tried to intercept the approaching Nationalists. But the Nationalists, stiffened by Franco's troops, turned back the militia.

As Franco drove closer to Madrid, Prime Minister Largo Caballero's main concern was to keep the city calm; even with the enemy barely 25 miles away, he acted as if nothing extraordinary were happening. Each night Largo retired at 10 p.m., leaving orders that he not be disturbed until 8 a.m.

By mid-October artillery fire from the outskirts could be heard in the city. Swarms of refugees—many of them accompanied by livestock—retreated into Madrid from the surrounding countryside. The government proclaimed an 11 p.m. curfew, and rationed water, food and milk.

Toward the end of October, Franco's troops were on the very rim of the city. Huge, frightening posters appeared in city squares: "At Badajoz the Fascists shot two thousand. If Madrid falls, they will shoot half the city." On November 6, the government transferred to Valencia, leaving Madrid in command of the War Minister, General Miaja. At 58, Miaja had the look of a benign grandfather. But he now called his deputies to his office and bluntly said: "The government has gone. Madrid is at the mercy of the enemy. The moment has come in which you must act as men! Do you understand me? As men! *Machos!* I want those who stay with me to know how to die." The 16 senior commanders said they were prepared to die, and as the Nationalists launched their assault into Madrid, Miaja's orders were dispatched to the streets: no retreat except to the cemetery.

Women took over the Quartermaster Corps and other service posts. Children threw up barricades in the streets while, in apartments above, their mothers prepared boiling oil to pour on any Nationalist troops who might penetrate the neighborhood. The labor unions mobilized their men with instructions that were chillingly direct: The supply of arms was limited; the supply of manpower was not. As those with guns fell, those who stood to the rear, unarmed, would have to come forward and take over the weapons.

On November 7, the Nationalists drove into the Casa de Campo, a park that ran from the western outskirts into the heart of the city. They were set back at one point when militiamen infiltrated and set off explosives among the attackers. When a bridge seemed to be in danger of Nationalist occupation, women passersby grabbed guns from a nearby supply depot, took up positions at the bridge and helped turn back the enemy. For one critical day Miaja was able to hold off the Nationalists until, on November 8, reinforcements from the International Brigades entered the city bearing Russian arms. The brigade commander was Lazar Stern, an able Hungarian professional. He mixed his 2,000 men in among the Republicans, one member of the brigade to every four from the militia—and the resistance hardened. And when Franco's men broke through into the academic enclave, University City, they encountered Brigade members who—according to one participant—"built barricades with volumes of Indian metaphysics and early Nineteenth Century German philosophy. They were quite bulletproof." At one point an important Loyalist line of defense seemed about to break, and Miaja himself abruptly appeared and reinforced the will of his men by going among them shouting: "Die in your trenches! Die with your General Miaja!"

Until the end of March, though Franco continued attacking the city, the battle was a stalemate. The Loyalists looked to Valencia, their new seat of government, for support and supplies, and received little. Exasperation mounted in Madrid, where horse meat was now a delicacy, while word spread that in Valencia 10-course dinners were common.

As Franco's troops struck on the ground, Hitler's bombers assaulted from the air. But the German bombs had the effect on Madrid that they would have later on other European cities; they did not cause morale and resistance to crumble, but in fact to stiffen. The Loyalist resolve was reflected in its slogan, *No pasaran!*—They shall not pass! Those words were chanted regularly over Madrid radio by Dolores Ibarruri, known as *La Pasionaria,* a fiery Communist who always wore black and was viewed by Spanish workers as a revolutionary saint. Formerly a devout Catholic, she now advocated free love and fiercely denounced the Church; there was a right-wing rumor that she had once killed a priest by tearing out his neck with her teeth.

In March the Italians announced their intent to achieve the conquest of Madrid that had eluded the Spanish Nationalists, even with German support. When 30,000 Italian troops went into combat from posts well north of Madrid, Mussolini announced, "I am certain that the dash and tenacity of our legionaries will sweep away the enemy's resistance." Instead, after an initial 20-mile breakthrough, the Italians were stopped, whereupon many of them surrendered, denouncing Fascism as they did so. Some Italian units managed to hold onto their gains; but German advisers to Franco sardonically observed that the International Brigades "might be made up of Jews and Communists, but they could fight like Germans and beat Italians."

At the end of March, Franco acceded to the stubbornness of Madrid and called off the attack. For nearly two more years he would continue to keep the city under siege. But he acknowledged that he had been turned back in his efforts for a quick knockout—and that he needed a new plan with which to try to win the war.

The strategy he chose was attrition. Franco's scheme was simply to swallow up territory until virtually all Spain was under his rule and he could overwhelm the remaining Loyalist strongholds with siege and concentrated attack. With much of the north already held by the Nationalists, he set the Basque and Asturian provinces as immediate targets; these, if conquered, would give his forces control of the entire north, a full one third of the nation. Moreover these provinces contained Spain's richest coal and iron mines, and more than 30 per cent of the country's industry. Bilbao, the region's largest city, was a very important industrial center, around which the Basques claimed to have constructed what they called their Iron Ring of fortresses.

In April the Nationalists moved north for a campaign that —under German influence—emphasized attack by air. The Condor Legion began using the Basque countryside as a testing ground for such new techniques as the combined use of incendiary and high-explosive bombs. Bilbao and the smaller industrial center of Durango were hit first. But a nearby town, Guernica, became the most celebrated bombing target of the conflict—and a symbol of total war.

Guernica was a town of about 7,000 people, located 18 miles east of Bilbao. It was a road and rail junction, and had other military targets—a bridge that might be useful in Loyalist retreat, and two small munitions plants. At 4 p.m. on April 26, 1937, two nuns began ringing a warning bell and calling out, *"Aviones! Aviones!"* (Planes! Planes!) Above was a group of Heinkel bombers, one of which dropped 550-pound bombs into the crowded plaza opposite the railroad station. "A group of women and children," according to one survivor, "were lifted high into the air, maybe twenty feet or so, and they started to break up. Legs, arms, heads, and bits and pieces flying everywhere."

Eight more waves of planes came over the town before dark. Some 1,600 people were killed and 900 wounded. Neither munitions plant was hit by the German bombers, whose equipment was too primitive to permit real accuracy. But Loyalist sympathizers outside Spain, shocked by news stories of the mass civilian deaths, brought charges of indiscriminate destruction. Berlin sent strict orders to the Condor Legion "to 'hush up' about the raid." Propagandists for Franco denied any Nationalist involvement, hinting that the town had been leveled by Basque dynamiters—a logical enough reaction by retreating troops. Indeed the Loyalists gave up the town two days after the raid. In Paris, Pablo Picasso began work on the classic painting, *Guernica,* still a talisman of the war for the adherents of Republican Spain.

Staring eyes and gaping mouths of Spanish children who were killed during a bombing raid on the city of Madrid lend a terrible reality to this Republican poster that says: "Assassins! Who upon seeing this would not take up arms to annihilate Fascism?" Atrocity scenes were also used as propaganda by Franco's Nationalists—who, for example, printed posters that showed priests and nuns being beaten by Republican thugs.

¡asesinos!
¿quien al ver esto, no
empuña un fusil para
aplastar al fascismo
destructor?
4 - 21
35
29
75 22
13
8 - 2
31
29 - 22
38
46 - 21
89
73 - 22
11
13 - 21
57

More immediately, the raid was confirmation of solidifying Nationalist power. The Iron Circle crumbled, Bilbao fell in June, and by the end of October 1937, after a seven-month campaign, Franco had captured the Basque and Asturian country. The Nationalists now held all of northern Spain, along with the western border and much of the south —a total of more than 60 per cent of the country.

The Loyalists now urgently needed some stroke of fortune to hold their cause together. It came in December. As Franco worked out plans for a renewed assault on Madrid, Loyalist spies in his entourage reported the scheme to their government, which decided to go on the offensive. On December 15, Republican forces hit the city of Teruel, standing between Madrid and Spain's eastern Mediterranean coast. The offensive coincided with the terrible winter weather for which the region is notorious; temperatures reached 18 degrees below zero, with winds that *The New York Times* described as "penetrating any amount of clothes." Beating back recurrent Nationalist counterattacks, the Loyalists captured the city in 26 days. But Franco maintained pressure on the victors, and after nearly two months more fighting, he recovered the town in late February 1938.

Franco's temporary difficulties at Teruel persuaded the Germans to involve themselves more actively in Nationalist strategy and tactics. General Wilhelm Ritter von Thoma, an armor expert, decided to experiment with a coordinated tank and aerial assault. Over Nationalist objections, the German tanks were to be thrown into battle as a unit instead of being split up among infantry divisions according to the old-fashioned military doctrine that Franco believed in. Moreover, Thoma was bold enough to aim his stroke at one of the Loyalists' stoutest remaining fronts.

Since the start of the war, the Loyalists had held a solid line along Spain's eastern coast, with strongholds in Barcelona to the north and Valencia to the south. The attack plan called for an assault on the route leading east from Teruel to the Mediterranean, and a breakthrough to the sea between Barcelona and Valencia. And that is exactly what happened. The German panzers tore through the Loyalist lines, and Nationalist troops reached the sea at Vinaroz on April 15. The forces of armor and infantry, supported by air, had overwhelmed the opposition. The German 88 mm gun, which was to earn a reputation as perhaps the most effective field weapon in World War II, made its debut in this battle against tanks and planes; in one encounter it knocked out three Republican tanks in three minutes.

Republican Spain had now been split and consisted, essentially, of two isolated wedges of land. One held the province of Catalonia and its key city, Barcelona. The other, larger triangle connected Madrid in central Spain, Valencia on the southeast coast and Almeria on the south coast.

As their holdings diminished with a renewed Nationalist advance toward Valencia, the Loyalists tried one more offensive in July, attacking from north to south across the Ebro River against the thin Nationalist line covering the rear of Franco's fresh offensive.

But the assault failed. Within a week the Nationalists had regained the initiative at the Ebro. Though not yet entirely beaten, the Loyalists were clearly on the ropes. In Madrid the daily food ration was two ounces of lentils, beans or rice per person. In Barcelona, which had recently become the seat of the Republican government, a newsman reported that "day after day, quiet women in black, with market baskets on their arms, stood in line at the stores, hoping to buy rice and beans from the limited stock. Alongside the wife of a textile worker might stand the elderly wife of a professor at the university, both with a little money; sometimes food cannot be had at any price."

On September 21, realizing the futility of further fighting, the Loyalist government announced that it was willing to withdraw all the International Brigades, and tried vainly to get the League of Nations to intervene with Franco for something other than unconditional surrender.

Three days later, the Lincoln Battalion withdrew from battle, and all across the remaining Loyalist territories, foreigners prepared to go home. During a farewell ceremony in Barcelona, *La Pasionaria* declared to the assembly of brigades: "We shall not forget you, and when the olive tree of peace puts forth its leaves again, mingled with the laurels of the Spanish Republic's victory—come back!"

Franco refused to offer any accommodation. By November, 70,000 Loyalists had been killed, wounded or captured during the Ebro fighting. Nationalist losses were less than half that. Moreover, the Nationalists had massed 300,000 well-armed soldiers in Catalonia. In opposition the Republic had 220,000 men with worn equipment and limited ammunition. And when Franco began a push toward Barcelona on December 23, he was able to sweep straight through.

A million refugees crammed into Barcelona, which could not provide sufficient food or housing. All males between the ages of 17 and 55 were ordered into service, but when Franco entered Barcelona on January 26, 1939, he found white flags of surrender hung from buildings—and a hungry city waiting for the convoys of food that his Nationalist radio had promised.

With the Republic near ruin, the Loyalists began fleeing to France. By February 10, when Franco sealed the border, 500,000 had crossed. President Azaña and his cabinet also left for France, assembling there to plan a course for the future. Most members of the cabinet now agreed that continued resistance could serve no purpose. And when some, notably the Communists, insisted on returning to renew the fight, Azaña would not accompany them. He said, "I refuse to help, by my presence, to prolong a senseless battle."

Colonel Segismundo Casado, Loyalist commander in the Madrid region, would have agreed. Madrid was hungry and cold; fuel supplies were virtually nonexistent. And Casado could see no chance to hold the city. His soldiers had only one rifle for every five men, and a total of 10 tanks.

On February 27, London and Paris recognized Franco's government. On March 5, Casado opened negotiations with Franco, hoping to stall a few days so that Army officers who had sided with the Republic could leave Spain.

Franco, meantime, continued to prepare a final assault, assembling a huge force on the edges of Madrid. But before the attack was fairly under way the Republican armies simply broke up, the exhausted men abandoning the front for home. At midday on March 28, the Nationalists entered the heart of Madrid. Abruptly, the streets filled with members of the Fifth Column, the city's clandestine Nationalist supporters. For years these Nationalists had been suffering *La Pasionaria*'s cry: *"No pasaran!*—They shall not pass!" As Franco's troops paraded through the city, the Fifth Column shouted: *"Han pasado!*—They *have* passed!"

Yet, not all resistance had ceased in Spain. Franco sat in Madrid while his forces confronted the holdouts, refraining from a proclamation of total victory. He was a tortuously methodical man—cautious, taciturn, solitary. (One day in 1940, he would sit with Hitler for hours, cold and unyielding, as the Nazi leader tried to persuade him to bring Spain into World War II. When later asked by an aide if it made sense to schedule another meeting, Hitler responded: "I'd prefer to have three or four teeth taken out.")

As Franco's units mopped up the Loyalist remnants, he silently awaited the capstone of three years' effort. On March 30, 1939, it arrived. Franco was notified by an aide that the last resistance had been snuffed out and he was in complete command of Spain. In celebration, he said, "Very good."

The Spanish civil war had caused over 600,000 deaths and cost more than $15 billion. It had produced still another totalitarian regime in Europe. The war had served Russia, Italy and Germany, providing not only military field experience, but also treasure—the $315 million in gold for Stalin, and free access to Spain's iron ore and magnesium deposits for Hitler's munitions manufacturers.

Among Western leaders, doubts grew about the wisdom of their policies toward the war. In the United States, President Roosevelt wondered if perhaps he should have helped prevent what he now viewed as a tremendous assertion of antidemocratic forces. In France, people began to perceive that their own vulnerability had increased: not only was their country bordered by Germany and Italy on the east, but Franco's Spain now cut it off at the south. And in Britain, Churchill brooded about the indifference that had greeted his attack, during the Spanish civil war, on his nation's reluctance to challenge Franco: "I fear that it will actually bring us nearer to all those dangers, which we desire, above all things, to withhold from our people."

On June 5, 1939, the Germans of the Condor Legion returned home to a triumphal parade in Berlin. The British author George Orwell, who had fought for the Republic, returned home and found no acknowledgment that there had been any war at all: "Here it was, still the England I had known in my childhood: the railway-cuttings smothered in wild flowers, the deep meadows where the great shining horses browse and meditate . . . the men in bowler hats, the pigeons in Trafalgar Square, the red buses, the blue policemen—all sleeping the deep, deep sleep of England, from which I . . . fear that we shall never wake till we are jerked out of it by the roar of bombs."

THE NAZIS' SEDUCTIVE RITUALS

At a table decked with Christmas greenery, feasting Storm Troopers celebrate the yuletide—and the ascending star of Adolf Hitler.

A CALENDAR OF WAGNERIAN HOLIDAYS

Nazism, a political movement in a great hurry, lost no time establishing its own glittering mythology, complete with a calendar of feast days. All these swastika-draped occasions were planned to coincide with the Reich's favorite old holidays—a congeries of Christian, pagan and plain old traditional German celebrations. So skillfully were the new orgies of Hitler worship grafted onto customary festivals that they seemed as appropriate to most Germans as did the moody Teutonic operas of Richard Wagner.

The biggest feast days blazed with the ancient pagan symbol of fire. Hitler's birthday, for example, was heralded by torchlight ceremonies like the one at right—and by nationwide daytime displays of his picture garlanded like an icon in shop windows. In the countryside, May Day Eve shimmered with fire as celebrants felled Maypoles and chose Kings and Queens of the May; next day, traditional dancing shared the program with banner-waving marching columns of workers. On the summer solstice, June 22, which had been celebrated in Germany since pre-Christian times, the Nazis lit great bonfires, and wreaths commemorating Nazi war heroes and martyrs burned in them. Then, to the banging of gongs, couples leaped across the fire.

At the annual Nuremberg Party Festival in September, roughly coinciding with the fall equinox, the Germans laid on a ritual that lasted a full week. Following Hitler's Opening Day address, successive extravaganzas included Worker's Day, for which 50,000 stalwarts performed intricate drills with burnished shovels carried like muskets; Hitler Youth Day; and Party Leaders' Day, when as many as 150,000 Nazi Party officers and militia paraded. On Brown Shirt Day, ranks of SA men goose-stepped past Hitler for five or six hours. During Army Day, combatants with rifles, machine guns, artillery and tanks fought mock battles. Closing Day was the climax—fireworks displays, torches, massed bands and banners, and hundreds of thousands of men marching in perfect unison. The total effect was menacing, yet moving. As one awed British observer put it: "For grandiose beauty, I have never seen a ballet to compare it to."

Uniformed youths mark the 10th anniversary of Nazi Party Day by a symbolic march of triumph through Weimar, the town in which Germany's short-lived republic was founded just after the conclusion of World War I.

German soldiers and sailors celebrate Adolf Hitler's 50th birthday with a ceremonial, torchlit midnight tattoo outside the old Chancellery building in Berlin.

torchlight parade through Nuremberg casts an eerie glow upon the medieval façades of the city.

Hitler speaks to an audience of Storm Troopers packed into the Munich beer hall where the abortive 1923 Putsch—a Nazi attempt to topple the Weimar Republic—had been organized.

At Stralau, near Berlin, girls dressed like sea nymphs lead a march. The party capitalized on an ancient folk festival that originally honored the year's most productive fishermen

Holding the Blutfahne, or blood flag—Nazi legend claimed these colors were stained with the gore of men killed during the Munich Putsch—Hitler ceremoniously accepts a "blood oath" of allegiance from an SS standard-bearer: "I vow to remain true to my Führer, Adolf Hitler. I bind myself to carry out all orders conscientiously and without reluctance. Standards and flags shall be sacred to me."

Novice SS men await swearing-in at the stroke of midnight in front of Munich's Feldherrnhalle, a shrine to fallen Nazis. During the staging of the ceremony no sound was permitted in the vicinity save the measured tolling of church bells; then suddenly Hitler himself strode onto the portico to administer the oath. In addition to relishing their pagan appeal, the shrewd Nazi leader preferred that spectacles be held at night because "In the evening the people's will power more easily succumbs to the dominating force of a stronger will."

7

ONE MINUTE TO MIDNIGHT

Three soldiers on bicycles came first. Below their steel helmets their faces were young, their figures brawny. Approving murmurs rippled through the crowds that were standing in Cologne's Cathedral Square. Then the sounds swelled to an ecstatic roar. Into the square marched line after line of German infantrymen, goose-stepping in perfect unison.

As the troops passed in review before their commanding general, the onlookers fell respectfully silent. They held off until a small girl handed the general a bouquet of red carnations. That ended the solemnities. Cheering, singing, surging through the square, the people of Cologne erupted in joy. A dignified businessman announced loudly: "The first soldier I get my hands on is going to get as cockeyed drunk at my expense as I did when I was a soldier in 1914—and I'm going to get cockeyed with him. Heil Hitler! Thanks be to God! *Deutschland über Alles!*"

Cologne was not the only German city in a fever of rejoicing on Saturday, March 7, 1936. Two other towns along the west bank of the Rhine saw similar scenes as German troops streamed across bridges from the river's east bank. The significance of their arrival was clear to the Rhineland's residents: Hitler was moving to remilitarize the region, bringing Germany's rapidly reviving armed power to the very doorstep of its once and future foe, France.

To statesmen around the world, the message was also clear: Hitler had torn up the Treaty of Versailles, the world's insurance policy against the threat of a revived and aggressive Germany. Few parts of the treaty had galled the Germans as much as the sections concerning the Rhineland. These terms required that all 9,450 square miles of the Rhineland west of the Rhine, and a 30-mile-wide zone east of the river, be permanently demilitarized to form a buffer between Germany and a perpetually wary France. Germany was not permitted to maintain any forces there; existing fortifications were to be dismantled and no new ones built. To ensure compliance, there would be a 15-year period of occupation by Allied soldiers.

The Allied forces were gone by mid-1930, four years ahead of schedule. By then the Germans seemed reconciled to the Rhineland's status; in fact, they had voluntarily renewed their pledge to keep it demilitarized under the terms of the Locarno Pact, the mutual-security treaty they had signed with the French in 1925. Hitler himself had since endorsed this action. As recently as May 1935, he had publicly hailed an unarmed Rhineland as Germany's "contribution" to European peace. Now, only 10 months later, German troops again patrolled along the Rhine—and Europe's leaders could not decide what to do about it.

The French began planning a military sweep into the Rhineland, then reconsidered and settled for a protest to the League of Nations. The League pronounced Germany guilty of violating the Locarno Pact, then failed to suggest any way to enforce it. In the end, a rationale was found for Hitler's coup—by the British. After all, the London *Times* noted, it was not as if the Führer were invading foreign soil: "He is only going into his own back garden."

The military units that marched into the garden for him seemed formidable—well-drilled, and ready for whatever might happen. In point of fact, they were but a token force, with little more to back them up than their leader's boldness. The troops were equipped only with rifles, carbines and machine guns. The planes that were sent up in a show of strength by the Luftwaffe, Germany's new air force, were not combat-ready; they lacked guns or ammunition or both, and the Luftwaffe pilots kept looking apprehensively westward, expecting a mass onslaught by French planes. Had France moved in, Hitler later admitted, "we would have had to withdraw with our tails between our legs."

Instead, the Rhineland provided Hitler with a wildly successful formula for future action elsewhere: An avowal of peaceful intentions followed by a lightning-swift military move—preferably made on a weekend, when most European statesmen liked to relax. The episode marked his first open display of force to gain an objective, stamping him as a consummate gambler, coolly ready for the ultimate risk—war. In the next three years Hitler was to place larger and larger piles of chips on this bet in places that could hardly be described as Germany's "own back garden." The places were Austria, Czechoslovakia and Poland.

In Paris and London and other capitals, despite the implicit threat of the Rhineland move, most officials were very slow to accept the vision of Hitler's Germany as a real menace to world peace. They were willing to concede that Hitler himself was troublesome, erratic, altogether an odd duck by conventional standards of statesmanship. But they found it inconceivable that he would want war, let alone relish the prospect. They preferred to believe that he was motivated solely by the desire to undo the humiliating damage that he felt had been done to Germany at Versailles—a feeling some of them had come to share.

Any of them could have known otherwise had they troubled to read *Mein Kampf,* the lengthy book of intent that Hitler had written in 1924. Few had read it and fewer still had taken it seriously. (Mussolini, in a triumph of illogic, dismissed it as "that boring book I have never been able to read.") But in it Hitler had clearly stated his aims for Germany, and not all of them involved rectifying Versailles. Hitler proposed not only to restore Germany's place in the sun, but to enlarge it—to make the German state, in his own grandiose words, "lord of the earth."

The march into the Rhineland was just one step in pursuit of his goal, and not the first step, at that. His first move, made within months after he came to power in 1933, had been to launch a campaign to absorb his native Austria into a Greater Germany—an objective recorded on the very first page of *Mein Kampf.* The operation began undercover; Hitler was not then prepared for overt military action. Instead he sent secret agents south into Austria. The agents had a potent, ready-made weapon at their disposal: hundreds of thousands of Austrian Nazis, belligerently asserting that their country was German by reason of racial ties and common language. Along with the Führer they passionately wanted what they called *Anschluss* —political union with Germany.

The chief obstacle to *Anschluss* was Austria's Chancellor, Engelbert Dollfuss. He was a tiny man, less than five feet tall; Viennese wags called him "Millimetternich," a miniature replica of his great 19th Century predecessor in diplomacy, Prince Metternich. But Dollfuss had a will out of all proportion to his size. He had clamped a lid on his country's seething politics by outlawing both its Nazi and Socialist parties and setting up an authoritarian regime. Italy was its model; to Dollfuss, Mussolini was not only mentor but acknowledged protector.

Driven underground, the Austrian Nazis resorted to terror tactics. In July 1934, after a bomb wrecked a power station and paralyzed Vienna's transport, Chancellor Dollfuss issued an ultimatum: a death sentence awaited any Nazi who was caught with explosives in his possession.

A few days later, the Chancellor was meeting with members of his cabinet when 10 men burst in, pistols in hand. Dressed in the uniforms of Austria's army and police, they had slipped in unchallenged by the sentries at the Chancellery entrance. Without saying a word, one gunman shot Dollfuss in the chest and neck; two others dumped him, bleeding, on a sofa. The Austrian cabinet members were seized as hostages while the Nazis occupied the building for six hours. Meanwhile, Dollfuss' agonized pleas for a doctor and a priest went ignored, and he slowly bled to death. Austria seemed ripe for Nazi plucking.

But at that moment the drama took a sudden turn, directed by the hand of one cabinet member the Nazis had failed to snare. Minister of Education Kurt von Schuschnigg had left the cabinet meeting for an early luncheon. When he discovered what had happened, he directed Austrian troops to lay siege to the Chancellery. Inside, the gunmen nervously telephoned the German envoy to Vienna, who arrived to arrange a truce. It lasted only until the gunmen emerged, expecting safe conduct to the German border. Instead, they were thrown into jail. Their leaders were promptly hanged, and the plot appeared to have collapsed.

Schuschnigg became the new Chancellor. The murder of Dollfuss sent shock waves around the world. In New York, stock prices tumbled as headlines blazoned the "war scare." The English press, lately fascinated by the exploits of an American gangster, dubbed Germany "the Dillinger of Europe." Even the London *Times* lost its usual air of detachment. The assassination of Dollfuss, the *Times* commented, "makes the name of Nazi stink in the nostrils of the world."

Officially, the British and French deplored the tragedy, declared that they stood ready to preserve Austria's independence from Germany, then made it plain that any action to be taken was up to Austria's best friend, Italy. In short, the buck was passed to Mussolini.

He took it. Mussolini had felt personally affronted by the assassination: Dollfuss had been killed while his young wife and two children were house guests of the Mussolini family at their Adriatic vacation retreat. The Duce's eyes brimmed with tears as he put the widow aboard a plane for Vienna. He then ordered 50,000 troops rushed to the Brenner Pass, on Italy's frontier with Austria.

Mussolini's ploy worked. The German government issued a denial of any connection with the Dollfuss murder. The Führer himself piously professed an earnest desire to restore relations with Austria "to normal and friendly paths." There was no confrontation with Mussolini's troops. For his decisive action in the crisis, the Duce was to earn an ironic sort of credit from history. He proved to be the only one among Europe's leaders to have faced Hitler down in the stormy era preceding World War II.

Hitler's embarrassment over the fiasco soon vanished. A final reckoning with Austria could wait, and meanwhile he had another move to make—this time entirely out in the open. In March 1935, he announced to the world that he was reintroducing compulsory military service and forming a new German air force. Until now, German rearmament had been accomplished by ruse and subterfuge, in order to get around the limits that had been imposed by the Versailles Treaty. Now Hitler was dropping all pretense. A new German war machine was going to be built, taking into full account the revolution in warfare that had been wrought by airplanes and by tanks.

The implications were staggering. Every country on the continent, and Britain as well, stood in potential jeopardy if Germany's dictator ever decided to send his new war machine on the rampage. The prospect looked grim enough to warrant a conference on the highest levels. A month after Hitler's announcement, Prime Minister Ramsay MacDonald of Britain and Premier Pierre Flandin of France journeyed to

On March 7, 1936, at Hitler's order, the first German troops to violate international agreement by occupying territory march across the Hohenzollern Bridge over the Rhine. The violation was the reestablishment of German arms in the Rhineland. According to the terms of the Versailles Treaty, the Rhineland, a part of the Reich straddling the Rhine River, had been made a demilitarized zone. By moving back in, Hitler was putting his guns and his men directly on the French border.

the little Italian town of Stresa for intensive talks with Mussolini. The result was an agreement that the three powers would use all suitable means to oppose any aggression by Germany. The agreement was nicknamed the "Stresa Front," and for a brief time it seemed solid.

Yet, within nine weeks it lay in ruins—wrecked by a new Hitler move, this one a masterpiece of political chicanery. Blandly ignoring Stresa, Hitler sent a private message to the British assuring them of his deep desire for their country's continued supremacy of the seas. Completely seduced by this appeal to their heart of hearts, the British, without consulting their Stresa partners, signed a pact fixing Germany's naval strength at one third Britain's. But what was presumably intended as a restraint on German naval expansion was in fact a green light. At the time of signing Germany had no navy to speak of; in order to reach the limit of 35 per cent, the Reich's shipyards would be kept humming for years. Moreover, the pact recognized the Germans' right to have submarines, expressly denied them by the Versailles Treaty.

Ten months later, Hitler's troops marched into the "demilitarized" Rhineland, tramping the remaining tatters of the treaty beneath their boots.

The Rhineland move paid a quick dividend. Reading the portents, the new Austrian Chancellor, Schuschnigg, sought an accommodation with his increasingly fearsome neighbor to the north. In the summer of 1936 the two countries signed an agreement by which Germany promised not to interfere in Austria's internal affairs and Austria pledged to conduct itself as a "German state" in foreign matters. But two secret clauses made a mockery of Germany's part of the bargain. Schuschnigg had to promise to grant amnesty to Austrian Nazis then in prison, and to make room in his government for Nazi sympathizers.

Austria's once staunch defender, Mussolini, showed no sign of alarm over this development. Instead, he accepted an assurance from Hitler that Germany would continue to respect Austrian sovereignty. This tacit approval of Hitler was a quick and dramatic bit of side-switching by Mussolini. He had been much impressed by the Führer's unopposed march into the Rhineland. The Anglo-German pact had shattered the anti-Nazi Stresa Front. And to Mussolini, Britain and France now appeared increasingly weak; neither nation had done anything about the Rhineland, and Britain had appeared almost servile in signing the naval agreement. If, as seemed likely, the Führer was on his way to upsetting the old balance of power in Europe, it could benefit Italy to be on the winning side.

Hitler encouraged this kind of reasoning by Mussolini. He went out of his way to feed the Duce's vanity, lauding him as "the leading statesman in the world, to whom no one may even remotely compare himself." The bond between the two men strengthened when each responded to a call for aid from a budding third dictator, Francisco Franco, after the start of the Spanish civil war in the summer of 1936. By autumn, the rapport between the Führer and the Duce was so firm that they agreed to synchronize their foreign policies. Speaking to a Milan audience, Mussolini coined the historic phrase "Rome-Berlin Axis" to describe the new relationship between the two countries.

The link was celebrated in spectacular fashion on a trip that Mussolini made to Germany in September 1937, the first time he had set foot outside Italy in 14 years. At the Munich railroad station, as a complimentary introduction to the Duce's visit, Hitler escorted him down a double line of busts of Roman emperors. In Essen the Duce toured Krupp's bustling steel foundries, now concentrating on the production of guns. Berlin was the next stop. As the separate trains carrying the Duce and the Führer neared the city, the engineers put on a demonstration of German precision: the two trains were made to run in precise alignment, at exactly the same pace. Reporting this marvel to Italian readers, Mussolini's newspaper, *Il Popolo d'Italia,* saw an obvious symbolism —"the parallelism of the two revolutions."

In Berlin the climax of the trip came when the two dictators spoke before a sea of people in a vast field on the city's outskirts. Mussolini was plainly overwhelmed; Hitler had assembled an audience of more than a million adherents, all roaring their acclaim. It was a great show. Unfortunately, however, in the middle of the Duce's speech a heavy thunderstorm broke, and the crowd began to run for cover. In the confusion Mussolini was inexplicably left unattended. His splendid uniform sopping wet, he had to find his own way back to his traveling companions.

His discomfiture was fleeting. Back in Italy, he radiated satisfaction over his journey. Hitler shared the feeling. Mussolini was now under control, and the Führer could turn his attention elsewhere. Five weeks later he called a top-secret meeting in his Chancellery to reveal a detailed plan for making the rest of *Mein Kampf* come true.

Of the six men summoned to Hitler's office on the afternoon of November 5, 1937, five were towering names in Germany: Field Marshal Werner von Blomberg, Minister of War and commander-in-chief of all Germany's armed forces; General Werner von Fritsch, Chief Admiral Erich Raeder and General Hermann Göring, respectively commanders-in-chief of the army, navy and air force; and Baron Konstantin von Neurath, the Foreign Minister.

The sixth man was Colonel Friedrich Hossbach, Hitler's military adjutant, who was there simply to listen and take notes. The meticulous memorandum he duly made turned out to be one of the most remarkable documents of its time: a brutally frank disclosure by Hitler that he was now ready to plunge the entire continent of Europe into war.

As his select audience settled at a big round table, Hitler launched on a four-hour exploratory discourse. It was not the usual monologue; some of his listeners made bold to raise a few points—to their imminent regret.

Germany's future, Hitler declared, entirely depended on meeting its need for more *Lebensraum*—living space; the German nation had a right to a larger share of land. The question was where the space could be acquired "at the lowest cost." The answer lay not in overseas colonies but in Europe itself, "in immediate proximity to the Reich."

Thus, Hitler continued, the "first objectives" were to be Austria and Czechoslovakia. The three countries joined would provide better strategic frontiers for a Greater Germany. They would free the Fatherland's military forces for "other purposes." And the annexed countries would be a source of food for five or six million Germans—once "compulsory emigration" had rid Austria of one million racially unsuitable persons and Czechoslovakia of two million.

Hitler shrugged off the fact that the coveted living space belonged to others. "The attacker," he said, "always comes up against a possessor." But he dwelt at length on the possible adverse reactions of Britain, France, Russia and Italy, particularly the first two. Britain and France were the "hateful enemies" that would have to be reckoned with. To both countries "a strong German colossus in the center of Europe would be intolerable."

If they moved to interfere in his plans, so be it: "Germany's problem can be solved only by means of force, and this is never without risk."

At least some of Hitler's listeners were stunned. What he was talking about was not just the old German dream of *Lebensraum*, which envisioned an expansion to the east. Hitler obviously was also prepared to wage war in the west, and thus to run a nightmare risk that any sensible German military planner hoped to avoid—conflict on two fronts.

Three of the men at the conference table found their voices. Blomberg warned that the German fortifications along the border with France were of "very little value." On Germany's eastern side, Fritsch pointed out, the Czechoslovakian defenses were extremely strong. These were Germany's two top-ranking soldiers objecting—and obviously in vain. Neurath fared no better when he argued that the entire plan would undo the carefully conservative foreign policy he had pursued.

The meeting ended after dark. Colonel Hossbach hurried away to transcribe his notes. The others went off into the Berlin night with a variously stated timetable from the Führer. He was going to put his plan into operation at the latest by 1945, but he might also move "as early as 1938"—a few short months hence.

The dissenters soon learned that they were to play no

Austrian Chancellor Engelbert Dollfuss lies on a divan in his Vienna office after he was shot in an attempted coup by local Nazis on July 25, 1934, and then allowed to bleed to death. To the surprise of the Nazis, the assassination did not lead directly to the fall of the Austrian government; instead, within hours of the murder, the leaders of the abortive coup were arrested by troops loyal to the Dollfuss regime.

major roles in either event. Getting rid of Blomberg and Fritsch without dangerously alienating the entire German officer corps posed a problem, but it proved easier than expected. Blomberg, a 60-year-old widower, unwittingly dug his own grave. In January 1938, he married a much younger woman. When police records disclosed that the bride had been a prostitute and a model for pornographic pictures, Blomberg's own mortified fellow officers insisted that he resign. Fritsch was framed by the Gestapo, the secret police, on a charge of homosexuality. Though he demanded and got a trial by a court of honor that eventually exonerated him, by then Hitler had compelled his resignation.

Neurath was replaced by Joachim von Ribbentrop, previously Ambassador to Britain. Ribbentrop was something new in the annals of traditional diplomacy—a onetime traveling salesman, his stock in trade the German champagne that was produced by his wealthy father-in-law. A reputable family name, a command of languages and the well-placed contacts Ribbentrop had made on his travels were his chief known assets, but there was one more of special value to Hitler. Beneath the polished veneer lay a total opportunist, ready to bend to the Führer's every whim.

The disposal of Blomberg, Fritsch and Neurath took just three months from the time of the fateful meeting in the Chancellery. On February 4, 1938, Hitler issued a decree that was broadcast to the nation. "From now on," it read, "I personally take over the command of all the armed forces." Henceforth Hitler was to direct Germany's military adventures by intuition, accepting less and less advice in policymaking from its professional soldiers.

People who observed Hitler at close range during this period agreed that there was only one way to describe him: he was in a state of exaltation. He had reason to be. It was five years since he had come to power. And he had now broken, forever, the old aristocracy's hold on both the Army and on the Foreign Office. He had successfully suppressed or intimidated other ideological enemies: he had not only extinguished the civil rights of the Jews but also deprived them of their livelihoods. The German Evangelical Church had been brought under state control; although Protestant pastors had managed to fight off proposals to remove crucifixes from their churches and to repudiate the divinity of Jesus Christ, hundreds of them had been shorn of their incomes or put in jail. In Catholic Bavaria, anti-Nazi priests had been tried on immorality charges.

Germany's laboring masses were also firmly in hand. Unions and strikes were banned. If the workers privately mourned these mementos of democracy, they were consoled by full employment. While Britain and France still floundered under the impact of the depression, with millions jobless, fewer than 200,000 Germans out of a total work force of over 25 million were idle. This rosy situation had been made possible by huge public-works projects and by the accelerating pace of rearmament.

Clearly, Hitler had little to worry him at home as he contemplated his new foreign adventures. Internationally, Brit-

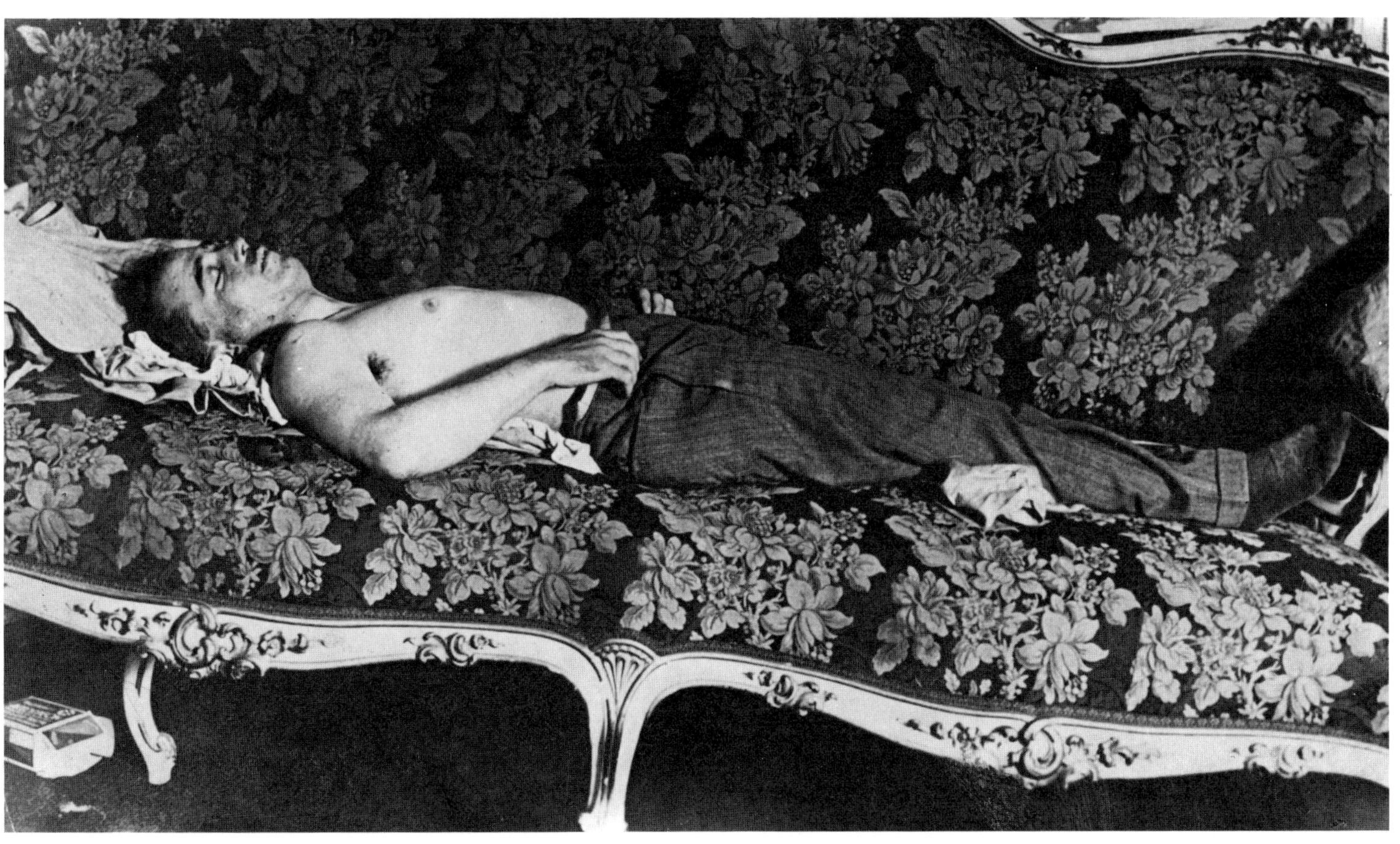

ain and France continued to be his major concerns, but he was also becoming increasingly aware of the rising power on his other front.

In Russia, an unprecedented bloodletting begun by Stalin in 1936 was still in progress. In a burst of psychotic ferocity equal to anything Hitler was capable of, the Soviet dictator was disposing of every last vestige of suspected dissent. The final toll was never to be known except in rough estimate: some eight million Soviet citizens executed, tens of millions more condemned to forced labor camps.

Though most of the victims were obscure, they included many who had labored faithfully in Stalin's service: two thirds of the members of the Central Committee of the Communist Party and some 35,000 Army officers—about one half of Russia's entire officer corps. Among the most prominent victims were Lev Kamenev and Grigory Zinoviev, Stalin's old colleagues in Lenin's first Politburo, and Marshal Mikhail Tukhachevsky, the Army's tank expert.

A select minority had been subjected to "show trials," making confessions of treason that appeared to have been extracted by torture or psychological duress. But in the type of treason charged against them lay a strong clue to Stalin's state of mind about the world outside his realm. The accused were alleged, among other things, to have conspired to partition Russia—in concert with either Japan or Germany. Each, in Stalin's view, was Russia's inevitable enemy, and his great fear was that he might have to fight both of them at the same time.

It was this fear of two-border confrontation that had motivated all of Stalin's moves in the foreign sphere for the past four years—ever since he had decided that Hitler was more than a passing phenomenon. In a major turnabout, Russian policy had changed from mistrust of Europe's democracies to cooperation with them toward the goal of collective security. In 1934, the Russians had joined the League of Nations; in 1935, they had signed mutual-security treaties

THE VENGEFUL VANDALISM OF KRISTALLNACHT

On November 7, 1938, a young Polish Jew named Herschel Grynszpan *(inset),* an unemployed 17-year-old, shot and killed the third secretary of the Reich's embassy in Paris. He did it, Grynszpan declared, to avenge Nazi treatment of his fellow Jews. On hearing the news Hitler flew into a rage and prepared to exact vengeance in the form of the worst pogrom that had ever taken place in modern Germany.

On Hitler's instructions, all German Jews were to be punished, and German non-Jews responded with terrible enthusiasm. Within 60 hours of Grynszpan's confession a wave of lethal vandalism swept through Jewish synagogues, homes and stores. In the course of their thuggish orgy, which came to be called *Kristallnacht* for the shards of glass that littered German streets, the Nazis by their own estimate killed 35 Jews, arrested many thousands, and levied against all German Jews fines that totaled one billion marks. They also wrecked 7,500 shops and 119 synagogues, and in a final insult added to injury, they confiscated the money that was later paid to Jews for insurance claims—five million marks ($1,250,000) for the broken glass alone.

Curious Germans peer at the gutted interior of a Jewish shop—one of hundreds the Nazis wrecked in retaliation for a political murder committed by a Jew. The destruction sped up a process that eliminated Jews from Germany's economic, social and political life.

with France and Czechoslovakia. And through agents of the Comintern, Stalin's international network, which kept Communists outside of Russia in tune with shifts in the Party line, new orders had gone out: In every country, Communists were given instructions to stop reviling socialists and bourgeois democrats and instead to unite with them in a "Popular Front" against Nazism and Fascism.

Although in the Western Democracies, support for the Popular Front was now rapidly waning in protest against Stalin's purges, his political machinations had bought him time for a steady buildup of Russia's war machine. Despite the blow the purges had dealt to military morale and efficiency, Stalin had 1.6 million men under arms in 1938, and his Army and Navy budget was 20 times larger than it was in 1933.

France, too, was beginning a belated reorganization of its defenses. During the early '30s it had spent huge sums to build an elaborate chain of steel-and-concrete underground fortifications along its border with Germany—the Maginot Line, named for the minister of war who was in office when construction started. The line was seemingly the last word in impregnability, and the expenditure had met with country-wide approval. Dread of a Germany once more on the loose was an emotion that was shared by most Frenchmen.

But on issues other than defense, they were anything but united. France's splintered party system spawned interminable factional quarrels, frequent changes of government, and recurring internal crises. Moreover, the scandal of the decade still haunted the French.

At the end of 1933 a promoter named Alexandre Stavisky had absconded with 200 million francs that investors had poured into his fraudulent bond issues. His subsequent death, supposedly by suicide, was widely believed to have been a murder by police to prevent the revelation that many prominent politicians and bureaucrats were involved in his scheme. In early 1934 the Stavisky affair sparked street riots in Paris by Rightist groups, climaxed by gunfire outside the parliament buildings. The violence, although put down, alerted the French to the growing power of Right-Wing militants—native species of Fascists.

Left-Wing factions had rallied in response. In June 1936, Socialists and Radicals—joined by Communists who were following Stalin's orders for a Popular Front—united to form a government. It was headed by the Socialist leader and one-time literary critic Léon Blum, who was promptly stigmatized by the Nazis, and by French Fascists, as the "Jew Blum." With the Left-Wing Popular Front's accession to power came a wave of sit-in strikes by factory workers demanding instant reforms, confirming the Right's fears that France was on the verge of revolution.

The Blum government managed to please some parts of the population and enrage others. Its enactment of a 40-hour week, minimum wage levels and the right to collective bargaining, although welcomed by workers, proved to be profoundly unsettling to owners of small, conservatively-run businesses. Its attempt to furnish aid to the anti-Franco forces in Spain was applauded by the Socialists in Blum's party, but was denounced by otherwise loyal pacifists. Although spending for armaments was increased—usually a popular measure—Blum's Right-Wing foes chose to see this increase not as a patriotic defense against Germany but as a plot to "provoke Stalin's war."

In June 1937, a discouraged and exhausted Blum resigned. His regime had survived for an entire year. But the old revolving-door pattern immediately reappeared: by the spring of 1938 three governments had been in and out of power.

Britain was enmeshed in its own difficulties. It was now obviously a small nation with a faltering economy, its strength sapped by World War I debts, by the loss of foreign markets and other drains. One effect of its dwindling wealth was a drastic cutback in military spending. A second effect was a reappraisal of Britain's responsibilities for the far-flung empire that had made it a world power; responsible Britons now had to face the fact that the tenuous ties of tradition and sentiment, instead of sheer economic and naval might, would have to hold the British Empire together.

A new war was clearly something for which the country was neither ready nor willing and its leaders were determined not to make a commitment that would place the decision for war or peace for their people in the hands of another nation. They made a show of backing the concept of collective European security, but any commitment that went beyond rhetoric was to be avoided. The most popular prime minister of the era, Stanley Baldwin, summed up the prevailing attitude: "I do not myself know what the word 'internationalism' means," he said. "All I know is that when I hear it employed it is a bad thing for this country."

When Stanley Baldwin stepped down in May 1937, he was succeeded by his Chancellor of the Exchequer, Neville Chamberlain, a member of a wealthy Birmingham mercantile family. Unlike the pink-faced, placid Baldwin, the new Prime Minister was a tall, gaunt, bleak-looking man whose infrequent smile reminded one critic of "the silver handles of a coffin." The forbidding exterior concealed a warmth that Chamberlain chose to reserve for the privacy of home. He liked to play the piano—Mendelssohn was a favorite—and he was a connoisseur of Negro spirituals, which he had collected while overseeing a family business venture in the Bahamas during his young manhood.

In his career in public service, both as Mayor of Birmingham and later in the national government, Chamberlain had gained a reputation for getting things done. Although he had neither training nor liking for problems of foreign policy, he had no doubt about his ability to handle them. Viewing the increasingly troubled international scene, he was convinced that it was time for a British initiative—for what he called "a general scheme of appeasement" to keep Europe at peace and secure. The term "appeasement" did not yet have the stigma that would soon be attached to it; what it meant, at the time, was a reduction of tensions. Chamberlain, a supreme rationalist himself, could see no reason why differences between nations could not be solved by rational men in calm deliberation. In this spirit he was determined to approach Hitler.

Unfortunately, certain strong prejudices he harbored affected his dealings with the Führer. Like Hitler, Chamberlain felt a fundamental distaste for both Russia and France. "I must confess to the most profound distrust of Soviet Russia," he once remarked. "Her motives seem to me to have little in common with our ideas of liberty and are mainly concerned with getting everybody else by the ears." As for France: "She can never keep a secret for half an hour or a government for more than nine months."

As it turned out, France was once more without a premier when, on March 12, 1938, Hitler suddenly moved to culminate his long-standing plan for *Anschluss*.

The final takeover of Austria was preceded by what was to become another familiar Hitler tactic: a confrontation designed to bully and soften up the adversary. In February, Austrian Chancellor Schuschnigg was invited to visit the Führer at his mountain retreat at Berchtesgaden. Schuschnigg had no inkling of what lay ahead. As he politely admired the magnificent view of the Bavarian Alps through the picture windows, Hitler rudely cut him short. "We did not come here to discuss the view and the weather," he said.

A two-hour tirade against Schuschnigg and his government followed, ending with an ultimatum. The concessions that Schuschnigg had made in the Austro-German pact of 1936 were not enough. The Austrian Nazi party, which was still technically outlawed, must be made legal. Arthur Seyss-Inquart, a pro-Nazi Viennese lawyer whom Schuschnigg had already made State Councilor in his Cabinet, must be promoted to the post of Minister of the Interior, in command of security. The cabinet ministries of defense and finance must also go to Nazis.

Schuschnigg was thoroughly browbeaten. His nerves were not improved by the fact that, although he was normally a chain smoker, he had been forced to do without cigarettes during the long session because of Hitler's aversion to the habit. He signed the ultimatum.

But on his return to Vienna, Schuschnigg proved both courageous and foolhardy. He decided to reaffirm Austria's independence, and scheduled a nationwide plebiscite for Sunday, March 13, to determine whether Austrians wanted a "free, independent, social, Christian and united Austria." Hitler's protégé, Seyss-Inquart, promptly presented Schuschnigg with another ultimatum: Postpone the plebiscite or face a German invasion. On March 11 Schuschnigg gave in and canceled the plebiscite. But by then it was too late: not only was Göring urging immediate action, but the general unrest in Austria had given Hitler the excuse he needed for invasion—the pretext of restoring order.

At the last minute he thought of Mussolini, and decided that he owed the Duce some explanation of what he was about to do in Austria. As his intermediary he used Prince Philip of Hesse, a German aristocrat who had married a daughter of the King of Italy. When Prince Philip telephoned from Rome to report that Mussolini had assented "in a very friendly manner," Hitler fairly burbled his gratitude: "Please tell Mussolini I will never forget him for this. . . . Never, never, never. . . . I shall stick with him whatever may happen, even if the whole world gangs up on him." It was one promise Hitler was to keep.

When German troops crossed into Austria on Saturday, March 12, they were welcomed with flowers and Nazi flags. Hitler arrived later that day to a rapturous reception in his hometown of Linz. A similar ovation greeted him in Vienna, scene of his dismal young manhood. As his big black Mercedes-Benz traveled the country's roads, adoring onlookers knelt to scoop up bits of earth the car's tires had touched.

Less well disposed Austrians soon learned what *Anschluss* held in store for them. Known Socialists and Communists were stripped to the waist and flogged. Jews were forced to scrub streets and public latrines. Schuschnigg ended up in a concentration camp from which he was not to be freed until 1945, by American troops.

Britain and France were rocked by Hitler's new coup. Chamberlain's Foreign Secretary, Lord Halifax, clapped his hand to his forehead, saying: "Horrible! Horrible! I never thought they would do it!" Both countries lodged protests in Berlin. The reply was icily insolent: German-Austrian relations were the sole concern of the German people.

On the night that German troops were advancing on the Austrian border, Air Force Commander-in-Chief Göring held a reception in Berlin at the Air Ministry's palatial new *Haus der Flieger* (Aviator House). Among the 1,000 guests present was Czechoslovakia's envoy to Germany. Clearly and understandably anxious, he approached Göring for a brief chat. Göring assured him in the Führer's name that events in Austria were in no way to be construed as a threat to his country. "I give you my word of honor," Göring pledged. "Czechoslovakia has nothing to fear from the Reich."

Few small countries seemed in a better position to withstand German pressure than Czechoslovakia. It had treaties of alliance with two great powers, France and the Soviet Union. It boasted the giant Skoda armaments works. Its common frontier with Germany was guarded by impressive fortifications. If necessary, its well-equipped, well-trained army could muster 44 divisions.

Czechoslovakia's weakness lay in the multiplicity of its ethnic groups. The Czechs, though predominant, numbered only seven and a half million, just about two million more than the combined total of other peoples—Germans, Slovaks, Ruthenians, Poles and Hungarians. By 1938, one of these groups—the Germans in the Sudetenland, the area closest to Germany—had become increasingly restive. Actually they had once been part of the old Austrian Empire of the Habsburgs, but the Sudeten Germans had now fallen for the siren song of Nazism, which had assured them that they all properly belonged in a Greater Germany. The

We, the German Führer and Chancellor and the British Prime Minister, have had a further meeting today and are agreed in recognising that the question of Anglo-German relations is of the first importance for the two countries and for Europe.

We regard the agreement signed last night and the Anglo-German Naval Agreement as symbolic of the desire of our two peoples never to go to war with one another again.

We are resolved that the method of consultation shall be the method adopted to deal with any other questions that may concern our two countries, and we are determined to continue our efforts to remove possible sources of difference and thus to contribute to assure the peace of Europe.

Neville Chamberlain

September 30, 1938.

The crowning irony of prewar efforts to appease Hitler was Prime Minister Neville Chamberlain's "triumphal" return from his negotiating mission with Hitler in Munich. At right, he stands before a welcoming British crowd and waves the so-called Anglo-German peace declaration (above) that Hitler had signed with Chamberlain that morning. The document was useless: Hitler had already secretly agreed with Mussolini that they would have to join in a future war against Britain.

leader of the Sudeten German party, Konrad Henlein, was on the Nazi payroll.

Two weeks after Austria was annexed, Henlein was called to Berlin and given a strategy lesson by Hitler personally. "We must always demand so much that we can never be satisfied," the Führer counseled. Henlein returned home understanding that on no account was he to propose any settlement of Sudeten grievances that the government in Prague could conceivably accept; Hitler had already begun laying plans to swallow Czechoslovakia whole.

The demands Henlein subsequently presented to Prague called, in effect, for the creation of a German state within the Czechoslovak Republic. The Czechoslovak government reported the proposals to its ally, France, noting that it was prepared to grant some concessions but not at the expense of its own independence. France was bound by treaty to come to Czechoslovakia's aid if the smaller nation's security was threatened. Were the French, Prague asked, prepared to fulfill their obligation now?

The French, having lacked a government when Austria fell, had managed by now to patch one together. Its premier was Edouard Daladier, a former professor of history who had been a member of most French cabinets since World War I. He had served gallantly as a sergeant in that war but had emerged from it resolved to do all in his power to prevent France from getting into another one.

Daladier and his Foreign Minister, Georges Bonnet, flew to London with a proposal for joint action: Britain and France would urge Prague to make maximum concessions in the Sudetenland and would simultaneously inform Berlin of Anglo-French determination to support Czechoslovakian independence. However, Chamberlain agreed to join the French in only the mildest of warnings to Berlin because he was not really convinced that Hitler intended to destroy Czechoslovakia.

Through the spring and summer of 1938, Hitler's propagandists stoked the fires of unrest in the Sudetenland. Broadcasts beamed from Germany told of horsewhippings and wanton killings of Sudeten Germans by Czechoslovakian police, and accused Prague of deliberate brutality to its German minority. The Sudeten German party organized a paramilitary force on the Nazi model and put on increasingly provocative demonstrations. By late August the situation had become ominous. Calculated rumors manufactured in Germany reported Czech troop movements along the common frontier. The stream of abuse aimed at Prague by Hitler's propagandists became a torrent.

Czechoslovakia's beleaguered president, Eduard Beneš, was under pressure not only from his enemies but also from his professed friends; Paris and London kept hammering at the need for concessions to the Sudeten Germans. In early September Beneš decided to try to satisfy his rebellious minority once and for all. The approach he used was decidedly novel in diplomacy—honest and direct. He invited two officials of the Sudeten German party to Prague; when they were seated across his desk, he took out a blank sheet of paper and placed it before them.

"Write down your party demands," he said. "I promise you in advance that whatever you write I will grant."

They sat transfixed, too astounded to speak.

"I mean it," said Beneš. "Write."

Still they made no move. Beneš took out his own pen.

"You tell *me* what to write," he said.

Forced at last to speak, the two men dictated party chief Henlein's latest terms. These now amounted to setting up, within the Czechoslovak Republic, not merely a German state but a German totalitarian state. Beneš wrote down the terms and affixed his signature.

At Sudeten Nazi Party headquarters, informed by telephone of the results of the encounter with Beneš, the reaction was not joy but consternation: "My God, he's given us everything we asked for." Beneš never received an answer to his offer. A week after the meeting in his office, sporadic outbreaks of violence by Sudeten Germans indicated that an open rebellion against Prague might be in the offing, and Beneš placed the Sudetenland under martial law.

War between Czechoslovakia and Germany seemed inevitable. France was now face to face with the question of honoring its pledge to defend the Czechs. Fearing to act alone, the French sounded out the Soviet Ambassador in Paris, noting that his own country's pact with the Czechs in 1935 had provided for joint Russian-French action to protect Czechoslovakia against Germany. The Ambassador replied that Russia would go to Czechoslovakia's aid if France also honored its agreement.

But indecision engulfed the French cabinet. Daladier telephoned Chamberlain to ask what he could do to avert the onrushing crisis. The Prime Minister had already decided to make a personal appeal to Hitler. On September 13 he telegraphed the Führer suggesting a meeting and offering to fly to Germany the very next morning. As it happened, the wire did not arrive until the 14th; Hitler quickly and affably consented to meet on the 15th.

Chamberlain's flight to meet Hitler at Berchtesgaden was only his second time in a plane; once, in 1923, he had ventured aloft to help promote a Birmingham trade fair. The journey from London, together with the long mountain drive from the Munich airport, took more than seven hours—no easy jaunt for a man of 69. Nor was he impressed by his first sight of the Führer. "Altogether he looks undistinguished," Chamberlain later reported. "You would take him for the house painter he once was."

They talked for three hours, alone except for Hitler's interpreter; apparently Chamberlain had not felt it necessary to bring his own. He was treated to a recital of an entire catalogue of complaints against the Czechs. After a while, extraordinarily patient as he was, he could take no more. He broke in to say—with "some asperity," he recalled—that he failed to see why he had been permitted to come so far since he was obviously wasting his time.

This remark had the effect of bringing Hitler to the point: If the British agreed to self-determination for the Sudeten Germans, he would consider the Czechoslovak matter settled. Chamberlain said he would have to consult the French. The two men parted with the understanding that Hitler would take no action until they met again.

The Anglo-French deliberations resulted in a joint recommendation to the Prague government that it cede to Germany all areas in which the Sudeten Germans were at least half the population; in exchange Czechoslovakia would get an Anglo-French guarantee of its new shrunken frontier.

Beneš and his cabinet rejected the terms. On orders from home, the British and French ambassadors in Prague hurried to see the President to urge him to reconsider. It was 2 a.m., and he had gone to bed; his visitors insisted he be roused. And so at dawn an exhausted Beneš, virtually sleepless for the past week, began a new round of consultations.

The Soviet Union reiterated its readiness to stand by Czechoslovakia if the French would also act. The French equivocated; despite their pledge to the Czechs, they had no desire to become Russia's ally in what seemed sure to expand into a Europe-wide conflict. The British had no formal alliance with the Czechs, and in any case it was their own Prime Minister who was pressing for concessions to Hitler.

Beneš now realized that his country stood totally isolated. At nightfall he gave in. He sent word to London and Paris that his country would accept the Anglo-French terms and cede the Sudetenland to Germany. "We had no choice," he told his colleagues. "We have been basely betrayed."

The next day, September 22, Chamberlain flew to meet with Hitler again—this time at the little spa of Godesberg on the Rhine, a less taxing flight from London than the journey to Berchtesgaden. The Prime Minister could not have been in better spirits when the conference with Hitler began. He outlined in detail the Anglo-French plan the Czechs had accepted for the transfer of the Sudetenland to Germany.

When he had finished there was a long moment of silence; Hitler seemed to be groping for words. Finally he found them. "I am extremely sorry," he said, "but that's no longer of any use."

He went on to give his reasons—all obviously improvised on the spot. The methods proposed for the transfer were too slow; the Sudetenland would have to be occupied by Germany immediately. Other areas of Czechoslovakia must be granted plebiscites to decide their own status. Moreover, Germany would not participate in any guarantee of Czechoslovakia's future boundaries.

Chamberlain's face flushed, reflecting his profound shock. He refused to entertain the new conditions. The discussion grew heated. Then came a touch of melodrama no proper Englishman could condone. From time to time messengers would enter with telegrams, and Hitler would shout: "Two more Germans killed! I will be avenged! The Czechs must be smashed!" Finally Chamberlain had enough; he announced he was returning to his hotel. As he rose, Hitler suddenly turned amiable host. He took the Prime Minister to the terrace outside the room, overlooking the Rhine. A late afternoon mist covered the river. "Oh, I am so sorry, Mr. Chamberlain," Hitler said. "I had so looked forward to showing you this wonderful view."

Hastily consulting by telephone, the British and French agreed to advise Beneš they would have no objection if he decided to mobilize. But overnight, in his hotel room, Chamberlain had second thoughts. He asked Hitler for a memorandum of his new terms.

That evening the two men met again. Chamberlain then discovered that something had been added to Hitler's demands: a deadline. The Czechs would have to evacuate the Sudetenland by September 28, only five days hence. Chamberlain declared this unacceptable; Hitler then agreed to extend the deadline to October 1, saying: "You are the only man to whom I have ever made a concession." What he did not say was that October 1 had long since been fixed as his target date for the start of *Case Green,* the code name for Germany's attack on Czechoslovakia.

Prague rejected the Godesberg proposals on September 25. The French affirmed that they would aid Czechoslovakia if it were attacked, and ordered partial mobilization. The British assured the French of Britain's support if they became involved in war with Germany.

Britain also began preparing for war. The fleet was mobilized. A few of the nation's pitiful supply of antiaircraft guns were mounted on London Bridge; workmen dug air-raid trenches in the city parks. Some 38 million gas masks were stocked in regional centers to be distributed upon the declaration of war. In a radio broadcast on September 27, Chamberlain confessed his despair: "How horrible, fantastic, incredible it is that we should be digging trenches and laying in gas masks here because of a quarrel in a faraway country between peoples of whom we know nothing."

Two hours after the broadcast the Prime Minister received a wire from the Führer indicating his willingness to have Chamberlain continue his efforts "to make the Czechs see reason." Several developments had given Hitler pause. His military attaché in Prague had estimated that combined Czechoslovak and French troops presently outnumbered German forces by two to one. His Ambassador in Washington had reported that in the event of war between Germany and Britain "the whole weight of the United States would be thrown into the scale on the side of Britain."

Chamberlain was overjoyed at Hitler's message. Without bothering to consult his cabinet, the French or the Czechs, he whipped off a reply saying: "I feel certain that you can get all the essentials you want without war and without delay. I cannot believe you will start a world war which may end civilization for a few days' delay in settling this long-standing situation."

The following afternoon Chamberlain addressed a packed and somber House of Commons. For 80 minutes the members heard a doleful recital of the Prime Minister's efforts to keep the peace. As he went on, a messenger entered and handed a paper to a cabinet member on the front bench, who thrust it at Chamberlain. He seized it, scanned it, smiled and said: "I have now been informed that Herr Hitler invites me to meet him at Munich tomorrow morning. He has also invited Signor Mussolini and Monsieur Daladier. Signor Mussolini has accepted and I have no doubt Monsieur Daladier will accept; I need not say what my answer will be." The House erupted. Members broke into cheers and applause, stamping their feet and tossing papers into the air.

The conference at the Führerhaus in Munich, the demeaning climax to the efforts at appeasement, lasted more than 12 hours and validated the surrender of the Sudetenland to Germany. Hitler dominated the proceedings. When Chamberlain brought up the question of compensation for the Czechs who would be forced to leave the Sudetenland, Hitler exploded, shouting that there was no time for "such trivialities." Chamberlain did not pursue the point.

The Czechs were not permitted to attend the meeting. Only after the agreement was reached were they handed maps of the areas to be ceded and a timetable for occupation. It was to begin October 1. *Case Green* was right on schedule—and without the need for firing a single shot.

Flying home to Paris, Daladier was deeply depressed. In abandoning the Czechs, France had gone back on pledges made as long ago as 1924. Daladier expected to be met by angry mobs. To his astonishment, the crowds at the airport and along his route into Paris gave him a noisy ovation. "Imbeciles," he muttered. "They are cheering me. For what?"

Chamberlain, on the other hand, was elated. He had stayed behind in Munich in order to present Hitler with a single-page document he hoped would guarantee the future. It was a declaration by the two men that the Munich pact was "symbolic of the desire of our two peoples never to go to war again." Hitler seemed delighted to sign, though

RED CARPET FOR INVASION

When Stalin decided in the spring of 1939 to offer a mutual nonaggression pact to the virulently anti-Communist Nazis, he knew that a successful approach to the Germans would astonish and outrage the world—especially his fellow Communists abroad. But he had cogent reasons for the move. He knew the Soviet Union was not prepared to fight a war against a rearmed, bellicose Germany; and he was prepared to roll out the Kremlin's reddest carpet for the Führer in exchange for the security of a treaty. But before Stalin could even open negotiations, he had to dispatch a clear signal to Berlin that Moscow was in earnest about making a deal.

Stalin's signal came in the form of an abrupt shift of key diplomatic personnel. He fired his able Commissar for Foreign Affairs, Maxim Litvinov, whom the Nazis hated as a Jew and a proponent of alliance with the Western powers. Underlining that message, negotiations for a defense pact with Britain and France collapsed within weeks of Litvinov's departure.

His replacement was Vyacheslav Molotov, a tough, effective old Bolshevik who had helped Stalin with the often dirty job of consolidating his power in the late '20s and early '30s. The Nazis were pleased with the switch; the German chargé d'affaires in Moscow noted that Molotov was "one of Stalin's closest and most intimate advisors, and not a Jew."

Though the new Soviet Foreign Minister had neither love for nor illusions about the Nazis, Molotov tackled his assignment with characteristic efficiency. In a series of talks with the German Foreign Minister, Joachim von Ribbentrop, he hammered out a treaty that, for the moment, at least, gave both sides what they wanted.

For Stalin, there was a guarantee of his borders against any intrusion, and recognition of the fact the Russians might want to move into the Baltic states. Hitler, in return, was free to invade Poland, without fear of Russian intervention. But, despite his satisfaction with the treaty, Stalin held one card in his hand in case the agreement fell apart; he did not shoot or imprison the displaced Litvinov, routine fates for unhorsed Kremlin bureaucrats. Sensing that one day he might well need to reactivate his contacts with the West, Stalin merely put Litvinov on a comfortable shelf in the Soviet foreign ministry.

Stalin shakes hands with Nazi negotiator Ribbentrop after they had signed the Soviet-German pact.

MAXIM LITVINOV

VYACHESLAV MOLOTOV

privately he was annoyed at Chamberlain for helping him procure his unwarlike victory at Munich. "That fellow has spoiled my entry into Prague!" he stormed.

In London, crowds massed outside the Prime Minister's residence at 10 Downing Street to cheer him on his return. He appeared at a window, flourished the agreement with Hitler and exulted: "My friends . . . there has come back from Germany peace with honor. I believe it is peace for our time." The House of Commons further buoyed him with a vote of confidence. He then departed for Scotland, for some restful days of salmon fishing on the River Tweed.

The Munich pact had spelled Czechoslovakia's doom. Loss of the Sudetenland not only stripped the country of its principal line of fortifications against Germany, but also whetted the appetite of Czechoslovakia's other enemies. Poland and Hungary simply walked in and took some 8,000 square miles of Czech territory. The provinces of Slovakia and Ruthenia demanded and got a large degree of autonomy.

Meanwhile President Beneš resigned and went into exile in England. His aging successor, Emil Hácha, had a weak heart and little skill in politics or diplomacy. In March 1939 he tried to halt his country's further disintegration by dismissing the fractious governments of Slovakia and Ruthenia. Slovakia, at Hitler's orders, proclaimed its independence; Hungary, posing as the protector of Ruthenia, demanded that province's evacuation by the Czechoslovak army.

In this new crisis Hácha and his Foreign Minister sought an audience with Hitler in Berlin. Hitler received them at one in the morning—an hour deliberately chosen with the thought that the ailing Hácha would be at his lowest ebb. Without further ado the Führer announced that he intended to impose German "protectorates" on Bohemia and Moravia, the two provinces remaining to Czechoslovakia. If Hácha did not sign by 5 a.m., the Führer shouted, German bombers would begin saturation bombing of Prague that morning. At 4 a.m. Hácha, near collapse, signed away his country's independence.

By daybreak German troops were in Bohemia and Moravia, and a few hours later a proclamation by Hitler informed the world that "Czechoslovakia had ceased to exist." That evening he personally arrived in Prague to impose the "protectorate" on his latest victims. To emphasize his new triumph, he chose to sleep overnight in Hradčany Castle, the traditional home both of the anient kings of Bohemia and their modern democratic successors.

With the final occupation of Bohemia and Moravia, the British and French could no longer continue to deceive themselves about Hitler. Here was a clear case of aggression involving peoples and territories that had never before been under German rule. But the two countries hesitated to act —and Hitler moved again.

Before March was out he forced the little Baltic republic of Lithuania to cede the city of Memel, once a part of German East Prussia. Next, he fixed his eyes on Poland. That shredded document, the Versailles Treaty, had carved a corridor out of Germany in order to give Poland an outlet to the sea; it had also given the former German seaport of Danzig the status of a free city. An overwhelming majority of Danzig's residents were Nazis, clamoring for reunion with the Reich. But the city lay within the corridor, at its very tip. Hitler ordered Foreign Minister von Ribbentrop to discuss a settlement of the questions of both Danzig and the corridor with Poland's Foreign Minister, Colonel Joseph Beck.

Chamberlain, still searching for ways to restrain Hitler, had also decided to approach Beck. But this involved some prior negotiating with Russia. Against his own deeply ingrained opinions about the Russians, Chamberlain proposed that they join with the British and French in a guarantee of Polish independence. But Beck declared he wanted no Russian guarantee whatever; he believed his country was best served by keeping both Germany and Russia at arm's length.

On March 31, Chamberlain made a move that was to stun his own countrymen. He offered Beck a unilateral British guarantee of Poland's security. This was too good for Beck to refuse. He accepted, as one observer put it, "between two flicks of ash from his cigarette." The unilateral guarantee —though France soon joined in it—was a complete reversal of the policy England had firmly maintained since the close of World War I: Chamberlain had, in effect, placed the decision for war or peace for his people in the hands of another nation. He had done so on the preposterous assumption that Poland was in no immediate danger and that it was militarily strong—an illusion Beck did his best to encourage. In any event, Britain was in no position to give any effective aid to its new ally if it were suddenly attacked.

Hitler knew this too, but the British guarantee sent him into a fresh fury against Chamberlain and his countrymen. "I'll cook them a stew they'll choke on!" he said. He was no happier with the Poles; they had rebuffed Ribbentrop's proposal to settle the questions of Danzig and the corridor. The German Army was alerted to prepare a new plan of operation: *Case White,* an attack on Poland. The date was set for September 1, 1939. This time, Hitler warned his generals, "We cannot expect a repetition of the Czech affair. We must prepare ourselves for conflict."

When Chamberlain informed an astonished House of Commons of his guarantee to Poland, he was barraged with shouts of "What about Russia?" Former Prime Minister Lloyd George had voiced the misgivings of many men: "If we are going into this without the help of Russia we are walking into a trap." Chamberlain had assured his listeners that Britain and France were still in touch with Moscow. In fact, talks with Moscow were stalled. Chamberlain had wanted Russia to give its own guarantee to Poland; the Russians preferred an Anglo-French-Soviet alliance that would also guarantee the Baltic states against German aggression.

Then, in May, Stalin made a move that portended no good for the British and French. He appointed Vyacheslav Molotov as his new Foreign Minister, replacing Maxim Litvinov, a staunch believer in collective security with the West. In Molotov's first public speech he criticized the British and French for their half-hearted efforts at rapprochement with the Soviet Union. But in any case, he added pointedly, continuing to negotiate with the Western Democracies in no way precluded the simultaneous strengthening of Russia's trade relations with Germany and Italy.

In July, prodded into action by Molotov's speech and by Polish intelligence reports that a German attack on Poland might come as early as the end of August, the British and French agreed to talks in Moscow between their military representatives and Russia's, as a preliminary to a military accord. But the Anglo-French mission took its time getting organized and elected to go to Russia by sea, taking a slow boat to Leningrad. Once in Moscow, the members of the mission proved unable to answer key questions of strategy posed by the Russians; for example, would the Poles allow the Red Army to cross Polish territory to make contact with the enemy? The talks adjourned, never to be resumed.

The Germans, meanwhile, had read Molotov's speech with great care. When the German Ambassador in Moscow asked him what he meant by his reference to improving trade relations between their two countries, Molotov replied that Stalin wanted to improve political relations as well. To Hitler this was a clear signal that Russia might be neutralized in the coming war with Poland.

Despite his long-time hatred of "Jewish Bolshevism," Hitler instructed Foreign Minister von Ribbentrop to express his willingness to go to Moscow to settle "all territorial questions" between the two countries.

On August 23 Ribbentrop landed at Khodynka airport at Moscow. After lunch he went to see Stalin and Molotov at the Kremlin and the three hammered out a mutual nonaggression pact that freed Hitler to invade Poland, and allowed Stalin to move as he chose, into Finland, Estonia, Latvia, the Rumanian province of Bessarabia—and the eastern half of Poland as well. Only the nonaggression pact would be publicly announced; the rest was kept in a secret protocol.

That night the conferees and their retinues celebrated with toasts in vodka and champagne to Russia, to Germany and to Stalin. Then Stalin rose to offer the final toast. "I know how much the German nation loves its Führer," he said. "I should like to drink his health."

The news of the Nazi-Soviet treaty burst over Europe like a clap of thunder before the deluge. But even now, a few ears refused to hear its real meaning. In France, there was talk of renouncing the guarantee to Poland: many feared that with Britain's army yet to be put into shape the brunt of war would fall on the French alone. In the end, however, they stood firm behind Daladier's determination that France would "be true to her solemn promises."

In Britain, the pact forged a unity of solemn, angry purpose that had been hitherto lacking. Conservatives, Liberals and Laborites outdid one another in denouncing Stalin's treachery. And the country braced itself.

On September 1, exactly as Hitler had planned all along, the German Army poured over the Polish border. The French and the British declared war on Germany on September 3. Chamberlain told Parliament: "Everything I have worked for, everything I have hoped for, everything I have believed in has crashed in ruins."

The prelude to war had ended.

THE FIRST BIG TAKE-OVER

Shocked and angry Czechs, some waving fists, watch German troops enter Prague on March 15, 1939, after the Czechoslovakian government capitulated.

AN EMOTIONAL WELCOME FOR THE FUHRER

The first solid indication of how the Nazis would treat occupied territories came in Czechoslovakia, and the auguries were both misleading and ominous. In 1938 Hitler's troops marched into the Czech Sudetenland; it was largely populated by Germans, who welcomed the invaders warmly. In most of the region, a carnival atmosphere prevailed. To greet the occupying troops, whom the Czech forces had been ordered not to resist, huge Nazi flags—smuggled in earlier by party agents—sprouted from buildings. Women wept or cheered at the sight of German soldiers, and garlanded them with flowers. One admirer was so carried away by excitement that a bouquet of roses she tossed to the Führer hit him in the face as he drove by into his new domains.

Behind these festive scenes were a few darker vignettes. A German mob in the town of Ceský Krumlov fired at the backs of retreating Czech soldiers; in other towns shops and homes belonging to Czechs and Jews were vandalized and ransacked; a railroad station ticket clerk was shot dead when he refused to turn his cash over to Sudeten freebooters. In Prague, veterans of the legendary Czech Legion *(pages 42-43)* were observed weeping. President Eduard Beneš despairingly left the capital of truncated Czechoslovakia for a self-imposed exile in England. No less despairing was Beneš's temporary replacement, General Jan Syrový, the head of the Czech Army, which had lost its main line of defense when the bristling fortifications in the Sudetenland slipped from Prague's control.

Even more ominous for Europe's immediate future were Hitler's words as he spoke at the Czech town of Cheb, congratulating his new subjects on their love for the Fatherland. He grandiosely assured them that "over the greater German Reich is laid a German shield protecting it, and a German sword protecting it!" Careful listeners noted that territory in German control for barely a day had somehow become part of the Reich, and clearly saw signs of the future in the words "greater" and "sword." As for Hitler himself, convinced that the mere threat of force could make him master of Europe, he began boldly to plot his next move.

Three Sudetenlanders, one overcome with emotion as she raises up a Nazi salute, pay homage as the Wehrmacht enters the border town of Cheb.

As jubilant Sudeten Germans line the road, Nazi notables triumphantly enter the Sudetenland under a banner proclaiming "One Folk, One Reich, One Führer."

Ecstatic Sudeten girls in traditional local costumes join in welcoming the German soldiers.

German troopers clutch belts to stop the happy throng from rushing parading comrades.

Sudeten boys peek through the boots and rifles of guards posted along the parade route.

Sudeten youngsters—some held in the arms of German infantrymen—become a proud part of the Wehrmacht's entry into the border town of Aš.

Aging Emil Hácha, hustled into the fast-rotating Czech Presidency, inspects an honor guard drawn up outside the Berlin railroad terminal. The President and his party went on to the posh Adlon Hotel, where the best suite had been reserved for their stay.

A gracious Hitler greets Hácha in the Reichschancellery. Moments later the Führer and his aides had bullied Hácha into signing Czechoslovakia's death sentence.

A NATION BULLIED INTO HELPLESSNESS

Most Czechs in the rump state still governed from the capital at Prague took scant reassurance from the love feast in the Sudetenland—and with reason. Within six months of Beneš' resignation, pressure from Berlin had persuaded the Czechs to accept as President 66-year-old Emil Hácha, the well-meaning, prematurely senile Chief Justice of the Czech Supreme Court. During the winter, the German pressure continued to mount until it was clear that Hitler was determined to dominate the remains of Czechoslovakia—perhaps even invade. In March 1939 an uneasy Hácha asked Hitler for an audience, which the Führer, with cynical grace, billed as a meeting between neighboring chiefs of state.

An honor guard, flowers and a box of chocolates greeted Hácha at the Berlin station, and a smiling, hand-pumping Hitler ushered the President inside the Reichschancellery. But once he was behind the closed door of the Führer's chambers, the old man heard from Hitler's own lips that, two days previously, the order had been given "for the invasion by German troops and for the incorporation of Czechoslovakia into the Third Reich." Whereupon Hitler turned and left the room.

Hácha fainted. Two of Hitler's ministers, left in the chambers with Hácha, panicked, fearing—as a German interpreter later noted—that "the whole world will say tomorrow that he was murdered at the Chancellery." But a physician revived Hácha with stimulants, and at four in the morning on March 15, he signed documents of complete surrender.

When spearheads of the German Army entered Prague *(right)* two hours later, the city's mood had changed forever. There was no cheering.

That evening, when Hitler himself rode through the capital in a light snow, the silence of despair had descended over the defeated Czechs. The gloom later intensified as the heavy but meticulous hand of German administration began rearranging various aspects of Czech life *(overleaf)*. Further disruption of the prostrate nation came with the establishment to the east of Prague of an "independent" Republic of Slovakia, which Hitler had forehandedly conceived as a base for his future designs on Polish territory to the north.

Reflecting a very different mood from that of the celebrating Sudetenlanders, a subdued crowd in Prague gets a look at the real face of Neville Chamberlain's peace as German columns roll in to occupy the Czech capital.

A German motorized unit clatters over snow-flecked cobbles in Prager Platz past Hradčany Castle, the ancestral home of Czech rulers. Although most of Prague's unarmed residents were embittered by the sudden occupation, the only resistance that Hitler's troops encountered was a few hurled snowballs.

Obeying German orders, a Czech policeman gets ready to change a street sign in the city of Brno from "Freedom Avenue" to "Adolf Hitler Place."

A stern notice from the German Occupation Army "Jüdische Geschäft"—Jewish store—warns buyers away from a Czechoslovakian radio shop.

A German official is flanked by Slovak customs guards at a border post. After the fall of Prague some Slovaks, like these men, continued to regard Hitler as a liberator. But they were permitted their illusions—and granted such posts—purely as a nod to the German pretense that there really was a self-governing Slovakia. Actually German troops were in command of strategic points all throughout the country.

Another new sign orders motorists to change over to German traffic patterns by driving on the right-hand side of the road ("Rechts fahren!") in Jihlava, a Czech town that lies 65 miles southeast of Prague.

A QUICK MEAL FOR THE NEIGHBORS

While sullen citizens in the Prague region watched the German military machine envelop the heart of Czechoslovakia, a tragicomic replay of the Sudetenland celebrations occurred in the easternmost Czech territory of Ruthenia. There, a dissident minority of Hungarians was agitating for their adjacent home country, which had already annexed the southernmost part of Ruthenia, to take over the whole area.

Hitler, of course, had counted on this to make the dismemberment of Czechoslovakia all the easier. He had already invited Hungary's Regent, Miklós Horthy, to share in the spoils by invading Ruthenia: "He who wants to eat at the table," Hitler wrote Horthy, "must help out in the kitchen."

"Heartfelt thanks!" Horthy wrote Hitler on March 13, 1939—two days before the Germans entered Prague. "The plans are already laid. On Thursday the 16th a frontier incident will take place, to be followed on Saturday by the big push."

The frontier incident went off smoothly —in fact, a day sooner than it had been planned—largely through the enthusiastic cooperation of the irredentist populace. As Horthy's troops continued to gobble up Ruthenia, however, they ran into a modicum of armed resistance—the only such incident during the entire Czechoslovakian occupation—from inhabitants of Ukrainian descent, who held up the banquet for 24 hours before being swallowed themselves. In a final irony, the greedy momentum of the Hungarian forces carried them not only across Ruthenia but also over the provincial borders into Slovakia—where fighting broke out between Horthy's men and startled Slovak soldiers. It required a point-blank order from Slovakia's German protectors to halt the Hungarian columns.

A Hungarian soldier wearing a German helmet carries a welcoming bouquet through the gleeful populace

of a Ruthenian border town. Hungarian infantrymen rolled triumphantly through the generally welcoming province, having had only one brief day of fighting.

BIBLIOGRAPHY

Aster, Sidney, *1939: The Making of the Second World War*. Simon and Schuster, 1973.
Baer, George W., *The Coming of the Italian-Ethiopian War*. Harvard University Press, 1967.
Barrett, Marvin, *The Years Between*. Little, Brown and Company, 1962.
Bendiner, Elmer, *A Time for Angels*. Alfred A. Knopf, 1975.
Benns, F. Lee, *Europe Since 1914*. Appleton, Century, Crofts, 1954.
Biagi, Enzo, ed., *Storia del Fascismo* (3 vols.). Sadea-Della Volpe (Florence), 1964.
Bianco, Lucien, *Origins of the Chinese Revolution, 1915-1949*. Stanford University Press, 1971.
Bischoff, Ralph F., *Nazi Conquest through German Culture*. Harvard University Press, 1942.
Bolin, Luis, *The Vital Years*. J. B. Lippincott Company, 1967.
Borgese, G. A., *Goliath*. Viking, 1938.
Bradley, John, *Allied Intervention in Russia*. Basic Books, Inc., 1968.
Brook-Shepherd, Gordon, *The Anschluss*. J. B. Lippincott Company, 1963.
Browder, Robert P., and Alexander Kerensky, eds., *The Russian Provisional Government*. Stanford University Press, 1961.
Buchanan, Sir George, *My Mission to Russia*. Little, Brown & Company, 1923.
Bullock, Alan, *Hitler: A Study in Tyranny*. Harper & Row, 1962.
Burlingame, Roger, and Alden Stevens, *Victory Without Peace*. Harcourt, Brace, 1944.
Carr, E. H., *The Bolshevik Revolution* (3 vols.). The Macmillan Company, 1951.
Cartier, Raymond, *La Seconde Guerre Mondiale*, Vol. I. Larousse, Paris-Match (Paris), 1965.
Cattell, David T., *Communism and the Spanish Civil War*. University of California Press, 1955.
Chilton, John, *Who's Who of Jazz*. The Bloomsbury Bookshop, 1970.
Churchill, Winston:
The Gathering Storm. Houghton Mifflin Company, 1948.
The World Crisis, Vol. IV. Thornton Butterworth Limited, 1929.
Clubb, O. Edmund:
China & Russia: The "Great Game." Columbia University Press, 1971.
20th Century China. Columbia University Press, 1964.
Del Boca, Angelo, *The Ethiopian War*. University of Chicago Press, 1969.
Deutscher, Isaac:
The Prophet Armed. Oxford University Press, 1959.
Stalin. Oxford University Press, 1967.
Eden, Anthony:
Facing the Dictators. Houghton Mifflin Company, 1962.
The Reckoning. Houghton Mifflin Company, 1965.
Eubank, Keith, *Munich*. University of Oklahoma Press, 1963.
Eyck, Erich, *A History of the Weimar Republic*. Harvard University Press, 1962.
Farnsworth, Beatrice, *William C. Bullitt and the Soviet Union*. Indiana University Press, 1967.
Fermi, Laura, *Mussolini*. The University of Chicago Press, 1961.
Ferro, Marc, *The Russian Revolution of February 1917*, trans. by J. L. Richards. Prentice-Hall, Inc., 1972.
Fest, Joachim, *Hitler*, translated from the German by Richard and Clara Winston. Vintage Books, 1975.
Fitzgerald, Charles Patrick, *Revolution in China*. Frederick A. Praeger, 1952.
Fleming, Peter, *The Fate of Admiral Kolchak*. Harcourt, Brace & World, 1963.
Friedrich, Otto, *Before the Deluge*. Harper & Row, 1972.
Fuller, J. F. C., *A Military History of the Western World*, Vol. III. Minerva Press, 1956.
Gilbert, Martin, and Richard Gott, *The Appeasers*. Houghton Mifflin Company, 1963.
Grunfeld, Frederic, *The Hitler File*. Random House, 1974.
Guillermaz, Jacques, *A History of the Chinese Communist Party, 1921-1949*, translated from the French by Anne Destenay. Random House, 1972.
Halliday, E. M., *The Ignorant Armies*. Harper & Brothers, 1960.
Harrison, James Pinckney, *The Long March to Power*. Praeger Publishers, 1972.
Heiferman, Ronald, *World War II*. Derby Books, 1973.
History of the USSR (in Russian). Nauka Publishing House (Moscow), 1968.
Ho, Ping-ti, and Tang Tsou, *China in Crisis*, Vol. I. The University of Chicago Press, 1968.
Hoffmann, Heinrich, *Hitler Was My Friend*. Burke (London), 1955.
Hoover, Herbert, *The Ordeal of Woodrow Wilson*. McGraw-Hill Book Company, Inc., 1958.
Hoyt, Edwin P., *The Army without a Country*. The Macmillan Company, 1967.
Hsu Longhsuen, and Chang Ming-kai, *History of the Sino-Japanese War (1937-1945)*. Chung Wu Publishing Co. (Taipei), 1971.
Huber, Heinz, and Artur Müller, eds., *Das Dritte Reich*, Vol. I. Desch (Munich), 1964.
Hughes, H. Stuart, *Contemporary Europe: A History*. Prentice-Hall, Inc., 1961.
Isherwood, Christopher, *The Berlin Stories*. New Directions, 1954.
Kaltenborn, H. V., *It Seems Like Yesterday*. Putnam's, 1956.
Katkov, George, *Russia 1917: The February Revolution*. Harper & Row, 1967.
Kennan, George F.:
From Prague after Munich. Princeton University Press, 1968.
The Decision to Intervene. Princeton University Press, 1958.
Russia and the West under Lenin and Stalin. Atlantic Monthly Press, 1966.
Russia Leaves the War. Princeton University Press, 1956.
Keynes, John Maynard, *The Economic Consequences of the Peace*. Macmillan and Co., Limited (London), 1920.
Knightley, Phillip, *The First Casualty*. Harcourt, Brace, Jovanovich, 1975.
Kochan, Lionel, *The Russian Revolution*. Wayland Publishers (London), 1971.
Langsam, Walter Consuelo, *The World Since 1919*. The Macmillan Company, 1954.
Laqueur, Walter, *Russia and Germany*. Little, Brown and Company, 1965.
Lehmann, Friedrich Wilhelm, *Berlin Kaleidoskop, 1910-30*. Heinz Moos Verlag, 1962.
Leventhal, Albert R., *War*. Ridge Press, 1973.
Liddell Hart, B. H., *Memoirs*, Vol. II, Cassell & Company Ltd., 1965.
Liepman, Heinz, *Rasputin and the Fall of Imperial Russia*, translated from the German by Edward Fitzgerald. Robert M. McBride Co., Inc., 1959.
Liu, F. F., *A Military History of Modern China*. Princeton University Press, 1956.
Lockhart, R. H. Bruce, *British Agent*. G. P. Putnam's Sons, 1933.
Lorant, Stefan, *Sieg Heil!* Norton, 1974.
Lu, David J., *From the Marco Polo Bridge to Pearl Harbor*. Public Affairs Press, 1961.
Luckett, Richard, *The White Generals*. The Viking Press, 1971.
Mack Smith, Denis, *Italy*. University of Michigan Press, 1969.
Maki, John M., *Conflict and Tension in the Far East*. University of Washington Press, 1961.
Manchester, William, *The Arms of Krupp*. Little, Brown and Company, 1964.
Manvell, Roger, and Heinrich Frankel, *Heinrich Himmler*. Heinemann, 1965.
Mavor, James, *The Russian Revolution*. George Allen & Unwin Ltd., 1928.
McAleavy, Henry, *The Modern History of China*. Frederick A. Praeger, Publishers, 1967.
McNeal, Robert H., *Bride of the Revolution*. University of Michigan Press, 1972.
Michel, Henri, *The Second World War*, translated from the French by Douglas Parmée. Praeger Publishers, 1975.
Montgomery, John, *The Twenties: An Informal Social History*. George Allen & Unwin Ltd., 1957.
Moon, Penderel, *Gandhi and Modern India*. W. W. Norton & Company, 1969.
Moorehead, Alan, *The Russian Revolution*. Harper & Brothers, 1959.
Morrow, Felix, *Revolution and Counter-Revolution in Spain*. Pioneer Publishers, 1938.
Mussolini, Benito, *My Autobiography*. Scribner's, 1928.
Nelson, Walter Henry, *The Berliners: Their Saga and Their City*. David McKay Company, 1969.
Nicolson, Harold, *Peacemaking 1919*. Houghton Mifflin Company, 1933.
Noguères, Henri, *Munich*, translated from the French by Patrick O'Brian. McGraw-Hill Book Company, 1965.
O'Neill, Robert J., *The German Army and the Nazi Party, 1933-39*. James H. Heinemann, Inc., 1966.
Paxton, Robert O., *Europe in the Twentieth Century*. Harcourt, Brace, Jovanovich, 1975.
Payne, Robert, *The Life and Death of Adolf Hitler*. Praeger Publishers, 1973.
Payne, Stanley G., *Politics and the Military in Modern Spain*. Stanford University Press, 1967.
Peers, E. Allison, *The Spanish Tragedy*. Oxford University Press, 1936.
Phillips, Cabell, *From the Crash to the Blitz 1929-1939*. Macmillan, 1969.
Picker, Henry, and Heinrich Hoffmann, *Hitler Close-Up*. Macmillan, 1969.
Pitt, Barrie, *1918: The Last Act*. W. W. Norton & Company, Inc., 1962.
Puzzo, Dante A., *Spain and the Great Powers*. Columbia University Press, 1962.
Renouvin, Pierre, *World War II and its Origins*, translated from the French by Remy Inglis Hall. Harper & Row, 1969.
Reischauer, Edwin O., *Japan, Past and Present*. Alfred A. Knopf, 1964.
Robertson, E. M., *Hitler's Pre-War Policy and Military Plans*. The Citadel Press, 1967.
Rowe, Vivian, *The Great Wall of France*. G. P. Putnam's Sons, 1961.
Rue, John E., *Mao Tse-tung in Opposition*. Stanford University Press, 1966.
Ryder, A. J., *Twentieth Century Germany: From Bismarck to Brandt*. Columbia University Press, 1973.
Schurman, Franz, and Orville Schell, eds., *The China Reader, Vol. II, Republican China, 1911-1949*. Random House, 1967.
Schwab, Peter, ed., *Ethiopia & Haile Selassie*. Facts on File, Inc., 1972.
Sedwick, Frank, *The Tragedy of Manuel Azaña*. Ohio State University Press, 1963.
Seydewitz, Max, *Civil Life in Wartime Germany*. Viking, 1945.
Silva, Umberto, *Ideologia e Arte del Fascismo*. Gabriele Mazzotta (Milan), 1973.
Shirer, William L.:
Berlin Diary. Alfred A. Knopf, 1941.
The Rise and Fall of the Third Reich. Simon and Schuster, 1960.
Shub, David, *Lenin*. Doubleday & Company, 1951.
Slezak, Walter, *What Time's the Next Swan?* Doubleday and Company, 1962.
Smith, Gene, *When the Cheering Stopped*. William Morrow and Company, Inc., 1964.
Snow, Edgar, *Red Star over China*. Random House, 1944.
Sontag, Raymond J., *A Broken World*. Harper & Row, 1971.

Speer, Albert, *Inside the Third Reich,* translated from the German by Richard and Clara Winston. The Macmillan Company, 1970.
Stallings, Laurence, *The First World War, A Photographic History.* Simon and Schuster, 1933.
Stein, George, *The Waffen SS.* Cornell University Press, 1966.
Sternberg, Josef von, *Fun in a Chinese Laundry.* The Macmillan Company, 1965.
Taylor, A. J. P.:
English History 1914-1945. Oxford University Press, 1965.
The Origins of the Second World War. Atheneum, 1962.
Taylor, George E., *The Struggle for North China.* Institute of Pacific Relations, 1940.
Taylor, Telford, *Sword and Swastika.* Simon and Schuster, 1952.
Thomas, Hugh, *The Spanish Civil War.* Harper & Row, 1961.
Thomson, S. Harrison, *Czechoslovakia in European History.* Princeton University Press, 1953.
The Times Atlas of China. Quadrangle/ The New York Times Book Co., 1974.
Tobias, Fritz, *The Reichstag Fire.* Putnam's, 1964.
Tuchman, Barbara, *Stilwell and the American Experience in China, 1911-45.* The Macmillan Company, 1971.
Ulam, Adam B., *The Bolsheviks.* The Macmillan Company, 1965.
Vita di Mussolini. Edizione di Novissima, 1965.
Werner, Bruno E., *Die Zwanziger Jahre.* Bruckmann München, 1962.
Wheeler-Bennett, John W.:
The Forgotten Peace. William Morrow & Company, 1939.
Wooden Titan. William Morrow & Company, 1936.
Wilson, Richard Garratt, *The Long March 1935.* The Viking Press, 1971.
Zeman, Z. A. B., *Nazi Propaganda.* Oxford University Press, 1973.
Zentner, Kurt, *Illustrierte Geschichte des Dritten Reiches,* Vol. I. Südwest Verlag (Munich), 1965.
Zweig, Stefan, *The World of Yesterday: An Autobiography.* University of Nebraska Press, 1964.

PICTURE CREDITS

Credits from left to right are separated by semicolons, from top to bottom by dashes.

COVER: Foreign Records Seized, 1941, National Archives.

WHEN THE SHOOTING STOPPED: 6, 7—Hugo Jaeger from TIME-LIFE Picture Agency. 8—K. Zentner Archiv. 9—Underwood & Underwood. 10, 11—U.S. Signal Corps, National Archives. 12, 13—FPG. 14, 15—Underwood & Underwood. 16, 17—FPG.

"A PEACE RESTING ON QUICKSAND": 20, 21—Heinrich Hoffmann, from *Hitler, wie ihn keiner Kennt* by Heinrich Hoffmann and Baldur von Schirach, published by "Zeitgeschichte," Berlin 1934. 22—Map by Nicholas Fasciano. 25—Bildarchiv Preussischer Kulturbesitz. 26—UPI (2); Harris & Ewing; Wide World. 29—Bildarchiv Preussischer Kulturbesitz.

KILLING GROUND IN RUSSIA: 32, 33—UPI. 34—Tass. 35—Sovfoto. 36, 37—FPG; Underwood & Underwood—Tass. 38, 39—The Bettmann Archive. 40 through 43—U.S. Signal Corps, National Archives.

THE SOVIET SPECTRE: 47—Aram Studio—Underwood & Underwood. 50—Culver. 52—D. Moor, Aurora Publishers, Leningrad, courtesy of Poster Originals Ltd., New York.

THE UNEASY RESPITE: 56, 57—Foreign Records Seized, 1941, National Archives. 58—UPI. 59—Roma's Press. 60, 61—MTI—courtesy R. Haliburton Jr., Northeastern Oklahoma State University, at Tahlequah; UPI. 62, 63—FPG. 64, 65—China Famine Relief—UPI (2). 66, 67—Wide World. 68, 69—UPI; Underwood & Underwood (2). 70, 71—UPI; Underwood & Underwood.

DIZZY DECADENT BERLIN: 72, 73—Steinfeld Archiv, Institut für Theater-Wissenschaft, Cologne University. 74—Bildarchiv Preussischer Kulturbesitz—From *Berlin Kaleidoskop 1910-30* by Friedrich Wilhelm Lehmann, published by Heinz Moos Verlag, Berlin 1962. 75—Ullstein. 76, 77—Ullstein (2)—Radio Times Hulton; Bildarchiv Preussischer Kulturbesitz. 78—From *Berlin Kaleidoskop 1910-30* by Friedrich Wilhelm Lehmann, published by Heinz Moos Verlag, Berlin 1962; Ullstein. 79—The Bettmann Archive—Landesbildstelle; Süddeutscher Verlag. 80, 81—Ullstein—From *Berlin Kaleidoskop 1910-30* by Friedrich Wilhelm Lehmann, published by Heinz Moos Verlag, Berlin 1962; Ullstein.

A NEW BREED OF CAESARS: 84—Foreign Records Seized, 1941, National Archives; Wide World; UPI (2); Heinrich Hoffmann from Zeitgeschichtliches. 86, 87—Roma's Press. 88—Rizzoli Press; Inset, Unedi. 91—Stefan Lorant Collection. 93—Bundesarchiv—Stefan Lorant Collection.

DEADLY GAME OF MAKE BELIEVE: 96, 97—Margaret Bourke-White. 98, 99—Margaret Bourke-White, courtesy Margaret Bourke-White estate. 100, 101—Margaret Bourke-White, courtesy Margaret Bourke-White estate—FPG. 102—FPG. 103—Margaret Bourke-White from TIME-LIFE Picture Agency—Margaret Bourke-White, courtesy Margaret Bourke-White estate. 104, 105—Margaret Bourke-White, courtesy Margaret Bourke-White estate.

THE THEATRICS OF POWER: 106, 107—France Presse. 108—Fototeca Storica Nazionale. 109—Bundesarchiv. 110—© Movietonews, Inc. 1935. 111—Heinrich Hoffmann from Zeitgeschichtliches. 112—UPI—Vitullo from TIME-LIFE Picture Agency; UPI. 113—Heinrich Hoffmann, from *Adolf Hitler,* published by Cigaretten-Bilderdienst, Altona 1936—Heinrich Hoffmann, from *Hitler in Seinen Bergen,* published by "Zeitgeschichte," Berlin 1935 (2). 114—Heinrich Hoffmann from Zeitgeschichtliches—Imperial War Museum; Heinrich Hoffmann, from *Adolf Hitler,* published by Cigaretten-Bilderdienst, Altona 1936. 115—Foreign Records Seized, 1941, National Archives. 116, 117—Wide World (2); Roma's Press—Interphoto; TIME-LIFE Picture Agency (2); Istituto Nazionale Luce. 118—Farabola. 119—Heinrich Hoffmann from Zeitgeschichtliches—Courtesy Enzo Nizza; Bildarchiv Preussischer Kulturbesitz. 120, 121—From *Ideologia e Arte del Fascismo* by Umberto Silva, published by Gabriele Mazzotta, Milan 1973—Süddeutscher Verlag; Farabola. 122, 127—Hugo Jaeger from TIME-LIFE Picture Agency. 123 through 126—Heinrich Hoffmann, from *Deutschland Erwacht* by Heinrich Hoffmann and Wilfrid Bade, pub. by Cigaretten-Bilderdienst, Altona 1933.

CONVULSION IN THE FAR EAST: 130—A. T. Steele from TIME-LIFE Picture Agency. 132—Map by Nicholas Fasciano. 135—Hugh Hutton, *The Philadelphia Inquirer.*

SAMURAI SLASH AT CHINA: 138, 139—UPI. 140—Tsuguichi Koyanagi. 141—UPI. 142 through 145—Y. Natori from Black Star. 146, 147—Paul Dorsey from TIME-LIFE Picture Agency.

DOWNFALL OF A FEEBLE LEAGUE: 150—Wide World; Insets, Keystone View; Erich Salomon from TIME-LIFE Picture Agency; Keystone View. 152—Cartoon by David Low, by arrangement with the trustees and *The London Evening Standard,* courtesy *The Devil's Decade* by Claud Cockburn, published by Mason & Lipscomb, New York 1973.

ROME'S NEW LEGIONARIES: 156 through 165—Caesare Bonvini, copied by David Lees.

DRESS REHEARSAL IN SPAIN: 168, 169—Courtesy Audio Brandon Films. 170—Maps by Nicholas Fasciano. 173—Amsterdam Institute of Social History, courtesy *20° Secolo,* Mondadori, Verona 1971.

THE NAZIS' SEDUCTIVE RITUALS: 176, 177—Hugo Jaeger from TIME-LIFE Picture Agency. 178—Foreign Records Seized, 1941, National Archives. 179—Hugo Jaeger from TIME-LIFE Picture Agency. 180, 181—Hugo Jaeger from TIME-LIFE Picture Agency—Bildarchiv Preussischer Kulturbesitz; Hugo Jaeger from TIME-LIFE Picture Agency. 182, 183—Hugo Jaeger from TIME-LIFE Picture Agency.

PACTS THAT UNLEASHED HITLER: 186, 187—Ullstein. 189—TIME-LIFE Picture Agency. 190—No credit; inset, Wiener Library. 193—Wide World; London News Agency. 197—FPG—Wide World (2).

THE FIRST BIG TAKEOVER: 200, 201—CTK. 202—UPI. 203—Hugo Jaeger from TIME-LIFE Picture Agency. 204, 205—CTK Heinrich Hoffmann, copied by Mario Fenyo, courtesy National Archives (2); Bibliothèque Nationale. 206—Ullstein—Stefan Lorant Collection. 207—Karel Hajek from TIME-LIFE Picture Agency. 208, 209—Wide World—Foreign Records Seized, 1941, National Archives; Wide World; Foreign Records Seized, 1941, National Archives. 210, 211—TIME-LIFE Picture Agency.

ACKNOWLEDGMENTS

Portions of this book were written by James P. Shenton and Geoffrey Field. The index was prepared by Mel Ingber. The editors of this book also wish to thank the following persons and institutions: Creed Black, Vice-President, *The Philadelphia Inquirer,* Philadelphia, Pa.; Professor Giovanni Barozzi, Museo Storico Italiano della Guerra, Rovereto, Italy; Colonel Rinaldo Cruccu, Lt. Nicola della Volpe, Ufficio Storico, Stato Maggiore dell'Esercito, Rome; Carolyn Davis, Syracuse University Library, Syracuse, New York; Fred Demarest, Chairman, Jim Caiella and Rob Heller, Department of Photography, Newhouse School of Communications, Syracuse University, Syracuse, New York; Hans Dollinger, Wörthsee, West Germany; Evelyn Farland, Poster Originals Ltd., New York City; Kenny Franks, Editor, *The Chronicles of Oklahoma,* and Martha Mobley, Oklahoma Historical Society, Oklahoma City, Oklahoma; Ed Griffiths, East Setauket, New York; Dr. Matthias Haupt, Bundesarchiv, Koblenz; Heinrich Hoffmann, Munich; Imperial War Museum, London; Dr. Roland Klemig, Bildarchiv Preussischer Kulturbesitz, Berlin; Vera Kovarsky, Purdy Station, New York; Noboru Kojima, Tokyo; Tsuguichi Koyanagi, Miyazaki Prefecture, Japan; Maria Pia Mariani, Archivio Centrale dello Stato, Rome.

INDEX

Numerals in italics indicate an illustration of the subject mentioned.

N

O

P

R

S

T

U

V

W

Y

Z

D. L. To. 1110-78.
Printed by Artes Gráficas Toledo, S.A.